JACK PARDEE · JOHN DAVID CROW · GRADY ALLEN · EDD HAR
ALL · MARK DENNARD · CODY RISIEN · JACOB GREEN · SCOTT
EY WASHINGTON · RICHMOND WEBB · W   RST ·
ARCUS BUCKLEY · GREG HILL · ANTONIO   HRIS
TT BUMGARDNER · BRANNDON STEWART · CHAD FRANTZEN ·
ITLEY · TERRENCE MURPHY · STEPHEN McGEE · MARK DODG
K PARDEE · JOHN DAVID CROW · GRADY ALLEN · EDD HARGET
MARK DENNARD · CODY RISIEN · JACOB GREEN · SCOTT POLK
ASHINGTON · RICHMOND WEBB · WARREN BARHORST · BUCKY
US BUCKLEY · GREG HILL · ANTONIO ARMSTRONG · CHRIS RUH
MGARDNER · BRANNDON STEWART · CHAD FRANTZEN · CHRI
Y · TERRENCE MURPHY · STEPHEN McGEE · MARK DODGE · JOE
PARDEE · JOHN DAVID CROW · GRADY ALLEN · EDD HARGETT
MARK DENNARD · CODY RISIEN · JACOB GREEN · SCOTT POLK
ASHINGTON · RICHMOND WEBB · WARREN BARHORST · BUCKY
US BUCKLEY · GREG HILL · ANTONIO ARMSTRONG · CHRIS RUH
MGARDNER · BRANNDON STEWART · CHAD FRANTZEN · CHRI
Y · TERRENCE MURPHY · STEPHEN McGEE · MARK DODGE · JOE
E · JOHN DAVID CROW · GRADY ALLEN · EDD HARGETT · ED SIM

WHAT IT MEANS TO BE AN AGGIE

WHAT IT MEANS TO BE AN
AGGIE

JOHN DAVID CROW
AND TEXAS A&M's GREATEST PLAYERS

RUSTY BURSON AND CATHY CAPPS

TRIUMPH
BOOKS

Library of Congress Cataloging-in-Publication Data

Burson, Rusty.
    What it means to be an Aggie : John David Crow and Texas A&M's greatest players / Rusty Burson and Cathy Capps.
       p. cm.
    ISBN 978-1-60078-369-2 (alk. paper)
1. Texas A & M University—Football—History. 2. Texas A & M Aggies (Football team)—History. 3. Texas A & M University—Sports—History. 4. Crow, John David, 1935– I. Capps, Cathy. II. Title.
    GV958.T44B88 2010
    796.332'630764242—dc22

                                                                    2010010478

This book is available in quantity at special discounts for your group or organization. For further information, contact:

Triumph Books
542 South Dearborn Street
Suite 750
Chicago, Illinois 60605
(312) 939-3330
Fax (312) 663-3557
www.triumphbooks.com

Printed in U.S.A.
ISBN: 978-1-60078-369-2
Design by Nick Panos
Editorial production and layout by Prologue Publishing Services, LLC
All photos courtesy of Texas A&M Sports Information unless otherwise noted

To my seventh-grade English teacher, Beverly Corzine, who pushed me to write and taught me to edit. And to my breakfast group—Bob Anderson, Mark Brauer, Chad Wootan, Dennis Fink, John Lampo, and Dallas Shipp—who prayed for me to receive more financial opportunities. Mentioning their names here may force them—even Lampo—to buy a book.

—Rusty Burson

Many Aggies have inspired me—none more than the former athletes I've been so fortunate to cross paths with over the years. Their stories are always rich and their friendships are priceless. I'm most proud of my Aggie family—all of them—but especially my children, Nikki Capps Norton, '04, and Jonathan Capps, '06. They have embraced the Aggie spirit and carry on the tradition.

—Cathy Capps, '85

CONTENTS

FOREWORD

What It Means to Be an Aggie

LOOKING BACK OVER MY CAREER as an athlete, coach, collegiate administrator, and fund-raiser, I've held many positions and been called many things over the past 55 years. Among my very favorite titles is this: an Aggie.

Texas A&M University has undergone remarkable changes since I first arrived on campus in 1954. It's gone from a small, all-male, military college to a bustling, vibrant, and diverse university with nearly 50,000 students. But the core system of values—honor, loyalty, duty, respect, commitment, patriotism, service, etc.—still remains today. A&M is still so unique among universities, and it gives me tremendous pride when I walk across campus and see the students who embody what first made me fall in love with Aggieland.

Ironically, I didn't know if I would love or loathe A&M when I first arrived in College Station. I didn't really know anything about Texas A&M, and I came to Aggieland for one reason: a coach. Probably not the coach you might suspect, though.

My hometown was Springhill, Louisiana, a very small community in northern Webster Parish along the Louisiana-Arkansas state line. My older brother, Raymond, played college football at a small school called Magnolia A&M, which was just across the state boundary in Columbia County, Arkansas. Raymond was on a football scholarship at Magnolia A&M, which later changed its name to Southern State College and is now Southern Arkansas University. He was particularly fond of his head coach at the time, Elmer Smith.

Smith was a great coach at Magnolia, compiling a 54–27–2 record from 1946 to 1953 and leading the Muleriders (that's not a typo) to conference championships in 1951 and '52. My family would go to Magnolia to watch Raymond play, and I would stand on the sideline during those games.

By my senior year at Springhill High, Raymond had graduated from Magnolia and gone into the military. Coach Smith, who became a tremendous friend of the family, called me one day and said he needed a favor. He said he wanted me to meet with a couple of businessmen who thought that Magnolia should be recruiting me.

So I went to Magnolia—I would have done anything for Coach Elmer—and met with the men, who talked to me about going to school there. They also said that I could have a part-time job. Those men really wanted me to go to Magnolia A&M, and I might have seriously considered it except for the fact that Coach Elmer Smith pulled me aside and said, "Look, these guys really want me to recruit you, but you need to go to a school on the next level."

I pretty much forgot about Magnolia, and I was looking at a lot of Division I schools. But then former Kentucky head coach Paul "Bear" Bryant took the job at A&M and hired Elmer Smith as an assistant. Not long after that, Coach Elmer knocked on our door. He said, "I told you that you need to go to a higher level of school. Well, that higher level school is Texas A&M."

That is the sole reason why I went to A&M. I had that much respect for Coach Smith. I didn't even know Coach Bryant at that time.

I do want to clarify one thing here. Back then, you could sign a letter of intent in each conference. I signed with A&M in the Southwest Conference; I signed with Oklahoma in the Big 8; and I signed with LSU in the Southeastern Conference. Initially, I really wanted to go to Oklahoma because they had been winning with Bud Wilkinson. But when Elmer Smith was hired at A&M, I knew that was the place for me. Of course, that didn't mean the other schools gave up on me.

I had a job with United Gas Company in Shreveport in the summer of '54, and about every week my boss would tell me there was a coach from LSU or OU there to see me. I would always visit with them, but I'd tell them the same thing: I'm going to A&M.

At one point, rumors started swirling that A&M had to come and get me off the campus of LSU. That's not true. I played in a Louisiana High School All-Star game in Baton Rouge, but A&M didn't have to come and get me. What really happened was Bobby Morris did go to LSU, and he checked into the dorm. But he didn't like it, so he left. He then drove to College Station. Somehow, my name became associated with that story.

I was bound for College Station all along. I married Carolyn, my high school sweetheart, on July 2, 1954, and she took a job at the campus bookstore and helped put me through school. We were able to make a little extra money by selling my football tickets, which was an accepted practice.

When we got to campus in 1954, it was like Mrs. Bryant once said. It was in the middle of a drought, and A&M looked like a prison camp. We moved into the College View Apartments, and we had quite a few roommates. We sprayed like crazy trying to kill the cockroaches, but they wouldn't die.

Coach Elmer paid us a visit at that apartment not long after we arrived. I had been very excited about going to a campsite out in the Hill Country with the rest of the football team and the coaches. But then Coach Elmer came over and said, "John, the rules say you can't go to Junction. None of the freshmen can."

I was some kind of disappointed. But that apartment left an impression on Coach Elmer. It was a furnished apartment, but we had no air conditioner. All we came with was our clothes and the cookware that Carolyn's mom sent. Coach Elmer was sitting in that apartment, sweating up a storm.

The next morning a delivery guy showed up with a water cooling fan. He asked where we wanted it. I said, "You've got the wrong apartment, because I cannot afford that." But the delivery guy said it was already paid for. I'm sure that was probably a violation. Just like selling our tickets was probably a violation. But that fan saved us.

Of course, you probably know what happened in Junction. That story has been told over and over again. When those two buses pulled out of College Station headed for Junction, they were pretty full. I remember wishing I could go with them.

Then one bus came back, and that bus wasn't too full. I don't recall hearing too much about Junction and how bad it was at the time. I wondered what happened to all those players, but there wasn't a lot of talk about it. And especially since I lived off of campus with my wife, I really didn't hear much.

What sticks out about my first year was that we had 109 guys on the freshman team. Some of them were walk-ons, many of them had one-year scholarships. I was told I had a four-year scholarship, but that first year was all about survival. Coach Bryant was trying to whip everyone into shape.

After accepting the Heisman Trophy at the Downtown Athletic Club in New York, John David Crow (44) chose to carry the trophy with him on the plane trip back to Texas instead of having it shipped home. *Photo courtesy of Texas A&M Sport Museum*

Later on, in talking to some of the older guys, I learned that the only major difference between Junction and the workouts we had on campus once school started was that in Junction they slept on cots; in College Station we slept on beds. We worked hard, but the varsity didn't have much luck in 1954. The Aggies won just one ballgame.

Things were not a lot better for me personally in the classroom. Springhill High School was a fine place, and I would never say anything derogatory about my teachers or administrators. But for me, personally, I was not prepared for the studies here at A&M. College classes were real tough on me, and I did not put enough effort toward them until my sophomore year. I thought I could do the same things I did in high school and get by. That was not the case. I got behind right from the start, and my freshman year was practically a blur. I worked really hard to catch up and took summer school.

We worked hard as a football team the next year, as well. I remember one practice, in particular, in the summer of 1955 where we had a scrimmage at Kyle Field. It was brutally hot. The first quarter was regulation, 15 minutes. The second quarter lasted a few more minutes, the third quarter lasted an extra 30 minutes, and then the fourth quarter lasted an extra hour. Coach Bryant didn't let anything end unless we did things the way he wanted them done.

xiii

We went to the locker room, and I immediately went to the shower, where I was sitting in a chair letting the cold water hit me. Then the manager came into the locker room and said, "Put 'em back on, boys." I asked him what he was talking about, and he said the man, Coach Bryant, wanted us back in our pads and back on the field.

So we all put our pads back on and were standing at the south end of Kyle Field. He was talking to us, but the whole time he was talking, I was looking at the ramp on the north end zone, thinking about leaving. But then I thought, *You might kill me, but you aren't going to make me quit.*

Well, he almost killed me. He put the ball on the 40-yard-line and then put the first team against the second team. We drove the ball down and scored and turned around and started back. I don't recall anything else. They said I came to the huddle, collapsed, and started having convulsions. They took me to the dressing room and iced me down. I was told that Coach Bryant was massaging me because I was cramping.

I woke up in the infirmary four or five hours later. Carolyn was sitting right there, and Coach Bryant was standing there. I remember him saying, "John, why didn't you tell me you were tired?"

When I came back to practice after a couple of days' rest, he told the team, "You know what happened to Crow, so if you get dizzy, just tell a coach you need to take a rest." No one was going to do that, because you would be gone the next day. But all that work paid off, as we were a much better team in '55.

The first team we played in 1955 was No. 1–ranked UCLA. We got on an airplane, which was my first time ever on a plane. They beat us 21–0, but we grew up a lot that day. That was my first varsity game, and I was scared to death. The L.A. Coliseum was huge.

We only lost one more game the rest of the year. I don't recall thinking that we were turning the program around. I just remember thinking that we were supposed to be good because Coach Bryant was preparing us to be good. We went 7–2–1 in 1955 and then really put it all together in '56.

We were on probation, so we didn't get to go to a bowl game, but we tied one and won every other game to win the Southwest Conference.

Of course, the highlight of 1956 was beating Texas in Austin. I didn't know anything about the rivalry, coming from northern Louisiana. But I quickly learned the Texas game meant a whole lot to Aggies. In '56 I scored a touchdown in the south end zone in Austin, and the Aggies in the crowd went absolutely crazy. I went back to the huddle and asked what was going on because it was only the first quarter.

Someone in the huddle said, "Hell, John, this is the first time A&M has ever scored in the south end zone." That was a big game and a great game to win. Before the game I had chipped a bone in my foot, my small toe. During the week preparing for Texas, I was told that I should get an X-ray. I told everybody that I was playing against Texas no matter what. So I didn't practice much that week.

Loyd Taylor had a bad calf, and Jack Pardee couldn't lift his arm, so we were pretty beat up. When the team went to warm up, the three of us went into the locker room for a shot that relieved the pain. No one made us do it, but we were going to be on that field. The importance of the game was great. It was amazing when we went back onto the field for the kickoff. My foot didn't hurt a bit; Jack's arm didn't hurt a bit; and Loyd was running like a deer. We played the game and beat Texas 34–21 that day to win the Southwest Conference title.

Carolyn was waiting for me in the parking lot. When I got in the car, I had to get in the back seat to prop my leg up because it was hurting so bad. We had planned on driving up to Fort Worth, but we finally had to stop in Waco, and she had to find some aspirin because I didn't have pain pills. We stayed the night in a hotel while everyone else was celebrating. I woke up the next morning, made a doctor's appointment, and got some medicine. It was pretty bad. The good news was that the doctor scheduled my surgery to remove that chip before spring practice, so I was in a cast for the spring and didn't have to go through practice.

Of course, when I talk to most people about my time at A&M, they want to talk about 1957 and what could have been. By early November, we were ranked No. 1 in the nation. We were 8–0 on November 9 after we beat SMU.

Many stories have been written about what happened next. According to many sources, the *Houston Post* released the news on the day of our Rice game—November 16, 1957—that Coach Bryant was leaving A&M after the season to coach at his alma mater, Alabama. According to many of the stories I've read, that was such a distraction that it caused us to lose that game.

Honestly, I can only speak for myself. I didn't pay attention to the papers then. That is probably why I didn't know anything about the Heisman Trophy back then, either. I tried to stay away from the sportswriters, so I didn't get quoted saying anything that would make Coach Bryant mad.

Anyway, back to the Rice game. Before a crowd of more than 72,000—still the largest ever to witness a game at Rice Stadium—and a regional television audience on KPRC-TV, we opened the game by driving deep into Rice territory. But then we had a pass intercepted at the Rice 9, and the No. 20–ranked Owls drove the length of the field to take a 7–0 lead after King Hill, Rice's All-America candidate, booted the extra point.

We finally answered that score on the first play of the fourth quarter, as Roddy Osborne lunged into the end zone to make it 7–6. But we missed the extra point. That didn't necessarily cost us the game. We mounted one more drive deep into Rice territory late in the fourth quarter, but the Owls stopped us on fourth down to preserve the win.

Years later, when I was an assistant at Alabama, Coach Bryant said to me, "John, if I would have let you go get Ken Hall and not allowed him to quit, and I would have moved Ken to halfback and you to fullback, and would have made a move here or there, we would have walked away with the national championship."

I said, "Hell, Coach, if you would've let Bobby Joe Conrad kick a field goal in the fourth quarter, we would have won it without all that other stuff." After I said that, I walked very fast to the locker room to get my clothes. I didn't want to see him again that day. He never brought it up again. But that was the truth.

We didn't win that game and then we got beat by Texas the next game. But I don't think the losses were because of distractions. We made some costly mistakes against Rice, and Texas was just better than us that day. Simple as that.

I owe Coach Bryant so much for so many things. I certainly owe him for me winning the 1957 Heisman Trophy. He'd mentioned to a bunch of sportswriters earlier in the year that if I didn't win the Heisman Trophy they should stop giving it. I had a good senior year, but I truly believe that is the reason I won the Heisman.

The funny thing is that, when I went to the Heisman ceremony, it was my second trip to New York in less than a month. I had been named to an All-America team, and I got sent to New York to be on a TV show with Bob Hope and Ed Sullivan. We got to New York early, and we were given tickets to go to a Broadway show, *My Fair Lady*. I thought some of my fellow All-Americans and I would leave at intermission and go see New York. But we didn't even leave our seats. That Broadway show was great.

After that trip, I came back to College Station and, a short time later, got a call from my mother telling me that the president of the college had called her. I wasn't there when she called, but I started thinking, *What did I do so wrong that the president of the university would call my mother?*

I was relieved to find out that I was not in trouble. Quite the opposite, in fact. The president of the Downtown Athletic Club in New York called the president of A&M and then called my mother to let her know I had won the 1957 Heisman. My mom said it must be a big award because they were flying her, Dad, and Carolyn to New York.

That trip was the highlight of my mother's life at the time. Coach Elmer also went with us because Coach Bryant was recruiting for Alabama. I also think he knew that Coach Elmer should go because he is the one who led me to A&M.

They took us to the 13th floor of the Downtown Athletic Club, which was the Heisman floor. As I was looking out the window at the Statue of Liberty

Crow, who grew up in Springhill, Louisiana, says the primary reason he chose to go to Texas A&M was because of his close relationship with Elmer Smith, who was hired by Bear Bryant to serve as an assistant coach in Aggieland.

and was surrounded by all the portraits of past winners, only then did I realize that winning the Heisman Trophy was a big deal.

The funniest story about that trip is that they asked me if I wanted to ship the trophy home. I said, "No, I will take it with me on the plane." It's a huge trophy, and I laugh at the thought of someone trying to carry that trophy onto a plane today.

The Heisman is a great individual honor, but I'd give it back if we could just replay those games against Rice and Texas in 1957. I would have loved to have given A&M another national championship.

Regardless, A&M gave me more than I could ever imagine. I was taken by the Chicago Cardinals in the first round of the 1958 NFL Draft and played 11 seasons in the NFL. When my playing career was complete, I was hired as a running backs coach at Alabama under Coach Bryant and then later worked as an assistant with the Cleveland Browns and San Diego Chargers. Then I was given the opportunity to return to my home state to become the head coach and athletics director at Northeast Louisiana.

In addition to all those roles, I had my real estate license and insurance license in Arkansas and Texas. As I said earlier, I have held many titles throughout my life.

But I was especially proud in 1983 when Jackie Sherrill offered me an opportunity to return to my alma mater as an assistant athletics director. When Sherrill left in 1988, I became the athletics director and was able to hire the person who would become the winningest football coach in A&M history, R.C. Slocum.

To this day, I take great pride in that decision and many other positive developments that took place at A&M when I was within the athletics department. Not because those things reflect positively on me but, rather, because they reflected positively on a place I have grown to love and cherish: Aggieland.

Through the years, I've run into many Aggies who still begrudge Coach Bryant for leaving A&M. But I totally understand why he left. To Bryant, leaving A&M meant going "home" to Alabama.

There is something magical about going home. I know. I was able to come home to Aggieland, and I've been here ever since 1983. This is much more than a place where I went to school or held a couple of jobs. This is where my heart has been ever since Elmer Smith first convinced me to come to school here. This is home.

—John David Crow

INTRODUCTION

A S KIDS, NEITHER ONE OF US could have possibly imagined that we would one day work so closely with Texas A&M athletics and former A&M athletes. Neither of us ever wore an Aggie athletics uniform; neither seemed destined for our current roles after college; and only one of us (Cathy) actually graduated from Texas A&M.

Yet both of us have found our professional niche working with former A&M athletes through the 12th Man Foundation or the Texas A&M Lettermen's Association.

We both feel blessed to be in these roles, and we feel like we have been adopted into the Aggies' athletics family. Our respective roles have become much more than careers; we are both passionate about promoting Texas A&M and recognizing the accomplishments of some of the greatest men and women who have represented the university in maroon-and-white uniforms. Many of the athletes featured in this book are so much more than historic names to us; they have become some of our closest friends.

So this book was certainly a labor of love for us. We both admire Texas A&M and all that this university represents. We appreciate its values and its ideals. We cherish its unique traditions and adore A&M's legacy of loyalty.

From its earliest and most humble days as an all-male military institution, A&M has been an extraordinary place: an institution where camaraderie is coveted, respect is revered, patriotism is applauded, and service—to others and to your country—is practically mandated.

The Corps of Cadets, the community, the demographics of the student body, the size of the enrollment, the constructional landscape of the campus, the reputation of the school's academic prowess, and so much more have changed dramatically over the years. But the core values, commitment to character, fundamental moral fiber, and most cherished traditions remain essentially the same today at Texas A&M as they were decades ago.

Texas A&M can best be described as today's students chasing tomorrow's breakthroughs while still embracing yesterday's values. At least that's our best attempt at a description. As the school's alma mater so eloquently states, "There's a spirit can ne'er be told. It's the spirit of Aggieland."

Perhaps that spirit is best defined, conveyed, and captured on Saturday afternoons and evenings in the fall. Texas A&M's traditions and values encompass far more than game days at Kyle Field. But if you want a snapshot of all that makes Texas A&M magnificent, the pageantry and passion of Kyle Field make a great picture.

Whether the A&M football team is awesome or awful, the Aggie student body—known nationally as the "12th Man"—can be counted on to camp out for tickets, yell for the home team, commiserate, and bond. And year in and year out, they show why this oak-lined, tradition-rich campus of more than 48,000 students—in good times or in bad—may be more spirited toward its football team than any other in the country.

Texas A&M is not steeped in decades of winning football tradition. At least not compared to some of the other powerhouse programs across the country. There have been some truly memorable moments in Aggie football history, however. For example:

- Beginning with his first game as head coach at A&M in 1917 and concluding with the final game of the 1920 season, D.X. Bible's A&M teams went 25 consecutive games without surrendering a point. During that span, the Aggies outscored opponents 771–0. Prison cells didn't contain like the A&M defense.

- En route to an 11–0 record and winning the school's only official national championship, the 1939 Aggies still hold an NCAA record for total team defense, allowing 76.3 yards per game. A&M also finished first in the country in rushing defense (41.5 yards per game) and scoring defense (1.8 points allowed per game) as the Aggies recorded six shutouts. Thanks to John Kimbrough's running and the dominating defense, the Aggies won eight of 10 regular-season games by at least 14 points. The closest game was in the Sugar Bowl against Tulane, a team that cut Kimbrough two years earlier. Kimbrough finished the day with 159 yards rushing to lead the Aggies to a 14–13 win.

- Bear Bryant arrived in College Station on February 8, 1954, and was startled by the colorless, womanless bleakness of the campus in the dead of winter. Bryant's first team at A&M went 1–9 in the 1954 season, which would turn out to be the only losing season in his 38 years as a head coach. But in 1956, the Aggies went undefeated (9–0–1) for the first time since the national championship season of 1939. And in 1957 the Aggies vaulted to No. 1 in the AP polls released October 28.

- The senior class of 1975—Emory Bellard's first recruiting class in 1972—helped transform A&M's football reputation from mediocre to meaningful. That class moved the Aggies from the obscurity of the SWC cellar to respectability in the national rankings. It certainly gave A&M a building block for a much brighter long-term future.

- Jackie Sherrill vowed to awaken Aggieland from its slumber, and A&M made national news when it hired him as head coach and athletics director on January 19, 1982. A&M awarded Sherrill a six-year contract worth $282,000 per year—an outlandish amount of money, according to a scathing *Sports Illustrated* commentary written shortly after the hire. After a couple of rough years to begin the Sherrill regime, A&M turned the corner. From 1985 to 1987, Sherrill's bunch went 29–7, claimed three straight SWC titles, won two Cotton Bowls, and placed A&M's name prominently among college football's premier programs.

xxi

- While Sherrill awakened the sleeping giant at A&M, R.C. Slocum nurtured it and transformed it into a menacing monster. A one-point loss to Arkansas in 1989 and a one-point loss to Texas in 1990 prevented the Aggies from winning conference championships in Slocum's first two seasons as head coach. Nevertheless, the Aggies ruled the SWC in the final years of the conference. A&M won three straight conference championships from 1991 to 1993 and would have won it again in 1994 if not for being on probation (as a result of a summer jobs scandal that had nothing to do with the coaching staff). The Aggies compiled amazing numbers under Slocum, winning 31 consecutive games at home from 1990 to 1995 and going 29 straight conference games without a loss (1991–1994).

For all the occasional brushes with brilliance, however, Texas A&M's football history is probably filled with twice as much heartache as heartfelt joy. Following the 1939 national title, the Aggies flirted with national championships in 1940, 1957, and 1975. Each of those seasons ended in demoralizing losses and broken dreams.

The Aggies have also endured long stretches of mediocrity...and misery. A&M did not produce a winning season from 1946 to 1949; or from 1958 to 1966; or from 1968 to 1973. Even in the modern era, times have occasionally been bleak. A&M is—at the time of this writing—in one of the longest droughts in school history in terms of not winning a conference title. The Aggies recently completed an entire decade (2000–2009) without winning a single league title. Or even a division title.

In good times or bad, though, the A&M football team generates incredible levels of passion among the students and former students. Game days at Kyle Field are breathtaking, exhilarating, intoxicating, and addicting. Looking across the stadium toward students on the east side of Kyle Field and watching them sway as they "saw Varsity's horns off" is mesmerizing. And ever since January 2, 1922, the Aggie fans have enjoyed a relationship with the players unlike any other university in the country.

On that day, Bible's Aggies faced the Centre College Praying Colonels. The Danville, Kentucky–based Colonels were the glamour team of college football, bringing an unblemished record to Dallas for the Dixie Classic (the predecessor to the Cotton Bowl). As the game began, injuries quickly mounted for the already depleted Aggies. Fullback Harry Pinson had broken his leg in the finale against Texas, and fellow fullback Floyd Buckner had seriously injured his leg in the pre–Dixie Classic practices. Captain Heine Weir, who missed much of the season with a broken leg, played against Centre...until he reinjured the leg on the third play. All-SWC halfback Sam Houston Sanders and Bugs Morris were also injured early in the game.

Bible realized that, at the current rate, he would not have enough bodies to finish the game. Then a thought struck him. One of his former players, E. King Gill, was working in the press box, serving as a spotter for Jinx Tucker of the *Waco News-Tribune*. Gill was quite an athlete, a multisport letterman who had been released at the end of the regular season to pursue basketball, his favorite sport.

So, with injuries mounting and Centre leading 7–3 early in the game, Bible called head yell leader Harry Thompson to the bench. He then sent

Thompson to the press box to retrieve Gill. Once Gill made it to the sideline, Bible asked him to dress in the uniform of an injured player.

"I'll never forget what Coach Bible said to me," Gill recalled years later. "He said, 'Boy, it looks like we may not have enough players to finish the game. You may have to go in and stand around for a while.' I don't guess A&M has ever played more inspired ball. All of our remaining players managed to survive from that point forward."

Not only did they survive; they thrived. In the third quarter, A&M's Puny Wilson connected with A.J. Evans on an end-around pass play to put the Aggies on top. Wilson scored later on a five-yard run, and Ted Winn intercepted a pass, returning it 45 yards for a score. It was enough to give the Aggies a stunning 22–14 victory.

Gill never played. Nor did he make much ado about his willingness to play. He had, after all, been on the team not too long ago. But Thompson, the yell leader, was so excited about the victory and so impressed by Gill's willingness to answer the Aggies' call that he scheduled a yell practice on the steps of the YMCA as soon as the team and students returned to campus.

At that yell practice, Thompson first used the words "12th Man" in reference to Gill. Ever since, Texas A&M has been known nationally as "the home of the 12th Man." From one generation to the next, students at A&M have stood throughout games as a symbol of their willingness to follow Gill's lead and answer the Aggies' call, if necessary.

It's that kind of passion that invites so many visitors to Kyle Field to learn more about becoming an Aggie. Contrary to what some fans at Texas, Texas Tech, Baylor, and so forth might want visitors to believe, you don't need an Aggie Ring to become part of the Aggie family. All you need to do is embrace the unique traditions and to explore the unique bonds of Aggieland.

Emory Bellard, one of the great coaches in A&M history, started his football career as a player at the University of Texas and enjoyed many successful seasons as an assistant or head coach at Texas, Mississippi State, and various high schools. But Bellard may be most remembered for what he accomplished at A&M. Bellard truly understands the allure of Aggieland, and he provided these stories when we asked what being an Aggie meant to him:

> What Texas A&M meant to me when I was in high school was simply
> that it was Texas' version of West Point. I knew that all the students wore

uniforms, that the student body was all male, and that John Kimbrough played football for A&M.

When I went to college, I decided to go to the University of Texas because I got a real nice letter from [former A&M coach] D.X. Bible inviting me to come to Austin and to play football. Freshmen were eligible in 1945 because of the war, which had just ended. We were scheduled to play Texas A&M in College Station that year, and practice took on a new intensity. I got a full dose of the A&M-Texas rivalry. During that week of practice, I broke the fibula and tibia in my left leg.

Therefore my first visit to Kyle Field was on crutches and on the sideline. But even then, I learned that the university was intense and real.

Later as an assistant at the University of Texas, I learned more about the rivalry and the uniqueness of Texas A&M. And after all those years of being on the Texas side of the rivalry, I was hired as the athletics director and head coach at Texas A&M. It was quite a change to be on the other bench.

Texas A&M was going through a gigantic change in those years, shortly after the admission of women.... I would like to think that the athletics program became very sound and competitive during this period, and I shall always take pride in Texas A&M University and my time in Aggieland.

I loved the traditions. I admired the work ethic of the young men we recruited. They became good students, they played hard, and they embraced what it means to be an Aggie.

There is so much to love when speaking of Texas A&M, and I loved the way so many people embraced me. But the athletes will always be my primary source of pride. They came to Texas A&M to compete and to get an education that would prepare them for their life after college. But they received more than they could have ever imagined. Not only did they earn a degree; they earned the right to call themselves "Aggies." And once you are an Aggie, you are part of a family unlike any other.

As you read through the chapters of this book, you will discover that theme over and over again. Some of the stories are on All-Americans who went on to fame and fortune in the NFL. Other stories focus on walk-ons who embodied the spirit of E. King Gill.

Regardless of what they accomplished on the football field, you will undoubtedly see that they all benefited from being part of the Aggie family and that they all still cherish the lessons learned and the values that were instilled during their time at Texas A&M.

We hope and believe that Texas A&M's best days as a football program are still ahead. Thanks to the generosity of former students, A&M now possesses some of the most extraordinary football facilities in the nation for student-athletes. A&M is now annually graduating as many students as most of the largest schools in the country nowadays—a far cry from a time as recently as the early 1960s when the school featured only about 10,000 students. As a result, A&M's resources are growing far more rapidly than those of most other schools around the nation.

In the near future, we believe all the pieces will fall into place, and A&M will consistently be in the hunt for division, conference, and even national titles. And when the Aggies truly start rolling, watch out. Because of its values, its traditions, and its people—people like the ones featured in the ensuing pages—A&M has staying power. Or perhaps more precisely, staying-on-top power.

The
THIRTIES
AND FORTIES

JOE BOYD

LINEMAN

1937–1939

Editor's Note: As told to Rusty Burson prior to Joe Boyd's death on June 1, 2009. For several years prior to his death, Boyd had been relegated to an assisted living facility in his adopted hometown of West Union, West Virginia. He had suffered several mini-strokes, limiting his communication skills, and his overall health had continued to deteriorate.

★   ★   ★

SERVING AS AN EVANGELIST for almost 70 years has provided me with many opportunities to see how God can use some of the most unlikely people for His glory. I've seen plenty of modern-day Sauls who have become Pauls on their own road to Damascus. For those not familiar with the New Testament, Saul grew up in Jerusalem and studied Jewish tradition, becoming a zealous Pharisee. He was at first an active opponent of the Christian movement, but on his way to Damascus to persecute Christian believers, he was stopped by a blinding light and the words of Jesus.

After being temporarily blinded, Saul's eyes and heart were opened to Jesus. He converted to Christianity, his name was changed to Paul, and he made missionary journeys around Asia Minor, Macedonia, and Achaia. He also authored 13 New Testament letters.

Joe Boyd was selected to six All-America teams following the 1939 season. Many years later, he was also named to *Sports Illustrated*'s 25-year All-America team.

Throughout the Bible and throughout history, God has used some of the coldest and most hardened souls for his glory through the ultimate transformative power of Jesus Christ.

I'm an example of that transformative power. Long before I experienced God's ultimate victory of salvation, I was what many people would label as a world-class loser. But the same God who saved a persecutor like Saul also used a renegade like me.

My unusual adventure began in Jacksonville, Texas, where I was born to some wonderful parents. Soon afterward, my family moved to Dallas, where my tough-guy image began to take shape. By the time I was a teenager, I was a member of one of numerous gangs in the Dallas area in the early 1930s.

The city's answer to the gang problem was to organize them into sports teams—the West Dallas gang, the Fair Park gang, and so forth. Each of the gangs had a football team, and it was there that my gridiron career began to flourish. But I didn't just leave my mark during the game.

Playing on those gang teams was so tough and rough that we drank wine at the half. All the games wound up in free-for-all fights, and I was at the center of many of those brawls. By the time I got to Crozier Tech High School, I was already tough, and I thought I could whip anybody—including my dad, who was a preacher.

I was a terribly sorry guy back then, much to the disappointment of my parents. They were sick of my attitude and my gang-related activities. When I was about 16 or 17, I had finally heard enough from my parents, and I even tried to fight my dad. He put me on the floor before I could even take a swing.

I was going to fight him in the kitchen, but I wound up on the floor real quick. He pinned me with his foot, took off his belt, and began to beat me with the buckle. I was bleeding, the belt was covered in blood, and my mother came running into the kitchen. She said, "Sam, you're going to kill him, you're going to kill him." He said, "I'm trying to, but he won't die." I can't say this strongly enough: I was mean and good for nothing.

Partly because of my troublesome reputation, I didn't have many collegiate suitors. But I liked football, and I wanted to keep on playing. That seemed to be one of the few good habits I had back in those days.

So I contacted Baylor, but the Bears had little to no interest in me. Several other schools had a similar response. Finally, Paris Junior College offered me a chance to play in 1936, and after a short stint at Paris, I contacted Texas A&M in College Station. I didn't know much about Texas A&M then, but I was willing to go anywhere I could in order to keep playing football—including an all-male, military institution pretty much in the middle of nowhere at that time.

I liked the contact; I liked the toughness of the game; and I liked hitting people without getting into trouble. The head coach at A&M, Homer Norton, was willing to give me a shot, but my stay in College Station was conditional. Coach Norton said he would take me. He also said that if I made the ballclub, I could stay. But he said that if I didn't make the ballclub, I would have to leave. They didn't want to keep troublemakers around.

Thankfully, God allowed me to make that football team. It was a real blessing being a part of that team for so many reasons. I met some great people who became friends for life. I also had some structure in my life during my time at A&M.

I still was a wayward soul, for the most part. In fact, I was one ornery, sorry guy off the field. There wasn't a whole lot to do in College Station back then. But if there was trouble to be found, I was usually in the middle of it. I was a real mess.

I also dabbled in boxing and wrestling during my A&M days. I became the school's heavyweight champion in both sports, never once losing a single bout in either ring.

But at least being part of those football teams made me finally realize that there was something admirable in being part of something that was much bigger than myself.

In 1937 we had a pretty good football team. We lost a couple games and tied a couple, too. But we finished that year by beating Texas and whipping San Francisco.

The next year started really well, but then we got beat by Santa Clara and absolutely ripped by TCU, 34–6, in Fort Worth. Looking back, it was no shame to lose to that TCU team coached by Dutch Meyer. By the end of the year, TCU's Davey O'Brien had won the Heisman Trophy, and the Horned Frogs were crowned as national champions.

The Heisman Trophy and the national championship are huge events nowadays, but I really don't recall them being that big of a deal in the late 1930s. Anyway, we finished that 1938 season by losing to SMU and Texas and then beating Rice in the season finale.

While we won that Rice game 27–0, it proved to be costly for me individually. I cracked vertebrae and broke some ribs in that game. I experienced temporary paralysis in my legs and was taken to Houston for X-rays.

A man came out of the X-ray room and told me my neck was broken. I said, "I knew there was something wrong with it."

I guess I was just a tough old bird, and it absolutely bothered me the next year. But the folks at Texas A&M hired a big, strong woman to massage my neck in between games in 1939 and to absorb the chips that came off that break. Then I would go back in and play on Saturdays. I ended up playing that whole year with a cracked neck.

Here again, I look back and thank God that I didn't do serious injury to my body back then that would have prevented me from becoming an evangelist and leading revivals around the world in the name of Jesus Christ. God was undoubtedly protecting me for my future mission. He also allowed me to have a taste of great victory in 1939.

Led by John Kimbrough, Marshall Robnett, Herb Smith, and a host of other great players, our 1939 team proved to be the best college team in the land. But, honestly, we didn't really know there was such a thing as playing for No. 1. We just went out there and played hard, and we were determined to beat any team that came to play us.

And we did just that. Our 1939 team still holds an NCAA record for total team defense, allowing just 76.3 yards per game. We also finished first in the country in rushing defense [41.5 yards per game] and scoring defense [1.8 points allowed per game] as we recorded six shutouts.

Thanks to Kimbrough's running and our dominating defense, we won eight of 10 regular-season games by at least 14 points. The closest game all year came in the Sugar Bowl against Tulane. Kimbrough's two-yard touchdown run in the first quarter gave us a 7–0 lead, but the Green Wave scored the next two touchdowns to take a 13–7 lead in the fourth quarter.

6

We then began a 70-yard scoring drive led by Kimbrough. His second scoring run and the ensuing extra point gave us a 14–13 victory and a perfect 11–0 record.

We were awfully proud that we won every game, and we painted the town maroon that night. We had dinner, we had champagne, and we dressed and met down in the lobby of the hotel and got on the bus to go to Antoine's for dinner. It was an eight-course dinner, but we couldn't wait to get through with that dinner so we could get out on the town. There was a party especially for us at this home out in New Orleans. We gathered there and then dispersed. We had a great time in New Orleans that night. We celebrated throughout the French Quarter, Canal Street, etc. We then got on a train and went back the next day to College Station and went back to school.

Honestly, it wasn't until we got on that train the next day that I realized we had won the national championship. Somebody came down in the train and said, "Y'all know we're national champions?" I said, "Great." Like I said earlier, it was not a big deal. The big deal was that we won every game.

After that season, I was selected to six All-America teams. I also earned the praise of the famous sportswriter Grantland Rice. Years later, I was also named to *Sports Illustrated*'s 25-year All-America team. And even with a cracked neck, I was selected by the Washington Redskins in the sixth round of the 1940 NFL Draft. But after doctors strongly advised me not to continue my playing career, I went to work in the Galveston shipyards.

I quickly rose to the top at Todd Galveston Shipyard, a company controlled by the Rockefeller family. In a short time, I was placed in charge of all the accounting, payroll, bookkeeping, and auditing for the shipyards. But as I climbed the corporate ladder, I became increasing involved in the numerous temptations Galveston provided in the early 1940s.

I was drinking, gambling, whatever. The higher I went in sports and business, the more I thought of myself and the less I thought about God or anyone else. I bought into all the good publicity I was getting for boxing, football, wrestling, and whatever. I was on the verge of being totally out of control.

I first heard God calling me when a hurricane blew through Galveston, taking the roof off Todd Galveston Shipyard. I heard an even louder voice following a car wreck in the early 1940s.

7

My mother had been constantly praying for me. After years of straying, I finally got a Presbyterian preacher to come to my house. I asked him, "Does God have anything for me?"

He quoted Isaiah 1:18—the exact same verse my mother had told to me time and time again. I fell on my knees and began to cry for mercy. God gave me mercy. My wife, Edith, had never seen me as defeated. She had always seen me as the champion, the one in control. She came and knelt beside me and got saved, and I got right with God. I have been going in his name ever since. That was 1943.

In 1947 I earned a master's in theology from Southwestern Baptist Theological Seminary in Fort Worth, and I received a doctorate of divinity from Hyles-Anderson College in '76. I also have written a number of books through the years, and in my mid-sixties, I founded the Mt. Salem Revival Grounds in West Union, West Virginia, in 1976.

Most of all, though, I have tried to be a light for Jesus through my revivals. I have trained hundreds of young men to do evangelistic, pastoral, and missionary work through the years, and I've held revivals all over the globe—

from Texas to Jerusalem. I've been in every state in the union, and I've been in many foreign countries in the name of Jesus Christ. I have been in almost all the Spanish-speaking nations. We preach to so many people in Mexico—5,000, 4,000, 6,500. It's been a real blessing.

I have had all kinds of wonderful experiences. I did the revivals in Jerusalem, and had a great many people saved. God's been good, and my life's been an adventure.

When my wife of 62 years died in 2000, I didn't slow down. In fact, I increased my travels. If I get to where I can't preach standing up, then I will preach sitting down. And if I can't preach sitting down, I will preach from the bed. God called me to preach, and I intend to end my life on this Earth preaching.

Joe Boyd was selected to six All-America teams as a senior at A&M in 1939 after leading the Aggies to the national championship. He was a sixth-round draft pick of the Washington Redskins in 1940, though he never played pro football. Boyd was later named to *Sports Illustrated*'s 25-Year All-America Team. After beginning an accounting career, Boyd chose to go into the ministry. In 1947 he earned a master's in theology and received a doctorate of divinity in 1976. He authored numerous Christian books through the years, and he founded the Mt. Salem Revival Grounds in West Union, West Virginia. Boyd led Christian revivals in every U.S. state and many foreign countries before his death in 2009.

ROY BUCEK

LINEMAN

1939–1941

SLEEP-DEPRIVED AND CHILLED to the bone by the bitter winds and freezing temperatures in the Ardennes Forest, I was merely looking for a foxhole to grab a few moments of sleep on the afternoon of January 19, 1945. I hadn't slept in three full days and, despite the threats of danger surrounding me, desperately needed rest.

A month earlier, German forces broke the thinly held American front in the Belgian Ardennes sector. Using the element of surprise, the Germans penetrated deep into Belgium, creating a "bulge" in the Allied lines and threatening to break through to the north Belgian plain and seize Antwerp.

By late January of 1945, when the German forces were destroyed or routed in what became known as the "Battle of the Bulge," approximately 82,000 Allied troops had been wounded or killed, and 100,000 Germans were killed, wounded, or captured.

I was one of those statistics from the Bulge. Following the instructions of a battalion commander, I searched for a specific location to grab some much-needed shut-eye. Instead, I lost my left eye.

I was behind a tree, and I heard machine-gun fire hitting the tree. They saw me. I got back on my belly and crawled 300 or 400 yards through the snow to another area, where I looked over the horizon to see if I could find the enemy. I couldn't see them, but they saw me.

Although he was injured in the season-opener at Oklahoma A&M (now Oklahoma State), Roy Bucek played in every game during the Aggies' 1939 national championship run. During his three-year career as a player at A&M, the Aggies went 29–3.

They fired a Howitzer, and the first explosion came within four or five feet of me. It knocked my helmet off and knocked me over. The next Howitzer explosion hit a tree, and the shrapnel from the tree hit me. It cut my left eye in two, and the metal went behind my nose. It is still lodged in my right cheek. It's a piece of metal seven-eighths of an inch long, but it doesn't bother me.

The mere thought of having your eye sliced in two instinctively causes most people to wince. But perspective is an interesting thing. I don't even bat my good eye at the memories of January 19, 1945. In fact, it is the happiest day of my life.

I lost my eye, but I got to go back to the United States. I went to a hospital in France, where I waited for a boat to take me back to the U.S. The soldiers there were injured—some with one arm, some with one leg, and so forth—but we were as happy as we could be to be going home. We would have loved to go home in one piece, but it beat the hell out of not going home at all. It's all about perspective.

I considered myself a lucky man. I've always been lucky, dating back to when I was growing up in Schulenburg. My father was a hard-working farmer, and nobody in our family had ever received an education beyond grade school. Money wasn't just tight for our family back then; we were poorer than church mice.

It was pretty much expected that after I completed grade school, I would go to work full time on the family farm. My life would have been so much different if a high school track coach had not seen me running. That coach ended up coming to our family farm and begging my daddy to let me go on to Schulenburg High School so I could compete on the athletic teams.

My daddy agreed to let me go to high school because my coach was convinced that I could have a brighter future because of my natural athletic abilities. That was one example of being truly lucky, and I guess that old coach of mine was right.

I ended up being a pretty good football player at Schulenburg, and I was an even better track man. As a senior in high school, I scored more points than any other competitor at the state track meet in the spring of 1938. The head football coach at Texas, D.X. Bible, saw me at that meet and was the first person who gave me a scholarship offer. I was tickled to death.

At that same meet, though, I also met Texas A&M trainer Lil Dimmit. And honestly, the idea of going to school in College Station was more appealing to me. Unlike many other high school boys, I thought one tremendous benefit of A&M was that—unlike Texas—it was an all-male school. I was a shy, timid, country boy who had never had a date in my life, and I was still intimidated about being around women.

Anyway, I won the high hurdles and took second place in the low hurdles at the state track meet, but I had what they call a stone bruise on the bone in my foot that I landed on. It hurt badly, and the University of Texas trainer wrapped it up real good so I could run. Then Lil Dimmit came by, and he didn't know a damned thing about wrapping my foot.

But I wanted to be an Aggie so badly, and I just felt like I would be more comfortable at an all-boys school like A&M. The Aggies' trainer wrapped my foot—it wasn't worth a damn, but I said, "Oh, that's wonderful." That was my first contact with A&M, and it led to me getting a football scholarship.

Of course, the number-one reason I became an Aggie was because I liked my high school agricultural teacher. My daddy didn't have a car, so he couldn't take me to A&M or any other university that was offering me a scholarship. But my high school teacher said he would take me to A&M, but not the four or five other schools that were offering me a scholarship.

After playing on the freshman team in 1938, I started at right guard in the season-opener at Oklahoma A&M in '39. But I separated my shoulder in that game, and my replacement, Marshall Robnett, went on to win All-America honors as our 1939 team won the national championship.

It wasn't until 1941, following Robnett's graduation, that I regained my starting position. But I still played in every game during the '39 national championship run, and during my three-year career as a player at A&M, we went 29–3.

More than all of the victories, however, my fondest memories are of spending time with a roster full of hungry, hard-nosed farm boys.

We were all so tired of farming that it was a joy to be at A&M. I never did leave campus. When we got up there we went into the mess hall, and that was some of the best food most of us had ever tasted. We were thankful. At that time, A&M was teaching more agricultural courses, so they attracted more students from the farm. Many of the boys on our team were farmers' kids and were used to working hard. We didn't have many distractions, either.

Most of us never wanted to go home because that meant working on the farm. So we hung around each other and made our own fun. One day Robnett said, "Let's go fishing." He had a car, so we bought a quart of shrimp and went fishing. We took shrimp and a case of beer, too. After about 40 or 50 minutes, we didn't catch a single fish. He said, "Forget this, let's go to a restaurant and have them fry these damn shrimp." That's what we did. We made a meal out of our bait and a case of beer. I guess you could say we were resourceful.

So was our head coach, Homer Norton. He wasn't the greatest of coaches, but he was a master motivator. And when all else failed, Coach Norton would occasionally arrange for Aggies living in Houston or Dallas to send our team telegraphs. But they weren't words of encouragement.

The telegraphs often belittled our team and—supposedly—they were sent by Texas coaches. Coach Norton hung the telegraphs on the blackboard in the locker room, adding fuel to our team's fire.

It wasn't until after I graduated that I finally figured out the telegraphs were from A&M fans, not dreaded rivals. But Norton's methods worked.

Following my graduation from A&M on May 16, 1942, I reported to an Army camp in Little Rock, Arkansas, where I served as a training instructor for two years. I was shipped overseas in June of 1944, and by September, I was in combat.

After losing my eye in the Battle of the Bulge, I was sent to a hospital in El Paso, where six operations were performed on my eye. I was given a marble eye, which has become a great icebreaker through the years. I sometimes will pop the eye out of my socket, and I've been known to place it in drinks at parties and social functions. As you might imagine, discovering my glass eye in your drink often produces a memorable reaction.

After leaving the service, I returned to A&M to serve as assistant director of student affairs. One of my only regrets was that I left College Station. I think I could have been more successful if I had stayed at A&M. Instead, I was persuaded after two years to come back to Schulenburg to run a meat-packing plant.

But I did just fine for myself back in Schulenburg. Following my stint at the meat locker, I became an appliance dealer and opened a feed store. I then opened 21 drive-in restaurants throughout Texas, and in 1966 I built the first of three Oak Ridge Smokehouses—one of which was in College Station. I also oversaw a cattle operation that included 244 registered cows and built a 72-unit motel in Schulenburg in 1976.

And, most significantly, my return to Schulenburg led me to meet my wife, the former Vera Veenstra. In January 2010 we celebrated our 59th wedding anniversary. We have two daughters, Beverly Bucek and Barbara Mollenbrandt; five grandchildren (Jennifer Mollenbrandt, Melissa Mollenbrandt, Julie Mollenbrandt, Chelsea Mollenbrandt, and Michael Mollenbrandt); and two great-grandchildren.

One of the reasons I left A&M was because I was single. When I moved back to Schulenburg, I talked to the school superintendent, and I told him that the next time he brought an attractive, young teacher into Schulenburg to let me know. So he called and let me know that they had a new teacher. I called her immediately and asked her to go out with me. She was 21 at the time. Sixty days later, we got engaged, and 60 days after that, we were married.

Vera and I have been together ever since. When we sold our College Station Oak Ridge Restaurant in 1995, I decided I wanted to give the proceeds to the school that helped me set the foundation for my successful business career. Even at 88, I am not completely retired. I now grow trees in Schulenburg, and I have 14,000 live oaks on my property.

But the seeds for all my success were planted at Texas A&M. I sold the College Station restaurant for $500,000 and gave all the money to the A&M Foundation. I put it in a charitable remainder trust. Upon the death of my wife and me, half of it will go to the 12th Man Foundation and the other half to the Corps of Cadets. A&M has meant so much to me. I love A&M, and other than finding my wife in Schulenburg, I wish I had never left College Station. It's still a very special place.

Right guard Roy Bucek was injured in the first game of the 1939 season, but he still played in every game that season. During his three seasons on the varsity, the Aggies went 29–3. Bucek lost his left eye in World War II, but he returned to his hometown in Schulenburg, Texas, to begin an extremely successful business career.

JESSE "RED" BURDITT

RECEIVER

1943 ★ 1946–1947

JUST BEFORE I WAS INDUCTED into the Texas A&M Athletic Hall of Fame in 2003, my oldest boy, Jess, summed everything up regarding my status as an A&M athlete when he looked me in the eye and said sincerely, "Daddy, just think. You're about to have your picture up there next to some real football players."

I've said for many years that I do not belong in the Lettermen's Hall of Fame. For that matter, I've joked with the authors of this book—Rusty Burson and Cathy Capps—that I don't deserve all the attention they have given me for many years. My greatest accomplishments in regard to Texas A&M athletics are that I was just talented to letter in numerous sports, and that I was the organizer of the various reunions held for one of the most overachieving and inspiring teams in Aggie football history.

As far as I can tell from the official A&M athletic records, I am one of only nine Aggies to letter in three sports, picking up varsity honors in football, basketball, and baseball. But I am probably best known as the historian and top promoter of the Kiddie Korps, a rag-tag group of youngsters who in 1943 captured the imagination of Texas A&M students and former students everywhere by overcoming the longest of odds to reach the Orange Bowl. In that game against LSU, I set an A&M bowl-game record by catching six passes against the Tigers. The record was finally broken in the 2009 Independence Bowl when Jeff Fuller caught seven passes.

I think it was about time somebody topped that record. After all, it's been a long time since the 1944 Orange Bowl, although I admit that I still vividly recall the six receptions I made that day. For that matter, there is very little about the entire 1943 season that I don't remember. I've replayed the moments and the magic of that season countless times in my mind.

Outside of my wife, family, and my coaching career, playing on the Kiddie Korps team was probably the greatest thing to ever happen to me. We waited 50 years and then had a reunion in '93. We had our 60th reunion during the 2003 season. We had a squad of 72 that year and had 27 here for the '03 reunion. We've lost some of those guys since the reunion in '03, and there aren't many of us left. But it was certainly a very special team. What most people find hard to believe is that we weren't surprised that we were that successful. No matter the circumstances, it never entered our minds that we weren't going to be good.

It entered the minds of virtually everyone else, though. Most sportswriters believed the '43 Aggies were destined for a devastating season, labeling the Aggies in the preseason as "the beardless boys of Aggieland" and a "glorified high school team." One writer even asked our head coach, Homer Norton, if the Aggies might be better off by following the lead of Baylor and sitting out the '43 season altogether. "Definitely not," Norton said at the time. "If I can find 11 boys on this campus who will suit up, we will have a football team."

Remember back then that the Aggies had established themselves as one of the nation's elite programs by winning the national title in 1939, claiming an SWC co-championship in '40, and winning another outright conference title in '41. But that began to change on December 7, 1941, when the attack on Pearl Harbor officially brought the United States into World War II. For the all-male military school in College Station, war would bring about many changes.

Among them was A&M's status as a football powerhouse. Through the Army's A-12 program and the Navy's V-12 program, thousands of A&M upperclassmen were drafted into officer training schools. By the spring of 1943 the A&M football roster was decimated by the draft. In fact, only one varsity player from the Aggies' 1942 roster returned for the '43 season.

I came to A&M in '43, and that was the year they cleaned out all of the upperclassmen because of the war. But here's the thing that is really

Jesse "Red" Burditt is one of only nine Aggies to letter in three sports, picking up varsity honors in football, basketball, and baseball.

interesting: if you were an upperclassman and a football player, you weren't going overseas directly.

They sent you to colleges that had the training schools for a couple of semesters first. So all of these other schools—Rice, Texas, and so forth—that had A-12 and V-12 programs would recruit the best players. We didn't have those programs at A&M. And ol' Earl Red Blaik really cleaned up at Army, picking up guys like Doc Blanchard, Glenn Davis, and Aggies like Marion Flanagan, Bill Yeoman, Hank Foldberg, and Goble Bryant. Military bases also picked guys up, and they played against college teams, too.

Randolph Field in San Antonio had 16 All-Americans on its team. And when we played Rice in 1943, there were seven guys on that team who had been playing at A&M in 1942. Practically all of our upperclassmen were gone.

But in the true spirit of the 12th Man, Coach Norton solicited what remained of the Corps of Cadets for football tryouts. When practices began in late July of 1943, 130 youngsters showed up for those practices, including me. The average age of the 1943 Aggies was only 17½ years old. But even as the sportswriters snickered, we began pulling off upsets. By the time we pulled off back-to-back road upsets at LSU and TCU, we were 4–0 and developing some legitimate star power.

18

We just believed we were supposed to be good because we were Texas Aggies. And for me personally it was a dream come true to be playing for the Aggies. My father was in the class of '21. From the day I can remember, the only thing I ever wanted to do was go to Texas A&M and play football. But coming out of Abilene High School, where I graduated at midterm, I arrived at A&M in the spring of '43 thinking I had no chance to play. I didn't even come to spring practice because I weighed only 158 pounds.

But that summer is when Coach Norton put an article in the paper saying that he needed football players. I was pretty cocky and said, "Hey, give me a uniform, and I think I can make your football team." I wasn't very big, but I had run a 9.7 in the 100-yard dash in high school. And I had a burning desire to prove I could play.

The rest of our boys had that same burning desire, and heading into the regular-season finale against Texas, we were 7–0–1. With the SWC title on the line, I accounted for a school-record 125 receiving yards against the Long-horns. Texas ultimately prevailed 27–13, but we were still extremely attractive to the bowl representatives. We accepted a bid to the Orange Bowl for a rematch with LSU, where Steve Van Buren proved to be too much for us to handle. Van Buren rushed for two touchdowns and passed for another as LSU beat us 19–14.

By 1944 many of the key contributors of our Kiddie Korps had been "drafted" into other lend-lease programs. After also playing basketball and baseball during my freshman year, I wound up playing football for North Texas Agriculture College in 1944, and then I was shipped to Pearl Harbor in 1945.

After serving my country as a radio man in Hawaii, I returned to College Station to finish my degree in physical education and married my high school sweetheart, Elinor. I lettered again for the Aggie football team in 1947 and '48 and also earned a varsity letter on the baseball team in 1948.

I then coached high school football for 12 seasons, compiling a 75–42 record and three district championships while at Hamlin [just outside Abilene], Lockhart, and Bryan High. If I had not been so competitive, I may have spent my entire professional career in coaching.

I loved high school football, and I still love it. But I quit in 1960 because I had asthma so bad in the fall from stress. I was my worst enemy. I just couldn't stand to lose. I got asthma attacks in September, and it wouldn't be until Christmas that I got over them.

When I hung up my coaching whistle for the final time, I joined the Jefferson Pilot Life Insurance Company as an agent and financial planner. I unofficially retired from that role in 1991, but I still go to the office in Bryan, serving my clients as an independent insurance agent and financial advisor.

The main point for me now is to work with people and to keep on the run. I'd go crazy and probably drive my wife crazy if I was just sitting around the house. I like to stay active, and I certainly like to help A&M in any way I can. I love that school. Aside from my own memories, I have two grown boys, Jesse III and Charles, and four grandchildren, two of whom graduated from Texas A&M.

So I am a proud Aggie in many, many ways. I am also proud of the fact that in 1997 I helped raise $35,000 from my teammates for a 12th Man Foundation–endowed scholarship. As far as I know, the 1943 team is the only A&M squad that has given such an endowment as a team.

So that's how I have helped to leave a legacy at Texas A&M. But even with as many donations as I have made through the years, I could never pay back

A&M for all that it gave me. I've always thought that far-fetched dreams were achievable because I was part of one of the most overachieving college football teams I've ever seen.

Red Burditt is one of only nine Aggies to letter in three sports, picking up varsity honors in football, basketball, and baseball. As a member of the Kiddie Korps football team in 1943, Burditt set an A&M bowl-game record by catching six passes against LSU in the 1944 Orange Bowl. The record was finally broken in the 2009 Independence Bowl. After a successful stint as a high school football coach, Burditt joined the Jefferson Pilot Life Insurance Company in 1960 as an agent and financial planner.

The FIFTIES

BILLY PETE HUDDLESTON

HALFBACK

1953–1955

O NE OF MY FAVORITE PLACES in the world is our 500-acre property just south of Navasota, called the Double H Ranch, located a couple miles off of Highway 6. When my wife, Flora, and I bought the property in 1986, there wasn't a blade of grass on it. Now the ranch features areas of lush sod, a man-made pond stocked with catfish and topped by black and white swans that we purchased, and about 60 life-sized, bronzed statues of animals that have been imported from around the world.

We've also added a cedar-lined barn that is perfect for hosting family, friends, and A&M gatherings. We're also very proud of the wildlife on the property, including black buck antelope, red deer, water bucks, addaxes, oryx, and rare breeds of sheep.

Right from the start, we built a game-proof fence. We grew up in the oil field and never had been in the ranching business, so we thought exotic wildlife would be fun. We've got about 200 exotic animals. We make money off of cows because we run about 150, but the exotics are just kind of fun. We had zebras out here at one time, but they killed everything in sight. They're gone now, but we've had a lot of fun raising and learning about the exotics and rare breeds.

Perhaps I've always been intrigued by rare breeds because I encountered so many one-of-a-kind individuals during my time at Texas A&M, beginning

Billy Pete Huddleston lettered in 1953 under coach Ray George and was a member of coach Paul "Bear" Bryant's famed "Junction Boys." He was a captain on Bryant's 1955 team that went 7–2–1, and Bryant later offered Huddleston a coaching job at the University of Alabama. *Photo courtesy of Billy Pete Huddleston*

with Coach Bear Bryant. My time at A&M gave me a great foundation for future success.

I've enjoyed a very prosperous career as an innovative petroleum entrepreneur, and I've brokered deals from Round Rock to Russia. I was raised in Iraan [pronounced "Ira Anne"], Texas, a town with no red lights, which is why I probably never learned the meaning of "stop." I've turned a profit with "junk oil properties," and I've built a great business after starting with virtually nothing.

The key to my success—if you want to call it that—is that work really has never been work for me. I don't get stressed out about work. It's easy for me to go to work every day. I still enjoy what I do. I do a lot of consulting work for different companies, and I still go to work at least four days a week.

When the *Junction Boys* movie was about to come out, ESPN came to the office in Houston and interviewed me, and the reporter asked, "Was Junction the toughest thing you ever did in your life?" I said, "Heavens no. The toughest thing was thermodynamics class at A&M."

They said, "Well, what did you learn from Junction?" I said, "I learned I could go a lot longer without a drink of water than I thought I could." Life

24

Huddleston lost 16 pounds at the famed Junction trip led by coach Bear Bryant in 1954, but he says he never even thought about quitting. *Photo courtesy of Texas A&M Sport Museum*

is about perspective; it's what you make of the situations you encounter. I've tried to look at everything as an opportunity to grow or prosper.

At Iraan High, I helped lead our school to second place in the Class B track meet. I actually scored every point by myself. I was also an all-state football player, and I played in the 1952 North-South All-Star Game and the Texas-Oklahoma All-Star Game.

All the major powers in college football, including Notre Dame, Texas, USC, Florida, and Oklahoma, expressed interest in me. Some even offered me plenty of monetary incentives to attend their schools. But my oldest brother, Kenneth, was A&M Class of '50, and a former student by the name of Murray Fasken punched all the right buttons to help lead me to College Station.

One school brought me a letter with a check for $2,500 and offered me two scholarships, one for myself and one for my fiancé. The next day, Murray Fasken, from the Midland National Bank, asked me, "Who are you going to sign with?"

I said, "I've got this offer here for $2,500, which is what my dad makes in a year." Murray says, "We didn't know you were for sale." I said, "For sale?" He said, "If you take that money, they bought you." I said, "I'm not for sale." So I signed with A&M without so much as a hamburger.

I played on the freshman team in '52 and lettered on the varsity in '53, as the Aggies went 4–5–1 under Ray George. Then in 1954 Coach Bear Bryant arrived in Aggieland, and everything changed.

Coach Bryant's spring training was grueling; and his legendary trip to Junction at the start of the '54 season was excruciating. But it has also been overblown and exaggerated.

Coach Bryant made us better football players, but we had character when we got there. I lost 16 pounds, but I never thought about quitting. It wasn't going to happen. But I believe everyone has had or will have a Junction in his or her life, a defining moment when you had to prove yourself—a time in your life where you had to reach down and dig a little harder.

Half the team quit in Junction, as everybody's heard, and we were dreadful that following season, going 1–9. I had to shoot up with novocaine to play because I had injured ankles. Years later, I read Coach Bryant's book, and he said one of things he was proudest of was that he never permitted drugs. So I found out that novocaine is not a drug. Coach Bryant was testing us, and what I remember from that whole experience has little to do with football.

25

My grades were really dropping, and I was in trouble academically because I was concentrating so much on football.

I was down by the engineering building and saw two guys in the Corps come by carrying their books. They had slide rules hanging off their belts. I was like Saul from the Bible on the road to Damascus. The light came down on me, and I said, "Boy, you're here to get an education, not just to play football." That's what I learned from Junction.

I was a captain on the 1955 team that went 7–2–1, and I went to work for Marathon Oil in Bay City after my graduation. Early on in my career at Marathon, I received a call from Coach Bryant, who offered me a job as the defensive backfield coach at Alabama. At the time, I was making $4,000 per year. Coach Bryant offered me twice as much.

That was tough to turn down. I had been working for a year, and I said, "Coach, I've worked too hard to get to be an engineer. I'm going to stick it out."

That was a good decision. I worked six years for Marathon Oil and was offered a promotion that would have moved me and my family to New York. But my wife decided against the move. So, with $2,500 in total assets, I went into business for myself.

I resigned in 1967, and we moved to Houston. I rented a storage closet as an office in a Class C building and said I was a consulting engineer. I didn't even know anybody in Houston. I had a folding card table, but I didn't have a chair. A guy on the same floor loaned me a chair. I didn't have any credit, so I couldn't get a commercial telephone. The geologist whose office backed into mine cut a hole in his office where I could reach over on his receptionist's desk and use the phone.

From those simple beginnings, I built a thriving business. In 1971 I started buying small interest oil properties known as "junk." The industry viewed the properties as the equivalent of slum housing, but I made a fortune on them. In about a decade, I'd made several million dollars.

Then Princeton University Endowment Fund came to me in '85 or '86 and said they wanted to join up with me as a partner. I already had some partners out in Atlanta, so we cranked our budget up big time. Now our partnerships run a net cash flow of about $100 million a year. No debt. Princeton and our original investors are still with us. We've never missed making money in any partnership we've had.

From 1981 to 1998, I also taught two three-hour courses at A&M. During that time, I taught more than 1,000 students, and I only had two that failed.

The only reason they failed is because they left school and I couldn't find them. If you got below a B in my class, you had to have make-up classes on Saturday. Nothing beats teaching. The fun of it is seeing where they are when they start and where they wind up. I got a long, handwritten letter from a young man named Don Gray, who said he kept the manual I wrote on the corner of his desk and read it almost every day. I had the guys at the office look him up on the Internet, and they discovered he had formed a company in Canada that is worth $200 million. I said, "Maybe I better go back and read that manual again. What did I miss?"

We actually haven't missed out on much. We have three very successful children and eight grandchildren; we have two thriving businesses [Huddleston & Co. and Peter Paul Petroleum Co.]; and we have donated more than 100 scholarships to aspiring students. I've also been honored as a Distinguished Alumni at Texas A&M, and in 2006 I was inducted into the Corps of Cadets Hall of Honor.

They key in life or business is to learn from your mistakes and to duplicate your successes. I've done that numerous times in my life, beginning with my days at Texas A&M.

After a stellar prep career at Iraan High School, Billy Pete Huddleston lettered on the varsity in 1953 under Ray George, and he was a member of Coach Bear Bryant's famed "Junction Boys." The hard-nosed Huddleston was a captain on the 1955 team that went 7–2–1, and he was offered a coaching job at Alabama by Bryant. Huddleston turned down the coaching offer and later started his own engineering consulting business in Houston. Through the years, he built two thriving businesses (Huddleston & Co. and Peter Paul Petroleum Co.) and has donated more than 100 scholarships to aspiring students. He was honored as a Distinguished Alumni at Texas A&M, and in 2006 he was inducted into the Corps of Cadets Hall of Honor.

JACK PARDEE

FULLBACK/LINEBACKER

1954–1956

I DIDN'T COME TO TEXAS A&M with visions of becoming a great football player, and winning a conference championship wasn't high on my priority list, either. To be honest, I came to Texas A&M with visions of air-conditioning.

I went to high school in Christoval, a tiny town approximately 20 miles south of San Angelo in southern Tom Green County. My dad had severe arthritis, and I had five brothers and sisters, so money was tight. During the summers—starting when I was about 14 and continuing on through high school—I'd work on these nasty, dirty, hot oil-field jobs, and every once in a while I'd see these guys drive up in a nice car or a nice pickup to give instructions to my boss.

What left the biggest impression on me was the fact that when they would roll down their windows, the air-conditioning inside the vehicle would pour out. It felt like a little bit of heaven, and it didn't take me long to figure out that I would rather be one of those guys inside the car as opposed to being on the oil-field crew. After asking a lot of questions, I discovered those guys inside the car were petroleum engineers.

I didn't know the difference between a petroleum engineer and a train engineer at that time, but it stuck in my mind that being an engineer might be a good thing. Several years later when I began being recruited by Texas A&M, I was pretty intrigued by the fact that A&M had a program to help you become an engineer.

Of course, it wasn't like I had a lot of other colleges beating down my door. At Christoval, we played six-man football. I scored more than 300 points during my senior year, and I played for a wonderful high school coach who left a lasting impression on my life.

There were only eight of us on the entire team, and we were not known as a college football factory back in those days.

But Coach [G.W.] Tillerson was our head coach and our school superintendent, and his wife was a teacher, too. He believed that we could achieve greater things in life by pursuing higher education, and I believe all eight of us ended up going to college. That was a pretty amazing thing back then. Coach Tillerson probably had the biggest influence on my life, maybe even more so than my parents at the time.

So I was open to the idea of going to college for many reasons. I also liked the structure of the military. And then there was a man named Jack Rollins, who was the manager of the Sears & Roebuck in San Angelo. I think he was A&M Class of '41. He was a successful guy who also refereed some of my six-man football games.

I was impossible not to notice. I was 6'2" and about 200 pounds, which made me a lot bigger than most of the boys I was playing with and against. Jack really began recommending me to the A&M coaches—Ray George was the head coach at the time, and Willie Zapalac was the freshman coach. Rice and a couple of other schools offered me scholarships, but Jack really sold me to the coaches at A&M. They offered me a scholarship, and that's where I wanted to go.

29

I had considered going to West Point, Navy, or one of the other academies, but A&M was a perfect fit for me because of its military structure and the opportunity to play football. My parents didn't have much money. They were great parents, but having the military furnish my clothes, putting food on the training table, and getting an education…it didn't get any better than that.

At the time, there were only about 6,000 male students at A&M, so it was a small campus. The friendliness of the campus made an impression on me right away. You'd be walking down the street, and you would hear students say, "Howdy." I felt like part of the A&M family right away because of that friendliness.

After my first year, I had literally met everybody on campus. That's just the way it was back then. Even though you were not best friends with everyone, it was a very friendly campus and was one of the big reasons I chose to

Jack Pardee went to Junction in 1954 as a fifth-team sophomore fullback and linebacker. After playing about eight different positions and losing more than 10 pounds during the camp, he returned as one of the Aggies' key players.

go there over the other schools. I also loved the traditions of A&M, especially Silver Taps and Muster. Those are the two traditions that I feel can never be replaced. They are unique to A&M and mean a lot to every Aggie out there.

I loved A&M right away, but coming from West Texas, I was in for a shock in terms of practicing. At first, I didn't know if I could make it with the heat and humidity of College Station. It was so humid and so miserably hot.

Coach Zapalac probably questioned whether I had the demeanor to play college football during my freshman season. When I arrived at A&M there were 110 freshmen on the team, give or take a few, and at that point I felt a bit lost in the shuffle. I was very quiet and reserved, and it took me a while to adjust to the game after playing six-man football.

During my first year at A&M, the varsity went 4–5–1 under Coach Ray George, who completed his third season with the Aggies in '53. That also turned out to be his last season. Texas A&M then brought in a new coach from Kentucky named Paul "Bear" Bryant.

Anybody who had followed college football probably knows about Coach Bryant, and anyone who knows about A&M has probably heard about Junction.

More than 100 players went to Junction for Coach Bryant's "mini camp," but after 10 grueling days of practice, only about 40 players came back as members of the team. I went into Junction as a fifth-team sophomore fullback and linebacker. After playing about eight different positions and losing more than 10 pounds during the camp, I returned as one of the Aggies' key players.

There was one heat stroke, and we were real fortunate no one died. But Coach Bryant believed one of the keys to winning was to be in better condition than your opponents and to be tougher than they were. Those of us who came back from Junction were certainly toughened.

A lot of boys quit during that time, but quitting honestly never crossed my mind. I was in good shape because I had been working in the oil fields, and I had those oil fields on my mind. If I quit football, I knew I was going to have to go back to those oil fields, and my momma and daddy would have been harder on me than Coach Bryant.

I also remember that when Coach Bryant came to A&M, I was living with Charles Hartley, a player from Odessa. We lived in Hart Hall on F Ramp on the second floor. There were four rooms and eight people to each ramp. After Coach Bryant got there, there were only two of us left, Billy Pickard and me. So we moved in together and became roommates because we were the last men standing on that ramp.

We had a miserable season in 1954, going 1–9. The only win of the season—a 6–0 victory at Georgia—was an anomaly of sorts. In reviewing films of Georgia, assistant coach Elmer Smith noticed that the Georgia quarterback tipped off the plays by how he aligned his feet. So I checked the quarterback's feet before I called the defensive plays, and we were usually waiting for the Bulldogs as the plays developed. It was the only highlight of A&M's second one-win season in a span of six years.

But we came back much stronger the next year and finished 7–2–1. It was obvious that Coach Bryant was building a good team with very tough guys.

Then in 1956 we rolled to an 8–0–1 record heading into the final game of the season at Texas. We had only beaten the Longhorns once since the national championship season of 1939 and had not won in Memorial Stadium in 16 previous trips.

But on November 29, 1956, we Aggies exorcised some demons and destroyed the Horns 34–21. Leading 21–14 at the half, we took complete control in the third quarter. I returned the opening kickoff of the third quarter 85 yards and scored two plays later on an eight-yard run. The victory gave us our first SWC title since 1941.

The Los Angeles Rams selected me in the second round of the 1957 NFL Draft, which was a thrill for me. Los Angeles was obviously a dramatic change for a country boy from a tiny town. But I felt right at home on the football field, and I played for Los Angeles from 1957 to 1970 and eventually became an All-Pro.

When I was 28, I was diagnosed with skin cancer. Fortunately, the doctors caught the cancer in time, but dealing with cancer really changed my perspective on life. Football had been so much of my focus up until that point, but I really began focusing more on my family and some long-term objectives.

I met my wife, Phyllis, on a blind date during my senior year at A&M, and we have been so blessed through the years with five wonderful children—Steven, Judy, Ann, Susan, and Ted.

After being diagnosed with cancer, I continued to play, and when head coach George Allen made the move to Washington, I moved with him, joining Coach Allen as a player/coach for the 1971 and '72 seasons. The final game I ever played was in Super Bowl VII against the Miami Dolphins.

Overall, I played 15 seasons in the NFL, and I enjoyed so many aspects of the game. First of all, I was exposed to so many great players, coaches, and people. It's hard to imagine a higher high or a lower low than life in the NFL. You can go from the mountaintop to the valley very quickly. But I had a lot of great times. And I always liked the challenges.

With my playing days behind me, I accepted the head-coaching position of the Florida Blazers in a 12-team confederation known as the World Football League in 1974. The league included teams such as the Philadelphia Bell, the Chicago Fire, and the Southern California Sun, and it had plenty of twists—such as seven-point touchdowns with an "action point" play to follow and goal posts at the end lines. Unfortunately, two months into the 20-week season of midweek games, the WFL was in major financial trouble.

But in my first head-coaching job, I led the Blazers into the championship game. We lost the title game, but I guess I had made enough of an impression to earn an opportunity as the head coach of the Chicago Bears the following year. I coached the Bears from 1975 to 1977 and then returned to Washington as the head coach of the Redskins from 1978 to 1980.

Following an ownership change in Washington, I was out of work. That's when I made a move that would eventually change my image forever. In 1981 I went to San Diego as an assistant to Don Coryell to learn how to win by throwing the football. Until that time, all I had really been associated with was power running offenses. It was a great experience, and I learned a lot.

After sitting out of football in 1982, I became the head coach of the USFL's Houston Gamblers in '83. With Jim Kelly at quarterback and a variety of other future NFL players on the roster, we introduced an exciting new offense known as the run-and-shoot. We never won a USFL title, but we were certainly exciting. And in 1987 the University of Houston called and asked if I would be interested in adding some excitement to its program.

The Cougars had finished the 1986 season with a 1–10 overall record and an 0–8 mark in the SWC. Our first season didn't start much better, as we went 1–6. But on November 7, 1987, we began to turn it around by shocking Texas 60–40. We didn't lose another game the rest of the season.

It was an exciting time. Then in 1988 we won nine games, finished in the top 20, and went to the Aloha Bowl. Although we were on probation and were unable to play on television, the 1989 season was even better. We went 9–2 in the regular season, losing only to A&M and Arkansas, and finished 14th in both polls. Furthermore, quarterback Andre Ware won the Heisman Trophy after producing some incredible passing numbers.

As a result of my success with the Gamblers and the Cougars, I was chosen to replace Jerry Glanville as the Oilers' head coach in 1990. I had a good time with the Oilers, taking the team to its first two divisional titles and making four straight playoff appearances [1990–1993]. Unfortunately, we could not press through the playoffs. We lost in the first round three times and lost a big lead in Buffalo in January of '93.

Then during the off-season in 1994, the bottom dropped out. The NFL's new salary cap cost us four Pro Bowl players, including quarterback Warren Moon. After we started 1–9, I was fired.

But I had a great run in football and have no regrets. I've always felt very blessed that I was able to do what I love to do as long as I did. Going all the way back to Texas A&M, I was very, very fortunate to be around some wonderful people. I was just a shy kid, barely 17 years old when I first came to Texas A&M.

Playing football and being a part of that university, with all the friendly people, kind of brought me out of my shell. I had a great career and gained a lot of great memories along the way. I don't get back to A&M much these days, as I choose to stay here on my ranch in Gause, which is just outside of Hearne. But I still think about all those times and great friends I met at A&M all the time.

Interestingly, people have asked me how I came up with the run-and-shoot concept. I tell them I credit Coach Bryant with providing me with the inspiration. Coach Bryant was never really into specific plays or systems. He always had the ability to adapt to his players and get the most out of them. He obviously didn't teach me the run-and-shoot. In fact, we always had three backs in the backfield at A&M. But we began running the run-and-shoot with the Gamblers in part because I learned from Coach Bryant that you don't have to be married to a specific system to be a successful coach.

We needed something that would help us compete, give us an edge. That's why I ran the run-and-shoot with the Gamblers, the University of Houston, and with the Oilers. But when I was the head coach of the Chicago Bears, we might run the ball 37 times a game because we had Walter Payton. Those people in Chicago didn't think I had a creative bone in my body. Still, it was what suited our team the best. That's what Coach Bryant always did, and that's what I always tried to do. From Coach Bryant, I learned you have to recognize what you have and make the most of it.

That's a great lesson for football…and for life in general.

Jack Pardee was an All-American in 1956 after leading the Aggies to their first Southwest Conference title in 15 years. The Los Angeles Rams selected him in the second round in the 1957 NFL Draft, and he played for Los Angeles from 1957 to 1970. Pardee joined George Allen in Washington as a player/coach for the 1971 and 1972 seasons. The final game he played in was Super Bowl VII. Pardee began his coaching career in the WFL in 1974, leading Florida to the championship game. He later coached the Chicago Bears from 1975 to 1977 and returned to Washington as head coach of the Redskins from 1978 to 1980. After sitting out of football in 1982, he became head coach of the USFL's Houston Gamblers in 1983. He also coached at the University of Houston and with the Houston Oilers, taking the team to two divisional titles and making four straight playoff appearances (1990–1993).

The SIXTIES

GRADY ALLEN

LINEMAN

1965–1967

L IKE SO MANY OTHER AGGIES, I have always enjoyed hearing the fascinating stories about Coach Bear Bryant's famed Junction trip of 1954. I've spoken with many of the survivors of that trip. I've also read numerous stories about how a 1956 championship team was formed on that trip to the drought-devastated town of Junction in August of '54.

Those hard-nosed young men who endured the hellish training camp helped Coach Bryant win a Southwest Conference championship just two years later.

It's a remarkable story. Magazine stories, books, and even a made-for-TV movie produced by ESPN have documented that trip. But what may not be as well known—even in Aggie circles—is that Junction had a sequel set roughly 10 years later in College Station.

It didn't involve a bus trip, and Coach Bryant didn't lead it, but the similarities were rather amazing. In December of 1964, following the release of A&M head coach Hank Foldberg, the Aggies hired Junction survivor and Coach Bryant disciple Gene Stallings to take over the slumping program.

Much as Coach Bryant first addressed his massive team, Coach Stallings gathered our team together, which numbered about 150, and told us to go enjoy the Christmas break. But when we came back, Coach Stallings warned us, it was going to be time to go to work.

Grady Allen was an All-SWC defensive end in 1967 and was the Aggie Heart Award winner that same year. His son, Dennis, played safety for A&M in the early and mid-1990s. Dennis was also a secondary coach for New Orleans when the Saints won Super Bowl XLIV.

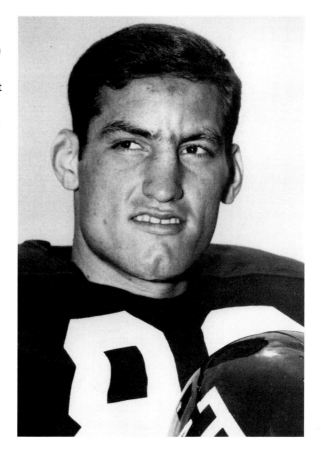

Little did we know at the time exactly what that meant. I had played on an unsuccessful freshman team in '64, and our varsity had gone 1–9 that same season. Furthermore, Coach Foldberg had a three-year record of 6–23–1, so we knew some changes were probably necessary.

On the first day after we came back from Christmas break, we were all gathered in this little workout room, wondering what to expect. Then, the assistants on Coach Stallings' staff came in carrying five-gallon buckets. I was thinking, *What are those for?*

It took me about 15 or 20 minutes to realize that those were depositories for what we had eaten earlier in the day. At the end of 45 minutes, I was just wondering if I could take another breath. It was grueling. And from everything I've been told and read about Junction, that off-season program was kind of a mini-Junction on campus.

It also had similar results. I think we began the 1965 season with approximately 65 players, down from the 150 who had started the off-season program.

We struggled initially, although we started the 1965 season with a 2–2 record. We lost 10–0 at LSU and were beaten 20–16 at Texas Tech. But we won at Georgia Tech and we came home to beat Houston 10–7.

Unfortunately, we just didn't have the depth to survive a long season. After our decent start, we lost 17–9 at TCU. Then we were shut out in our next three games. Baylor, Arkansas, and SMU outscored us by a combined score of 72–0. We finished the year at 3–7.

But we continued working, and we took a step in the right direction in 1966. We finished the year at 4–5–1, but there were signs that we were getting much better. For example, we whipped Texas Tech and TCU, and tied LSU in Baton Rouge.

We were all very excited about the 1967 season, but then it started disastrously for us. We lost the season-opener 20–17 to SMU on the very last play of the game. We might have still been thinking about that SMU disappointment during the next game when Purdue beat us 24–20.

We then had to go to LSU, where the Tigers were looking for revenge after we had tied them in '66. They got their revenge, beating us 17–6. Then we came home and lost 19–18 to Florida State in a pouring rain. We could have easily been 3–1 at that point, but instead we were 0–4.

We had worked way too hard to give up on the season, though. And even though Texas Tech took a late 24–21 lead in the fifth game of the season in Lubbock, we rallied for a thrilling victory when our quarterback, Edd Hargett, scored a touchdown on the last play of the game.

That win was just the confidence boost we needed. After starting the season 0–4, we rolled off six consecutive victories to win the 1967 Southwest Conference title. All that hard work had paid off. All the times we had deposited our lunch into the five-gallon buckets was worth it.

Our mini-Junction had produced the desired results. Ironically, our reward for winning the SWC was a trip to the Cotton Bowl to face Coach Bryant's Alabama Crimson Tide. Alabama, led by quarterback Ken Stabler, was ranked No. 8 in the nation. While they may have been a better team than we were, we were on a mission.

We converted an interception and a fumble into a 13–10 halftime lead and took control in the third quarter when our fullback, Wendell Housley, bulled in for a touchdown. Stabler engineered one more scoring drive for the Tide, but our defense stiffened in the fourth quarter to preserve a 20–16 win.

For me, that is still probably the best birthday present I ever received. That was a fantastic game and a season I will never forget.

Coach Stallings used to joke with me, saying I was probably the slowest defensive end in America. But he toughened me up and helped turn me into an All–Southwest Conference performer in '67. But the bigger honor for me was when my teammates chose me as the Aggie Heart Award winner in 1967.

I owe Coach Stallings so much. Playing for him, and having endured the mental stress and strain that he demanded of us, gave me the opportunity to play five years in the NFL with the Falcons. After going through Coach Stallings' workouts, it made it a lot easier for me to make it in Atlanta. Training camp in Atlanta was a cakewalk compared to the off-seasons and two-a-day practices I went through at A&M.

Playing for Coach Stallings, under those circumstances, really shaped my football career. I think it probably also helped shape my life in terms of understanding and applying discipline, dedication, and perseverance.

Like the Junction boys, most of the men who endured "Camp Stallings" have thrived in their professional lives after football. So many of my A&M teammates have enjoyed wonderfully successful careers.

39

After a knee surgery cut my NFL career short, I worked in the life insurance industry for a year and then opened a restaurant in Atlanta before finding my niche in the industrial chemical business. In sales or management, I was involved in that industry for more than 25 years, building a successful and strong business reputation in the Dallas–Fort Worth area. In many ways, my football experiences were largely responsible for my business success.

I love the sales nature of the business because it keeps my competitive juices flowing. I learned right away that being behind a desk would drive me insane. And I would estimate that 50 percent or more of my business was directly or indirectly related to my having gone to Texas A&M. And that could be as high as about 75 percent. Obviously, A&M has meant the world to me.

And I have shared my love for A&M with my family. All three of my children attended A&M, and two graduated. Geoff attended A&M for three years and left with a 4.0 GPA for Southwestern Medical School. He is a pediatric intensive care specialist at Children's Hospital in Dallas.

Our youngest child, Ann Marie, is also an A&M graduate and is now working for a law firm in Dallas. And our middle child, Dennis, followed in his father's footsteps, lettering for the Aggies from 1992 to 1995. Of course, Dennis was blessed with a little more speed than I was.

Dennis started 21 consecutive games in the A&M secondary and helped the Aggies win two SWC titles. Now Dennis is the secondary coach for the New Orleans Saints, and he is celebrating their victory over the Indianapolis Colts in Super Bowl XLIV—the team's first trip to the big game and first NFL title.

Fortunately, Dennis received some of his mother's athletic genes. If I was an architect or engineer, I couldn't build or design a better mother and wife than Kay. She deserves all the credit for raising three outstanding children, of whom I am very proud.

One of my proudest parental moments came at Kyle Field in late November of 1993. With the Longhorns driving for the potential go-ahead score and the conference title at stake, Dennis intercepted a Shea Morenz pass in the end zone late in the fourth quarter. The Aggies then marched the length of the field for a game-icing field goal, an 18–9 victory and their third consecutive SWC title.

Words can't express how thrilled I was to be able to witness that in person. Here we were playing our hated rival, and my son made the key play to beat those SOBs. It was something I will never forget. When I was a player at A&M, I didn't think anything could top the feeling of beating Texas at Kyle Field for the conference championship in 1967. But that ranks right up there with it. My maroon blood was really pumping that night.

Hopefully, I have many more magic maroon moments ahead of me. I'd love to see some of my grandchildren at A&M one day, too.

Grady Allen was an All–Southwest Conference defensive end in 1967, the same year he won the prestigious Aggie Heart Award. Allen played five years in the NFL with the Atlanta Falcons. He then began a highly successful career in the industrial chemical business. All three of his children attended A&M, and two graduated from A&M. One of his sons, Dennis, was a defensive back for the Aggies from 1992 to 1995. Grady Allen attended Super Bowl XLIV in 2010, where he watched Dennis serve as the secondary coach for New Orleans when the Saints won their first Super Bowl.

EDD HARGETT

QUARTERBACK
1966–1968

THROUGHOUT THE YEARS, I've probably received way more recognition from Texas A&M fans and former students than I ever deserved. For example, I was inducted into the Texas A&M Lettermen's Athletic Hall of Fame in 1974, and I have been honored numerous times since then by my alma mater in various ways.

I've also been included in books about A&M like this one, as well as magazine stories, television reports, and so forth. I really am grateful for the tributes and honored by the praises, and if you only paid attention to the glowing stories about me you might be led to believe that I was a remarkable quarterback on a sensational team.

But here's the truth: I was a pretty good quarterback on a pretty good, overachieving 1967 team. Period.

I'm convinced that the reason I have continued to receive attention from Aggies 40 years later—and the reason I've been asked to be included in this book, as well as others—is because we were so bad for so long before and after that one shining season.

Following the departure of Bear Bryant after the 1957 season, the Aggies began one of the most forgettable stretches in school history. With the exception of 1967, A&M did not win more than four games in a season from 1958 to 1970. Included in that stretch were two seasons [1960 and 1964] when the Aggies only won a single game.

Edd Hargett scored the game-winning touchdown as time expired against Texas Tech in 1967. That victory turned the season around and propelled the Aggies to the SWC title.

My older brother, George, played football and baseball at A&M from 1961 to 1963. There was also a big A&M supporter, Tom Lanier, from my hometown—Linden, in far northeast Texas near the Arkansas and Louisiana state lines—who owned a Chevrolet dealership and regularly took me to College Station to see games.

I really loved A&M, and I bled maroon as a student-athlete at Linden-Kildare High School. But honestly, the Aggies were so bad back then that I nearly went to Arkansas. The distance from my hometown to Fayetteville, Arkansas, was about the same as to College Station, and my head was telling me it would be wiser to be a Razorback.

Even Elmer Smith, who had first been an assistant coach at A&M under Bear Bryant in 1954 and stayed in Aggieland for the next 18 years as an assistant, couldn't muster much excitement regarding A&M's program when he was recruiting me in 1964. At the time, Hank Foldberg was the head coach, and Smith had a hard time looking me in the eyes and promising me that things would be any better.

In three seasons, Foldberg won only six games. Fortunately, A&M made a coaching change following the '64 season—the Aggies' seventh straight losing season—and brought in a former player, Gene Stallings, as head coach.

Coach Stallings had been a part of Coach Bryant's famous "Junction Boys" team, and Elmer Smith came back to Linden early in 1965 far more optimistic than he had been on previous trips. Not long after that, Coach Stallings came to visit my home, and I decided to follow my heart to Texas A&M.

Just because Coach Stallings brought a new approach and old-school toughness to A&M didn't mean that we turned things around right away.

I had been injured during my senior football season at Linden, and I hurt my knee again playing baseball in the summer of '65, so I wasn't able to play freshman ball my first year at A&M. Meanwhile, the varsity went 3–7 in Coach Stallings' debut season. We showed signs of progress under Coach Stallings, but we were also shut out three consecutive games.

In 1966 we slowly began to turn things around. After dropping our first two games, we played really well in our next four games, beating Texas Tech, TCU, and Baylor, and tying LSU in Baton Rouge. But we lost three of our last four games to finish 4–5–1 for the Aggies' ninth straight losing season.

This is why our 1967 season is still remembered and revered by so many. Even though we only won seven games, the mere fact that we won the SWC championship and played in the Cotton Bowl—where we beat Alabama— makes that season stick out like a beacon in a sea of bleak years.

Of course, the '67 season started out more like a continuation of lean times instead of a breakthrough year. We lost to SMU in the season opener, 20–17, on the last play of the game. Purdue then beat us 24–20, and then we went to LSU. The Tigers whipped us, although the final score was only 17–6. Then we came home and played Florida State in a driving rain. The Seminoles squeaked out a 19–18 win that left us 0–4.

We had worked so hard in the off-season of 1967, and we really believed we had a solid football team. We easily could have been 3–1 as we headed to Lubbock for our October 14 game against Texas Tech, but it seemed like we were snakebit or haunted by the ghosts of A&M's wretched past.

And even though we played well against the Red Raiders for much of that game, it once again appeared that we were being governed by Murphy's Law

43

when Tech scored a late touchdown to take a 24–21 lead with 53 seconds left in the fourth quarter.

We moved the ball to the Tech 43, but we faced fourth-and-15 with just 11 seconds left. At that point, it was going to take a minor miracle for us to win, and that's just what Bob Long produced when he out-leapt three Tech defenders to make a sensational catch at the Tech 15.

Three seconds were left on the clock when we called a timeout, and Coach Stallings decided to go for the win as opposed to attempting a 32-yard field goal. We called the play—pass 62—where I would fake a handoff to the tailback and then look for my receiving options: the fullback would release into the flats, the tight end would run a crossing route, and our split end would run a curl.

No matter what, though, we knew we had to get the ball into the end zone. Just before the center snapped me the ball, one of Tech's defenders jumped offside, so I knew we had a free play. I rolled out and noticed that Tech had our receivers blanketed.

I then looked back to my right and saw that Larry Stegent had just one defender on him. So I decided to tuck it and run for it. Stegent made a great block, and I ran into the end zone and kept on going into the locker room because the final gun had already sounded.

That victory was a huge one for us because it lifted our spirits, raised our confidence, and generated tremendous momentum. We then rolled past TCU, Baylor, Arkansas, and Rice to set up a Thanksgiving Day showdown against Texas. If we beat Texas, we were going to the Cotton Bowl, but if we lost, I think Tech would go to Dallas.

We got off to a good start and took a 3–0 lead into the locker room thanks to a 32-yard field goal by Charley Riggs in the second quarter. Then at the start of the second half, Texas lost Chris Gilbert, the leading rusher in the SWC, to a hip pointer. The Longhorns also were turning the ball over at an alarming rate. We intercepted Texas four times and recovered two fumbles.

That was another key to our season. That whole year I think we had 40 takeaways and only 14 turnovers.

But early in the fourth quarter, Texas finally put a complete drive together, and with 11:11 left in the game, Texas quarterback Bill Bradley scored on a two-yard run to put the Longhorns up 7–3. Kyle Field grew eerily quiet, as 50,000 spectators looked on and tried not to think, *Here we go again*. But it was difficult not to think that way. We had not beaten Texas at Kyle Field since 1951. And it had been 11 years since A&M had beaten Texas anywhere.

Fortunately, 11 years of frustration would be put to rest—ironically—11 seconds later. Following Texas' go-ahead touchdown, we started at our own 20. I threw an incompletion on first down, and the next play was designed for a short pass to tight end Tom Buckman—the exact same play we had run one series earlier. But on the earlier play, Bob Long noticed that Texas safety Pat Harkins was cheating up, looking for the tight end and leaving the deeper route open.

Harkins had intercepted one of my passes earlier in the day, and Bob told me in the huddle that he could get behind Harkins. I just laid it up there for Bob, who caught the ball at around the Texas 45 and outraced the Longhorn defenders into the end zone to give us a 10–7 lead that we would maintain.

Looking back, that pass to Long in the Texas game and the run at the end of the Texas Tech game were my highlights. Those victories, along with our win in the Cotton Bowl over Alabama, were so stunning that I was named to the All–Southwest Conference team in 1967 and again in '68.

When I ended my career, I had passed for 5,379 yards, which was the all-time school record. But that record has been broken several times, and it will be shattered in the future.

45

I view all the honors I received then—and now—as team awards. What we accomplished in 1967 was rewarding to all of us players and shocking to everyone else. Unfortunately, we were not able to build on it. In 1968 we went 3–7, and the Aggies would not produce another winning season until 1974.

One winning season in a span of 16 years. That's why '67 is still remembered so glowingly by so many Aggies.

Don't misunderstand me. I am certainly grateful for that one season, but more than that, I am thankful for my entire time at A&M. I developed some lifelong friendships while at A&M, and I learned a lot about myself. Coach Stallings was so intense, and he expected so much of us.

I remember working extremely hard in the off-seasons, going through workouts that would literally make us throw up on a daily basis. Coach Stallings made us tough and made us believe that we could be tougher than any circumstance that life threw at us. In that regard, my time at A&M had a tremendously positive impact on the rest of my life.

I managed to play five seasons in the NFL—first with the New Orleans Saints and then with the Houston Oilers, and I later played in the WFL in Hawaii and Shreveport. I then put my electrical engineering degree to use, and I currently serve as the manager of the East Texas Electric Co-Op in Nacogdoches.

Throughout the years, my wife, Shirley, and I (we were married during my final two years at A&M) have returned to College Station hundreds of times to watch the Aggies play and to share our passion for A&M, first with our kids and now with our grandchildren.

Our daughter, Amy, attended A&M for a while but left. She is now going back to school. Our two boys, Tedd and Thadd, are both graduates of A&M. Thadd played on the football team for several years as a walk-on quarterback, and Tedd worked in the video lab for several years.

During their time as students at A&M, I'm sure my kids heard about 1967—from well-meaning fans, students, and former students—more times than they could ever possibly recall. But it obviously didn't hinder them too much.

All three of our kids are doing exceptionally well in their personal and professional lives, and they have given Shirley and I eight wonderful grandchildren. Hopefully, many of our grandchildren will attend A&M, as well.

It's an incredible place that still teaches and appreciates old-school values. And I'm living proof that old-school quarterbacks are remembered at A&M, as well.

Edd Hargett was a two-time All-SWC quarterback in 1967 and 1968 and left College Station as the leading passer (5,379 yards) in school history. Hargett played five seasons in the NFL—first with the New Orleans Saints and then with the Houston Oilers, and he later played in the WFL in Hawaii and Shreveport. After hanging up his cleats for good, Hargett put his electrical engineering degree to use, and he currently serves as the manager of the East Texas Electric Co-Op in Nacogdoches. Hargett, who was inducted into the Texas A&M Lettermen's Athletic Hall of Fame in 1974, and his wife, Shirley, have three grown children who all attended A&M.

The SEVENTIES

ED SIMONINI

LINEBACKER

1972–1975

M Y FATHER WAS IN THE MILITARY for 30 years as a Navy pilot. During the early 1960s, he was the commanding officer for the recruiting station in Abilene, Texas, and it was during that time that my brothers and I began to play organized football. My oldest brother, Frank, played for Abilene High School and was good enough to earn a football scholarship to New Mexico State University.

At that time, Emory Bellard was the head coach at San Angelo Central High School. He became head coach at Texas A&M in 1972, the same year I graduated from high school in Las Vegas, Nevada.

John Paul Young was the linebackers coach at A&M, and he was responsible for recruiting the West Texas area. Coach Young had graduated from Abilene High School and knew many of the former students from Abilene, as did my father from his time in the military.

From our friends and contacts, the coaches at A&M learned about me. I'm sure Coach Young thought they were playing a joke on him coming all the way from Las Vegas, but he discussed the prospect of recruiting me with Coach Bellard. I'm also very sure that Coach Bellard had a lot of doubt about the stories Coach Young was telling him in order to extend his recruiting territory to include Las Vegas.

But Coach Bellard remembered having coached against Abilene High and my brother, and agreed to bring me in on a recruiting visit. I've told the story

Ed Simonini (77), shown here on the sideline with running back Bubba Bean (44), anchored the No. 1–ranked defense in the nation in 1975.

many times that I agreed to sign after Coach Young visited our house the first time, but for some reason he told me to wait…so he could make a second trip to Las Vegas.

The first time I ever saw the Texas A&M campus was during my recruiting trip in late February 1972. After landing at Houston Intercontinental Airport, I was picked up by one of the players. We got back to campus a little late and went straight to G. Rollie White Coliseum, where the basketball team was playing Rice.

Although neither team was near the top of the conference standings, the arena was packed, and during halftime all the football recruits were introduced. The announcer would describe each recruit's athletic accomplishments, and the crowd would give a big "Whoop!" After all the recruits were at center court, the "Spirit of Aggieland" and the "Aggie War Hymn" were played.

When the crowd sawed varsity's horns off, swaying back and forth, G. Rollie looked like it was moving. At that point, I was ready to come to A&M. Years later, the NCAA decided this type of event—where recruits were announced before the crowd—provided some schools too much of an advantage, and it was stopped.

During the early 1970s, a military career was not as valued as it had been before. At A&M, the military heritage has always been an integral part of the school. But even with a war in Vietnam and the antiwar movement throughout the United States, the people associated with A&M maintained tremendous pride in the school's military tradition.

I never had a desire to join the service, but because of the military background in my own family, I was always especially proud to be associated with Texas A&M's commitment to the Corps of Cadets.

In my first two years at A&M, the football team lived in Henderson Hall. Our team went 3–8 in my freshman year and 5–6 in my sophomore season. It helped that Henderson was the football dorm because it made the team closer during a rough time. It allowed many of us to form the friendships with our teammates that continue today.

We were not "kind" to Henderson since everyone knew we would soon be moving into the new Wofford Cain Athletic Hall. There were many times when you would open the wooden door to your room and discover that it had been covered in lighter fluid and it lit on fire. Or a fire extinguisher was placed under the door jam and turned on. Or, while walking down a dark hallway, a tennis ball would explode toward you from a canister at the far end (another use for lighter fluid).

I am truly amazed that no one ever was seriously injured from all of the pranks, but all of those experiences brought us closer together.

In my junior and senior years, we moved to Cain Hall, where all the sports teams were housed. Cain Hall was a great place in its day, featuring a terrific dining hall and a training and treatment facility to go along with rooms that had cable, phones, private bathrooms, etc. Today, that may seem trivial, but coming from the barracks-style housing we'd been in previously, it was big deal.

My last two years at A&M, we went 8–3 and 10–2, and the team's accomplishments mirrored the improvement on campus. In addition to the new dorm, the Memorial Student Center was completed, as well as other important projects bringing A&M more national attention.

Kyle Field became a menacing place for visiting teams those last two years, as A&M did not lose a home game during the 1974 and '75 seasons. In early October my junior year, Texas Tech came to town after beating Texas and looking very strong.

The temperature at kickoff was somewhere in the 90s, and the humidity was most likely the same. We had scored midway through that first quarter, and when they got the ball back, I intercepted a pass in their end of the field, and we scored a second touchdown soon after. At halftime, we were up 21–0, and we knew Tech was not going to win the game. Their players were drained, and I recognized the look, having felt the same during many of our practices on the stifling Astroturf of Kyle Field.

My favorite memory of Kyle Field was from the last game during the '75 season against Texas. The game had plenty of significance, as the Longhorns could win the conference title outright with a win. For our senior class, it was also the last chance to defeat the Horns, as A&M had not beaten Texas since 1967.

With time running down, we led 20–10, and the Aggie Band began to play the "War Hymn." When the crowd began to "saw varsity's horns off," I looked into the stands and was reminded of my recruiting visit with the stands filled and everyone swaying back and forth.

The team would also use Kyle Field and the track around the field for the spring and off-season conditioning drills, one of my least favorite memories. One of the drills was to pair up by position and run halfway around the track [220 yards] before walking across the field and repeating this anywhere from 15 to 20 times.

51

This became especially difficult when Lester Hayes came to A&M. For some reason the coaches felt it appropriate that he play linebacker, and worse still was when they paired him with me or anyone else to make these runs. Lester was a 220-yard state champion and a future star defensive back in the NFL. I was quick, but never fast beyond five yards.

The coaches would be yelling about giving 100 percent, running faster, and other "words of encouragement," as Lester would finish 40 yards ahead of me and any other linebacker, while not looking as if he had run at all. Meanwhile, my tongue was hanging out.

While those are some of my worst memories, some of my favorites involve traditions like Bonfire, Midnight Yell Practice, and Muster. My first Bonfire was unforgettable, especially because it was so cold that night. The students and Corps of Cadets had worked on it for weeks, and we were told that they soaked the wood with jet fuel. When the fire was lit, you could feel the heat from more than 100 yards away.

One thing I most regret during my time at A&M was not getting to go to Yell Practice. With curfew, you weren't supposed to be out past 10:00 PM during the season, and on Friday night before the game, we were either in a hotel or shut down in the dorm. Sometimes you could still hear the yells from Cain Hall, and it never failed to get you in the mood to play on Saturday.

Another regret I have is not getting my undergraduate degree from A&M, instead receiving a B.S. in engineering from Johns Hopkins. Having played as a freshman, I had four years to complete my degree. At the end of those four years, I was a little over a semester short of graduating. Once I went into the NFL, it became more and more difficult to complete the work. If I hadn't got married to my wife, Karen, after my third year in Baltimore, I'm sure I'd have never gone back to school.

The best thing about going to Texas A&M is going back. The school has grown, the student body has grown, but there is still the same spirit and feeling of togetherness—seeing the former players and students and reliving our time together.

After seven years in the NFL, in 1986 I went to work for the Hilti Company, a Swiss-based manufacturer of construction-related products such as drills, hand tools, fastening systems, etc. I started as a field engineer in Dallas and then worked as a sales manager in the Southwest United States and then went to work in our Latin American region. I lived in Caracas, Venezuela, for three months and learned Spanish. I started to work for them in January of 1994. In January 1996 I opened up Hilti Peru, so I took my wife, daughter, and son down there and lived in Lima for two and a half years.

Today my wife and I are empty-nesters in Tulsa, where Hilti's Western Hemisphere headquarters are based. We have traveled many places and called many places home. But no matter where we have gone, part of me has always felt like my home away from home is right back in Aggieland.

Ed Simonini was a consensus All-American in 1975, the same year he was selected as the SWC Defensive Player of the Year. Simonini anchored the No. 1–ranked defense in the country in 1975, and he finished his A&M career with 425 tackles, the most in the history of the school at the time. Simonini was a third-round draft pick by the Baltimore Colts in 1976, and he spent seven years in the NFL. In 1986 he went to work for the Hilti Company, a Swiss-based manufacturer of construction-related products. He and his wife, Karen, now live in Tulsa, where Hilti's Western Hemisphere headquarters are based.

BUBBA BEAN

RUNNING BACK

1972–1975

ANYBODY WHO KNOWS ME realizes that I love construction. I like working with my hands; I thoroughly enjoy the challenge of designing plans and following a blueprint; and I receive a tremendous amount of fulfillment from completing small and large projects that involve sawdust, elbow grease, and old-fashioned sweat labor.

For many years, I ran my own business in the Bryan–College Station area—Bean Construction—and I am now the project manager for CME Testing and Engineering in College Station.

I know there are many former star athletes who miss the roar of the crowd. Some find it difficult to work without the constant affirmation of fans and high-fives of teammates. But I've long been content with the satisfaction of a job well done. No standing ovations are necessary. No pats on the back are needed.

I enjoy the physical side of construction. I've pretty much been at it full-time since 1995 in one form or another, but I have actually been doing this stuff since I was about 12—even in the off-seasons. I can just see a sense of accomplishment every day when I leave a construction site.

Aside from my family—my wife, Kathy, and I have two grown children (Nicki and Jarrett) and three wonderful grandchildren (Madison, Matthew, and Mackenzie)—construction gives me the greatest sense of accomplishment.

Bubba Bean appeared on the cover of *Sports Illustrated* in 1975 after the Aggies shredded Texas to move to 10–0 for the season. The only A&M football player to ever be featured on the cover, he led the Aggies in rushing three consecutive seasons, from 1973 to 1975, averaging a career-best 6.6 yards per carry in 1975.

I love it. I can't emphasize that enough. Building is in my blood, and it has always been.

I suppose that is also why I am so proud of my time as a student–athlete at Texas A&M. I was part of a pretty remarkable construction/renovation project in Aggieland that was orchestrated by an outstanding gentleman, Coach Emory Bellard, and his exceptional staff.

I was part of Coach Bellard's first recruiting class in 1972, and I played a role in helping the Aggies go from SWC also-rans to national championship contenders during my four seasons. That is still meaningful to me because somebody had to make the first move to come to A&M. I came here the same time as Ed Simonini, Garth Ten Naple, Skip Walker, Carl Roaches, Richard Osborne, Pat Thomas, and that group.

It turned out to be a terrific recruiting class that helped transform the image of A&M as an athletic program. And I am certainly one proud Aggie. But what's ironic is that, if Colorado had gotten back to my house before A&M, I would have signed with Colorado.

Fortunately, my mom and my dad, who did not want me to go out of state, kind of intervened and called R.C. Slocum, who was recruiting me at the time. I was with Coach Slocum the day he took the A&M assistant coaching job. He was recruiting me for Kansas State while we were having a barbecue at his brother's house in Orange. We were sitting out in the yard when he got a phone call from Coach Bellard; he walked in, came back, and said, "Well, Bubba, you know all that stuff that I was telling you about K-State? Forget it. Think Texas A&M." I didn't know what the future would hold, but it turned out to be a really good move for me.

By the time I was finished at A&M, I had rushed for 2,846 yards. But more than the yards, I was proud that we came miles in terms of our overall national perception.

In my first two seasons at A&M, we struggled to records of 3–8 and 5–6. But by the start of 1974, it was apparent that Coach Bellard's first recruiting class would form the nucleus of something special.

In Coach Bellard's wishbone attack, I led the Aggies with 938 rushing yards in 1974, as we posted our first winning season in seven years. Then in 1975 things truly came together as we rolled to a 10–0 start and were ranked No. 2 nationally with one game left to play.

Following the 1975 win over Texas, I even appeared on the cover of *Sports Illustrated* under the headline: "A&M Stakes Its Claim. Bubba Bean Shreds Texas."

Thanks in large part to the nation's stingiest defense, we looked as if we might have a shot to win it all in '75. But a made-for-TV move changed the date of the Arkansas game from November to the first weekend of December.

After the emotional victory over Texas, we showed up in Little Rock a little flat. We left flattened, as Arkansas rolled to a 31–6 win in what can probably be considered one of the most disappointing losses for A&M in a long time.

I have replayed that game in my mind a time or two. But it no longer causes me the anguish that was once associated with it.

I learned a long time ago that you can't go back and dwell on things. Sports are fun, but also fickle. If you play them long enough, if we continued to play TCU long enough, we're going to eventually lose to them. It's the law of averages. So I don't jump off the deep end simply because you lose a football game, even when it might have meant as much as that Arkansas game.

If we had won that game, it might have changed some things for A&M's future. But on the other hand, it's not the cure to cancer that we've all been looking for. I don't lose sleep over it.

Following the disappointing end to 1975, I was a first-round draft pick of the Atlanta Falcons in the spring of '76. Along with quarterback Steve Bartkowski, a first-round selection in 1975, I again was part of a construction project of sorts. We helped the once-lowly Falcons reach the playoffs in 1978 and again in 1980.

Both playoff trips, however, were ended by heartbreaking losses to the Dallas Cowboys. In the latter loss, the Cowboys overcame a 24–10 fourth-quarter deficit and won on a dramatic Drew Pearson reception in the corner of the end zone.

That second loss to the Cowboys pretty much reminded me of Arkansas. Pearson made a dramatic catch just like the Arkansas receiver caught a fluke pass over Lester Hayes right before halftime in college. It just kind of fizzled out from there.

I played a couple more seasons of pro football and eventually moved back to the Bryan–College Station area in 1986. I began working in the athletics department under Jackie Sherrill and then moved to career planning and placement, where I stayed until 1995.

I enjoyed working with the university. But I was just not a desk person. The itch for construction wasn't being fully scratched by my weekend projects. So I started my own business in 1995, and I have enjoyed so much of the process ever since.

My athletic connections did help me in getting started in my new business. When I went back to work for the university, former athletics director Wally Groff was the first person for whom I did some construction work. He asked me what I had been doing since I quit playing football. I told him, and he said he had some work at his house. I wound up doing some work for him. Then current A&M athletics department administrator Penny King, who was

Wally's secretary at the time, said she had some work at her house she wanted done. It kind of snowballed from there.

The bottom line is that I enjoy the hands-on part of construction. It's really my dream job. And I am just so glad that I played part of a construction job of sorts when I played at A&M, as well. We didn't use the tools I do today, but we hammered some opponents along the way.

Bubba Bean rushed for 2,846 yards in his career at A&M, which was the most in school history when he left Aggieland in 1975. Bean was a two-time All-SWC selection, and he led the Aggies in rushing three consecutive years (1973–1975). Bean is the only A&M football player ever to be featured on the cover of *Sports Illustrated*. He was a first-round draft pick of the Atlanta Falcons in the spring of 1976. After his NFL career, he eventually moved back to the Bryan–College Station area in 1986. He worked in the athletics department under Jackie Sherrill and then moved to career planning and placement, where he stayed until 1995. He then began a career in construction, and he is now the project manager for CME Testing and Engineering in College Station.

PAT THOMAS

Defensive Back

1972–1975

AS A YOUNGSTER GROWING UP in Plano, I never gave any thought toward pursuing a career in professional football or even playing on the college level. Many of my childhood and adolescent dreams involved making sales contacts, not gridiron contact. And one of my earliest role models was known for covering his sales territory, not wide receivers.

Eventually, I earned All-America football honors at Texas A&M and made two Pro Bowl trips during my seven-year career with the Los Angeles Rams. But those accolades were merely a by-product of my major childhood dreams.

As a kid, I wanted to go to college; I wanted to get a degree; and I wanted to be in industrial sales. There was a gentleman in Plano named Terry Ziegler, who sold furniture for a major manufacturer. He drove a little Mercedes, had a big, beautiful house, and lived a charming life. That's who I wanted to be, and that's what I wanted to do.

Football success—both as a player and a coach—altered and rerouted some of my initial plans. But now—in my mid-fifties—I am basically doing exactly what I planned to do all along.

I am the owner and president of a company called L&P Group, LLC, which I named after my wife, Lenith, and me. The business—a certified 8A company in commercial construction—is headquartered in Buffalo, New York. But I spend most of my time in Texas, selling furniture and more

Cornerback Pat Thomas was a two-time All-American at Texas A&M in 1974 and 1975. But Thomas says his proudest accomplishment in Aggieland was being a part of a 1972 recruiting class that began changing the ethnic diversity of Texas A&M.

through a branch of the company called L&P Interiors. And, honestly, I am still as excited about landing contracts today as I was on the day I signed my first NFL contract in 1976.

We started the company in Buffalo in 2002 after I was released from the Bills' coaching staff. My youngest son is still freezing in Buffalo, running the company, while my wife and I settled in Galveston, opening up a division of the company in the Houston area. I'm really excited about being here because I had always planned on moving back to Texas one day.

And, although I grew up in North Texas, I strategically chose to open a division of the company in the Houston area to take advantage of the numerous Texas A&M connections in the region.

I am regularly reminded by A&M fans and former students I come in contact with today why I first fell in love with A&M. Aggies never forget your name and never cease to amaze me in how they look after their own.

I didn't know a lot about A&M prior to arriving in College Station in 1972. I had been a pretty good running back at Plano High School, where I rushed for two touchdowns in our 1971 Class 4A state championship victory over Gregory-Portland. I had a good high school athletic career in Plano. In fact, I was inducted into the Plano ISD Athletic Department Hall of Honor in 2005.

My parents were proud of my athletic accolades, but they were most pleased that my accomplishments on the field earned me numerous scholarship offers. My parents' inability to pay for college was truly the only reason I was such a dedicated high school athlete. Football was a means to an end for me.

But playing for Plano and growing up in a predominantly white, upper-income community in the 1960s prepared me for going to a place like Texas A&M, which didn't have many African American students in the early 1970s.

Of course, my grandfather was a great role model for me in terms of seeing past the color of a person's skin or in breaking down racial barriers. They named a school in Plano after my grandfather, James Thomas Elementary. He was a very special man, and he really helped the minorities in the community. He bridged the gap between blacks and whites when nobody else could at that time. He had made a living in downtown Plano by shining shoes. But he left his legacy because of the way his heart shone.

He always made sure that the people who were in most need were able to have things that they needed to survive. During the Depression, he would get things from the richer, more influential white people that he had grown up with, and he would give things to others. He was honored for his giving, his charity, and his kind heart. There were a lot of rich, white kids who would run away from home and run to my grandfather's house. He was beloved by many in Plano, regardless of the color of their skin.

So I think coming from Plano and being a product of my grandfather's genetic makeup made the transition to A&M easier for me.

I chose A&M then for the very reason that I'm back in Texas now, which is the alumni base that takes care of its own. The camaraderie of A&M made me believe that if I went to school in Aggieland, I would be a part of something very special. That proved to be the case. I went to college thinking, *Hey, I did what my mom and dad asked me to do in earning a scholarship. Now I'll just get my education, play ball, and then be able to go into industrial sales.* But I wound up being All-America and was lucky enough to get drafted to play in the NFL. But, truly, that was never an aspiration of mine. It just kind of worked out that way.

In fact, lots of things worked out for me at A&M beyond some of my wildest expectations. I was part of Emory Bellard's first recruiting class in 1972. During my first two seasons, we suffered through losing seasons, going 3–8 and 5–6. But in '74, we posted the school's first winning season in seven years. Then in 1975 we rolled to a 10–0 start and a No. 2 national ranking. One of the amazing things about our '75 team was that 21 of 22 starters went on to play in the NFL.

But for all the magical moments and defining games that I was a part of at A&M from 1972 to 1975, it was the role that several of my teammates and I played off the field—not on it—that ranks most prominent in my memory bank. I am definitely proud of becoming an All-American, but I am more proud of becoming a trendsetter for African Americans at A&M.

There was some racial unrest at that time, and we were the first real wave of minority students, especially in football, to come through A&M. We had a group that stood out and stuck up for each other. There was no question that we were trendsetters, and I was proud to be a part of that effort. I felt a kindred bond with my grandfather in that regard.

61

We had eight freshmen who started in 1972, and five of them were black. So it was an opportunity for us to prove that we could thrive at a place like A&M.

Because of my background, I was able to communicate and to get along with people of all ethnicities. That's the way I was brought up. It wasn't a strange environment for me, which was the case for some of the other black players who had not experienced what I had. It maybe helped me to bridge the gap a little between some of my fellow black athletes and the predominantly white student body at that time.

Following my playing career at A&M and in the NFL, I landed my first assistant coaching job with another former A&M standout, Jack Pardee, who was the head coach of the USFL's Houston Gamblers in 1984. From there, I also had coaching stints with the University of Houston, the Houston Oilers, the Indianapolis Colts, the Buffalo Bills, and an arena team in Dallas.

But now that I am out of the game, I am finally following my heart's true desires. I love being back in Texas, love being back around Aggies, and love the challenges of the business. My wife and I wanted to have a place where all of our relatives—we have four grown children and two grandchildren, along with nieces and nephews—could get away and come visit. So we chose a house in Galveston, and we are really having a good time on the island, renewing Aggie contacts and enjoying life.

I am so grateful to be an Aggie. Not just a former A&M football player, but an Aggie. We Aggies come from all backgrounds and we have varied skin colors. But we're really all one family, and the only color that matters when we get together is the color of our blood: maroon.

Pat Thomas was a two-time All-America cornerback for the Aggies in 1974 and 1975, as he picked off nine passes during those two seasons. Thomas was a second-round draft pick of the Los Angeles Rams in 1976, where he played in two Pro Bowls and Super Bowl XIV in 1980. Following his playing career, he coached with the USFL's Houston Gamblers in 1984. He also had coaching stints with the University of Houston, the Houston Oilers, the Indianapolis Colts, the Buffalo Bills, and an arena team in Dallas. Today he is the owner and president of a company called L&P Group, LLC, a certified 8A company in commercial construction that is headquartered in Buffalo, New York.

CHARLES L. "TANK" MARSHALL
DEFENSIVE END
1973–1976

I HAVE MANY CHILDHOOD MEMORIES of my mom, dad, brother, and me, loading up the family car in our Dallas Oak Cliff neighborhood and traveling south for the weekend to Washington on the Brazos [now known as Navasota], which is where my father was raised. Back then, there was not an outer loop to Highway 6, so we had to take what is now called Business 6—or Texas Avenue—to get to Navasota.

Traveling that route took us directly in front of Texas A&M's campus, and I would look out the car window and see a particularly awesome building that grabbed my attention every time. That building is the old administration building, which stood out on campus. It was quite impressive to a youngster in his preteens.

As I looked at the building from the back seat of the family car, I would tell mom and dad that I was going to go there someday. Since I was so young at the time—and since that was during the early 1960s when A&M and many other large universities were essentially segregated—my parents didn't take my comments too seriously. As time passed, I began playing football, and I became quite good at it, according to my coaches. All I knew was that I thoroughly enjoyed playing the game.

I also enjoyed many of my coaches, and I remember that my high school head coach often told us to always give your absolute best because you never know who will be watching. That later proved to be quite prophetic for me.

During my senior year at Roosevelt High School, we were playing against Kimble—our big rival—when my coaches asked me during halftime to leave my normal defensive end position to play defensive tackle. Apparently, one of my teammates was consistently being beaten at the tackle spot. I agreed to move to tackle and began to have an outstanding game.

Little did I know at the time that a college assistant coach by the name of R.C. Slocum was watching. Coach Slocum was in the stands scouting the young man who wound up being lined up right across from me in the second half. I later found out that Coach Slocum changed his mind based on my performance that night. He began recruiting me to attend Texas A&M University and was no longer interested in the other guy.

Slocum's change of mind that night dramatically altered my life forever. It took me on a course that God definitely had planned for me—and one that I had planned on taking many years earlier when my family was driving past the A&M campus.

64

Unlike the recruiting process today, when young men sometimes choose colleges solely based on their chances of immediate playing time, recruiting in the early 1970s involved more personal connections than checking out this website or that one. In my time, the potential student-athlete got to know more about the institution, the people connected to the institution, and how you fit into that environment.

As I investigated Texas A&M, I met people who have had made a tremendous impact on my life because they cared so much about me as an individual. I know that's not the case everywhere. In fact, I've read numerous stories through the years about young men and women who have been recruited by various institutions that had little to no interest in the student-athlete's home life, future plans, or character development.

At A&M, however, character has always counted. As far back as I can remember, A&M has attempted to recruit individuals with integrity and moral values. Not just in terms of finding student-athletes, but also students in general.

My mother and father recognized that trait about Texas A&M right away. They could tell that A&M was interested in me as a person and not just as a football player. During the recruiting process, my family and I became quite close to the Aggie coaches, men who expressed a genuine and sincere interest in my development as a player and as a young man.

In other words, they were sincerely interested in helping me obtain a degree from Texas A&M University. That may not sound unusual today, but in the early 1970s, it meant the world to my family and me.

Remember that I was a young African American from Oak Cliff, which was—and still is to this day—a predominantly African American neighborhood where there wasn't much to look forward to beyond high school in terms of education. The future for so many of those Oak Cliff kids was filled with considerable uncertainty in those days. Many of them merely hoped to get out of high school and find a job as a laborer. If they were lucky, they could scratch out a living until God called them home.

Hope was a precious commodity for people in my neighborhood. But Texas A&M University gave me the opportunity to hope for a bright and prosperous future—one far beyond the typical expectations in Oak Cliff.

Many universities offer students hope, and many institutions at that time were providing African Americans like me with an opportunity to be the first member of their family to earn a degree. But A&M offered even more. It provided a loyal network of Aggies, and it offered the chance to earn an Aggie Ring, which is recognized and revered virtually anywhere in the world.

Although I had many offers from other schools, I wanted to be part of the Aggie network and the A&M family. My decision to attend Texas A&M University was the beginning of a very special relationship that had first been envisioned by a young boy in the back seat of the family car.

Upon arriving on campus, it was evident very early on that I was in a completely new environment. Everywhere I went on campus, I heard the word "howdy." That was not a common word that was heard on the streets of South Dallas. Nevertheless, I knew people were being sincerely friendly toward me. It was a major culture shock for me, but a good one nonetheless.

There were many challenges in the early 1970s for an African American student at A&M, but the positives greatly outnumbered the negatives, and I was made to feel welcomed. That meant a lot to me, as I began to first understand what it meant to be an Aggie.

The football practices were long and hard. I was accustomed to the duration, but not the intensity of practices I experienced during those first few weeks of my freshman year. But to this day, I remember the buzz on campus

Tank Marshall was an All-SWC defensive end for the Aggies in 1975 and 1976. He returned to A&M many years later and finished what he started, earning his degree in 1986. *Photo courtesy of Charles L. Marshall*

the night before the first home game as cars, motor homes, and even private jets cruised into College Station. It was unlike anything I'd ever experienced before.

I recall my fellow teammates and I getting pumped up because of all the activities outside the dorm the night before game day. And the morning of the game was even more exciting as we exited the dorm and walked to Kyle Field, seeing thousands upon thousands of people lined up all the way to the stadium to support us. You could feel the passion and pride our fellow Aggies had for us. And we, as football players, felt the pride, as well. We did not want to let our great fans down, and we wanted to represent them—and our university—with integrity and passion.

Today, far too many student-athletes are wrapped up in themselves and concerned primarily about using their colleges as a stepping stone to the next level. I acknowledge that many of us were thinking about the next level, too, but we were tremendously proud of our institution and were intent on not letting our fans down.

I also recall the feeling of arriving in the locker room and knowing it was time to get down to business. You'd look around and see your fellow teammates—guys you sweated and bled with in grueling practices. It was comforting to know that we could rely on each other, and the guys in that locker room were essentially your immediate family for the next 60 minutes. Ethnicity and background didn't matter at that point. Neither did a disagreement earlier in the week.

At that point in the week, there were no black or white players. Only Aggies united together.

The coaches were also part of that family, and my position coach, R.C. Slocum, was especially important to me. Coach Slocum recruited me, coached me, and mentored me. As in any relationship, we had our ups and downs and differences of opinion. But Coach Slocum has always had a sincere and genuine interest in the development of young men.

For many years, he's also had a real love for Texas A&M University, which continues to this day. He was a blessing in my life. So was former head coach Emory Bellard and assistant coach Melvin "Mad Dog" Robertson. Coach Robertson always had encouraging words for me, and he pushed me to the limit on the field and in the classroom. I will forever appreciate their patience and be grateful to them for in instilling in me what it meant to be an Aggie.

While I played in many memorable games during my career at A&M, my junior and senior years [1975–1976] were especially exciting due to the amount of success we had in both years. And being on the A&M defense at that time was something really special. We finished the '75 season with the No. 1–ranked defense in the country.

As I look back over the many years that have passed since I first left A&M and concluded a short career in the NFL, my one regret is that I didn't return to College Station to build my family and my career. But I didn't even give that much consideration at the time.

Although I didn't graduate after my senior season, I did return to finish what I had started academically. My folks, Coach Slocum, and my lovely wife, Chandra, whom I married during the summer after my freshman year, all encouraged me to return to A&M to finish my degree. It would have been easier to finish my degree plan at a school in the Dallas–Fort Worth area, since that is where my family settled.

But I didn't want any degree; I wanted a degree from Texas A&M University. Most of all, I wanted that prestigious Aggie Ring.

When I finished my degree in 1986 and slipped that ring on my finger, I felt blessed beyond my dreams. And to this day I still view Texas A&M University with honor and pride.

Although I don't attend as many of the games as I'd like, I still fire up whenever I hear the Aggie Band. In fact, I wouldn't mind the "Aggie War Hymn" being played as my memorial when God calls me home. I am not planning on leaving anytime soon, but A&M means that much to me.

Texas A&M shaped my life in many ways, further teaching me the values that my parents had first instilled—discipline, sacrifice, dedication, determination, perseverance, and commitment to doing things the right way. These are qualities I've passed along to my own two sons.

It's difficult to put into words what it means to be an Aggie. In fact, I think it is practically impossible to explain; it has to be experienced. But I am so grateful that so many people in my life took the time to help me experience it for myself. People like Robert "Bob" Mohr, J.L. Huffines, Harvey R. "Bum" Bright, Tom O'Dwyer, and Thomas R. "Bob" Frymire continued to teach me about the Aggie spirit even after I left school.

Once you experience Texas A&M's tradition, honor, integrity, and loyalty, it remains with you forever. That young African American boy who dared to dream in the back seat of his family car many years ago can say that Texas A&M exceeded his lofty expectations.

And now, with the better part of my life behind me, I dare to dream again. Someday, I hope to return to Texas A&M and College Station not just as a visitor, but as a resident of the community that is home to an institution I still cherish so much.

Charles "Tank" Marshall was a two-time All-SWC defensive end for the Aggies in 1975 and 1976. Marshall was drafted in the third round by the New York Jets in 1977. He and his wife, Chandra, whom he married during the summer after his freshman year, have two grown boys. Marshall fulfilled a promise to his parents by returning to A&M to earn his degree in 1986.

MARK DENNARD

OFFENSIVE LINEMAN

1974–1977

FOR ME, BEING AN AGGIE seems effortless because it is so engrained in my life. It is my past, present, and, hopefully, my future. It encompasses athletics, education, friendships, family, and business. It was athletics that almost directed me away from Texas A&M, but fortunately for me, it was athletics that ultimately took me to Texas A&M.

I had grown up being a big fan of Southwest Conference football, and I followed all the teams. In the early 1970s I played football at Bay City High School, and I was thrilled when I had the opportunity to take a recruiting trip to the University of Arkansas.

The Razorbacks, led by Coach Frank Broyles, had some great teams in the 1960s and early '70s. I was excited about seeing the Arkansas campus, and even more excited about taking my first plane trip. It was a charter flight out of Houston, and I got to visit with other recruits on board, including Steve Spitzenberger from Spring Branch. We became friends during the recruiting trip, and we vowed to keep in touch during the whole process.

I had made a verbal commitment to Arkansas, but Texas A&M assistant coach Paul Register continued his recruiting efforts and kept in touch long after I had visited Aggieland—something the Arkansas coaches didn't do. My interest in A&M grew with the continued communication with Coach Register.

I had been to a couple of A&M games, and I was always impressed with Kyle Field. I had a good friend who was a senior in the Corps of Cadets in

1973 and another high school friend, Ricky Seeker, who was already playing center for the Aggies.

All of these things made me reconsider my earlier decision. I still remember Spitzenberger's call at home. He asked, "What are you going to do?" I told him I was seriously considering going to A&M. He said, "I think that's what I'm going to do, let's be roommates." That was it. Our decision was made.

I was so excited about attending Texas A&M, but my enthusiasm was soon tempered when I saw the size of the players I would be going against. When I first stepped on the scale in the summer of 1974, I weighed 218 pounds.

Obviously, I was overwhelmed and undersized. Fortunately, Ricky Seeker, who was a senior in '74, took me under his wing. He gave me help and guidance, but I was still a freshman and a world away from a senior in many ways, as I would soon find out.

At that time, upperclassmen tested underclassmen on and off the field. Spitzenberger and I made many trips for fast food for Ricky and his senior buddies. What they didn't know at the time was that we worked out our reluctance and aggravation by enhancing their food before they got it. You will have to use your imagination in regard to what we actually did to that food.

As freshmen, we were really tested when the weather turned cold. I vividly remember one time when the temperature was about 15 degrees outside. The seniors had us shower at Cain Hall and walk over to the old outdoor swimming pool in our bathing suits. We had to climb up the high dive platform and jump into the freezing water. When we climbed out of the pool, we had to stand and sing the "Aggie War Hymn." It was freezing, but fun.

It's disappointing to me that the NCAA outlawed athletic dorms like Cain Hall. I absolutely loved Cain Hall, which opened my first year at A&M. As athletes, we ate together, watched game films together, studied together, and bonded together. The camaraderie we developed was in large part due to the dorm.

In 1974 under Coach Emory Bellard, we went 8–3—the first winning season for the Aggies since 1967. Heading into my sophomore year, the coaches made me take the center position on the offensive line. Seeker had graduated, and I began the '75 season as a backup to senior Henry Tracy, who was a very solid player.

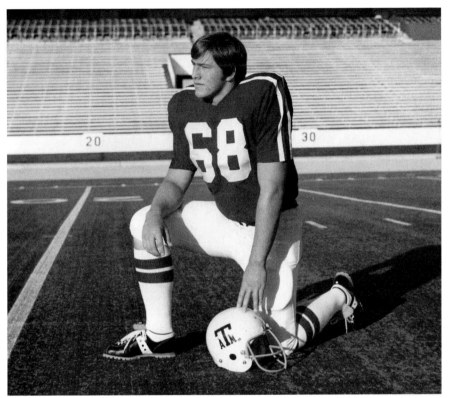

Mark Dennard first left his mark in College Station as a standout offensive lineman for the Aggies in the mid-1970s. After a stellar NFL career, he came back to the area and started an extremely popular restaurant business that has become a College Station landmark.

We rolled through non-conference play in 1975, beating Mississippi, LSU, Illinois, and Kansas State to move to 4–0. We then beat Texas Tech, TCU, and defending SWC co-champion Baylor to improve to 7–0.

On the Friday evening prior to our eighth game, some guys were playing catch, and the football hit Tracy in the eye. He suffered a detached retina, and his collegiate career was over in an instant. That put me in the starting lineup against SMU, and they had an outstanding defensive line.

I was so nervous before kickoff, but I played pretty well in the game. I started having serious cramps in my calves, and I could hardly walk. With Tracy hurt, I knew there wasn't a backup, so in between plays, my fellow linemen would literally massage my calves to help me get through the next play. It wasn't pretty on my part, but we beat SMU 36–3.

The next week we beat Rice and moved to 9–0, setting up a showdown against the Longhorns on Thanksgiving Day in 1975. The game was at a sold-out Kyle Filed with a national television audience.

Coach Bellard gave me the honor of being a co-captain as a sophomore with David Shipman. To this day, that game—a 20–10 victory for the Aggies—is my fondest memory as a Texas A&M football player. It was the first win over the Longhorns since 1967, but we still had one game left to finish the season.

Originally we were supposed to play Arkansas early in the 1975 schedule, but TV executives asked us to move the game to early December in order for it to be broadcast nationally. I really believe that if we had played the schedule as originally planned, we would have won the 1975 national championship.

We were emotionally flat after beating Texas on Thanksgiving Day. After a close first half, Arkansas hit a big pass that turned the momentum of the game, and the Hogs cruised to a 31–6 win. We settled for a SWC tri-championship and a trip to the Liberty Bowl, where we were blasted by USC and Ricky Bell, 20–0. The only regret that I have for my college football is not finishing the job in 1975.

My final two years at A&M were good ones. In 1976 we went 10–2 and soundly defeated Texas in Austin, 27–3. We finished off the season by beating a very good Florida team in the Sun Bowl, 37–14.

As a senior in 1977, we went 8–4 and played USC in the Bluebonnet Bowl. In my four seasons, the Aggies went 36–11 and played in four bowl games. I earned first-team All-SWC honors in 1977.

Not bad, but I would have loved to have won that 1975 championship for my school, my teammates, my own selfish reasons, and, most of all, for my head coach, Emory Bellard.

Along with assistant coach Dan Lagrasta, Coach Bellard was a tremendously positive influence in my life. They both transformed me as a player and a man. I owe them both a huge debt of gratitude for helping me become an NFL prospect.

In April of 1978 I was selected by the Miami Dolphins in the 10th round of the NFL Draft. This was truly a dream come true for me. I was coached by the legendary Don Shula and played with great players such as Bob Griese, Larry Csonka, and Dan Marino.

We made it to one Super Bowl in January 1983, but there were many great games and memorable times. One game, in particular, was my first start in the NFL, and it was on *Monday Night Football* in Miami against the Houston Oilers.

I was lined up against All-Pro Curly Culp, and on the third play of the game, he stuck his thumb through my face mask and jabbed me in the eye. It cut my eye, which was about three-quarters shut the rest of the game. To make it even more memorable, with about four minutes left in the fourth quarter, he stuck me in the other eye. I had triple vision, but luckily not a detached retina. Welcome to the NFL.

My farewell to football was equally painful—both physically and emotionally. After starting every game for the Philadelphia Eagles in 1984 and 1985, I was released by the new head coach, Buddy Ryan, in 1986.

Fortunately, or unfortunately, I wound up back in Miami. But a preseason ankle injury and an attempt to come back before it had healed earned me a trip to Coach Shula's office. I had torn all the ligaments in my ankle earlier and tried to come back way too soon.

With about three games left in the season, Coach Shula said, "I think you've lost a step." I said, "No kidding." I had planned on retiring after that season, but it was disappointing that the option of retiring as a Dolphin wasn't given to me, and I was let go.

The Cleveland Browns were in need of help at that time. Their center, Mike Baab from the University of Texas, was injured, and I was offered full playoff benefits and the opportunity to play for Coach Marty Schottenheimer. I stood on the sideline with fellow Aggie Cody Risien and watched John Elway conduct "the Drive."

He went 98 yards to score and defeat the Browns. Unfortunately, that was my last football game. Coach Schottenheimer invited me to camp the next year, but I thanked him and told him it was time to retire. My family was ready to be back in Bryan–College Station on a full-time basis, and I was ready to get started in the restaurant business.

This idea came while playing for the Dolphins. After the home games, the players would relax outside of the stadium and someone would bring buffalo wings. I had never heard of them, but I became a big fan. My wife was reluctant to try them, but once she did, she was hooked. My children soon followed.

I opened my first Wings 'N' More in Houston on Highway 290 in 1986. The first College Station restaurant debuted across from the A&M campus

73

in 1988. We opened a second College Station location in Southwood Valley in 1994. We now have our largest restaurant on University Drive, which replaced the location across from campus, and a new location on Highway 21 in Bryan. I'm so thankful to the people of Bryan–College Station, along with the current and former students of Texas A&M University, who have helped us make Wings 'N' More a permanent part of Aggieland.

My Aggie past has wonderful memories of school, football, and friends. My wife and I met at A&M, and I watched both my children graduate from the university.

My Aggie present is spent watching my grandchildren learn the traditions and values of Texas A&M, and I am proud and deeply honored to have been inducted into the Texas A&M Lettermen's Association Athletic Hall of Fame.

I hope the future holds opportunities for my grandchildren and even great-grandchildren to be able to write about their Aggie memories, because time will never change the unique spirit and integrity of Texas A&M. This is what it means to be an Aggie.

Mark Dennard was an All–Southwest Conference center for the Aggies in 1977, and he was a 10th-round draft pick of the Miami Dolphins in 1978. Dennard played six full seasons in Miami, two in Philadelphia, and ended his career with the Cleveland Browns. He opened his first Wings 'N' More restaurant in Houston on Highway 290 in 1986, and the first College Station restaurant opened across from the A&M campus in 1988. The restaurant chain has been extremely popular in College Station ever since.

CODY RISIEN

OFFENSIVE LINE

1975–1978

O N THE FIRST DAY OF PRACTICE during my rookie season with the Cleveland Browns, I received the phone call I feared would come. When I had departed Houston in the summer of 1979 for my first NFL training camp, I knew it was a strong possibility, but I had not envisioned it happening so soon.

I had hoped my father, George, would be able to see me play in the NFL. I had hoped for a miracle recovery.

But after my very first practice of two-a-days, my brother, Flint, called me and said I needed to come home immediately. My father was very ill with cancer, and his doctor believed he would not make it through the night. Fortunately, I was able to return to Houston and be at his bedside before he died.

Unfortunately, my dad never got to watch me fulfill one of my childhood dreams of playing in the NFL, as I played 11 seasons with the Browns. For that I am sad. But making it into the NFL was never really my number-one dream, anyway.

From the time I can first remember, my dream was always to play football for Texas A&M. And my father, who was a student at Texas A&M when I was born, proudly witnessed that dream come true beyond his wildest expectations.

George Risien raised me and my brother, Flint, to be Aggies. In fact, I have always jokingly referred to it as "brainwashing" in the purest sense.

Cody Risien and his brother, Flint, both fulfilled lifelong dreams by playing at Texas A&M. During Cody's time at A&M, the Aggies went 36–12 and played in four straight bowl games.

76

All I ever wanted to do was to be a Texas Aggie football player. I wore maroon-and-white diapers and drank out of Texas Aggie baby bottles. I said, "Gig 'em, Aggies," before I said, "Mommy," or "Daddy." Fulfilling my life-long dream has been very rewarding to me, and my dad was as proud as a father could be that both my brother and I went to Texas A&M and played football.

I remember the joke my dad used to tell people when I was being recruited. People would ask him where I was going to school, and he would say, "I raised him to stand on his own two feet and make his own decisions. So he can go anywhere he wants. But if he doesn't go to Texas A&M, he will have to change his last name!" It was a joke (I think), but he had an enormous love for Texas A&M.

So he was not only glad that I played at A&M; he was thrilled that my brother and I played significant roles in Aggieland. During my tenure at Texas A&M [1975–1978], the Aggies went 36–12 and attended four consecutive bowl games. Up to that point, it was the most successful four-year stint in Aggie football history in terms of total number of wins.

I was a backup in '75, and I earned a surprising amount of playing time primarily because we were destroying many of our opponents en route to a 10–0 start and a No. 2 national ranking. By my sophomore year—the Aggies' second straight 10-win season—I was starting at left tackle.

I won All–Southwest Conference honors in 1977 and 1978, and I helped to open holes for our wishbone attack for talented ball carriers such as George Woodard and Curtis Dickey.

Knowing the rather bleak history of the Texas A&M program up to that point, I took a great deal of pride in being a part of the revival of Aggie football that has, for the most part, continued to thrive ever since.

That was a fun time for me and for the program as a whole. I had so much respect for Coach Emory Bellard and the way he handled himself in meetings, on the field, and in the public. He was a gentleman, he was tough, and he had so much personal charisma.

A&M had a couple of good seasons under Coach Bear Bryant in the 1950s, one in '67, and the national championship season [in 1939], but we really didn't have a real accomplished history.

Did Emory put us back on the map? I think he might have put us on the map. I think he deserves a lot of credit for starting Texas A&M football back in the right direction.

After leaving A&M, I was selected by the Cleveland Browns in the seventh round of the 1979 draft. Following the death of my father, I contemplated not returning to the Browns. I missed the whole first week of training camp, which is most important for rookies.

Cleveland had selected two other offensive linemen ahead of me, and after missing time at training camp, I doubted my overall chances of even making the final roster. Nevertheless, following my father's funeral, I boarded the plane back to the Browns' training camp uncertain of what awaited me.

On the way back to Cleveland, I prayed about my circumstances and decided to put my faith in God. I made a decision to put my football future and my life in the hands of God and take it one day at a time. When I got there, I found I had a lot of support in Cleveland.

Coach Sam Rutigliano was very supportive of me. Every day he would look in my eyes and make a point of asking me how I was doing. A lot of the veteran players were very supportive, as well. Although I missed my dad, and training camp was tough, things went well for me as I got the chance to start against the Baltimore Colts in my second preseason game. I had a great game, made the team, and seven games into my rookie season I was in the starting lineup.

Playing in a lineup that featured stars such as Brian Sipe, Greg Pruitt, and Ozzie Newsome, I made the All-Rookie team, and the Browns affectionately labeled me "the find of '79."

Except for 1984, when I blew out my knee in the final preseason game, I was a steady figure in the Browns' starting lineup for a decade. I was a two-time Pro Bowl selection, and I was part of seven playoff appearances, including three AFC Championship Games.

Unfortunately, two of the title game appearances—in 1986 and 1987—ended in heartbreaking losses to the Broncos. Those two losses helped to create the aura of John Elway and cost me a shot at the Super Bowl.

78

Next to Texas Aggie fans and Kyle Field, Cleveland fans and the old Cleveland Stadium were the best of the best. We had the "Dawg Pound" and incredible support. My only regret is that we didn't have a chance to play in the Super Bowl. Those losses to the Broncos were heartbreaking, and they still hurt. But I would have rather had the opportunity to play in games of that magnitude than not to have ever gotten to play in them at all. I've learned how to deal with disappointment.

I also learned to deal with the scars of an 11-year NFL career. I had 12 surgeries during my time in pro football. Most of the operations were minor in the off-season and were primarily for maintenance purposes. But I still feel the pain of the game.

Some days are better than others. It's also helped my knees and joints quite a bit that I have slimmed down over the years. When I left the NFL in 1990, I was 285 pounds, and I was still one of the biggest linemen in the league. That's small compared to the size of these guys now.

I look at the size of these guys in the NFL today—and the guys coming into A&M, for that matter—and I'm not so sure I would have been big enough. It's a good thing I came through when I did. To play 11 years in the NFL was hard work, but it was also very rewarding. But the highlight of my football career was playing at Texas A&M. That was the real dream come true.

Playing at A&M and earning a construction science degree also played a large role in my finding a job after I was done in the NFL. Today I am married to a wonderful woman named Linda, and I have four daughters: Jenlizbeth, Cassidy, Jessica, and my step-daughter, Natalie. I am the project manager for Austin Commercial, a Dallas-based general contractor, and I work in the Austin office.

After I retired from the Browns, I got into the construction business in Cleveland and worked for a general contractor. Before my oldest daughter was going to be in the eighth grade, we decided we needed to get back to Texas. Once we made that decision, I called Dr. Marsh in the construction science department at A&M and asked him what I should do. I told him I was ready to get back to Texas.

Coincidentally, they had a career fair scheduled for the following week, and he told me to get down here to interview. All the top contractors from the state were scheduled to be there. The construction climate was really good at that time, and they were looking for good people.

So I got to the career fair, and as soon as I walked in the door, I saw one of my former classmates, Jack Archer. He asked why I was there, and I told him I was there to find a job and move back to Texas. He signed me up for an interview, and I landed a job with Austin Commercial. My second career is a direct result of the power of the Aggie network.

I get back to Aggieland as much as I can these days. Whether it's to interview students in the Construction Science department for positions at Austin Commercial, attend Aggie football games, or to just hang out with my Aggie buddies…I just love being there.

Cody Risien was a two-time All-SWC offensive lineman for the Aggies in 1977 and 1978. He was selected by the Cleveland Browns in the seventh round of the 1979 draft. He made the All-Rookie team, and the Browns affectionately labeled him "the find of '79." He played in Cleveland from 1979 to 1989 and was a two-time Pro Bowl selection. He was part of seven playoff appearances, including three AFC Championship Games. He has four daughters: Jenlizbeth, Cassidy, Jessica, and stepdaughter Natalie. He is the project manager for Austin Commercial, a Dallas-based general contractor.

JACOB GREEN

DEFENSIVE LINEMAN

1976–1979

As a student-athlete at Texas A&M, I would frequently stop by the old offices of the Aggie Club on my way to football practice. At the time, I didn't know much about the Aggie Club, which became the 12th Man Foundation in 1988, but I did enjoy the people in the office.

Curtis Dickey and I would stop by those little offices—which were leveled in 2000 to make room for construction of the Zone Plaza—and visit with former Aggie Club executive director Harry Green. I couldn't have told you all of the specifics of what Harry did, but I knew he loved A&M athletics, and I knew he was a real people person. Little did I know that I would one day come full circle.

Nowadays, I am no longer a visitor in the offices of Texas A&M's fundraising organization; I am a full-time employee.

I accepted the position of assistant director of major gifts in February of 2006, and I love working with former A&M students and former athletes across the great state of Texas. And I most certainly enjoy the fact that I have an office inside Kyle Field—the place where I was first able to establish a name for myself many years ago.

Growing up in Houston, I didn't know too much about Texas A&M or any other college as a youngster. But I did know that I wanted to eventually go to college so that I could one day run a business like my dad, Jacob Carl

Jacob Green still holds Texas A&M's single-season sack record with 20 in 1979. Green remains closely tied to the athletics department today, serving as a fund-raiser in the major gifts department of the 12th Man Foundation.

Green, who was known to practically everyone as "J.C." My father owned Green Brothers Dirt Yard in Houston, and I worked for him throughout my teenage years, driving dump trucks and tractors.

My mom, Tommie Mae, and my dad stressed the importance of working hard and getting an education to my sister and me throughout our childhood. So, by the time I started gaining the attention of college recruiters because of what I was accomplishing on the football field at Kashmere High School, earning a degree was a top priority.

Ultimately, my decision came down to A&M or Texas, which was recruiting another really good player at Kashmere by the name of Eddie Day. Eddie was a more complete player than I was at that time, but he broke his leg as a senior. Texas immediately stopped recruiting him. I knew right then that Texas was not the place for me.

So I came to Texas A&M, which proved to be one of the best decisions of my life. We had really good teams in 1976 and 1977, going a combined 18–6 in my first two years in College Station. We also started the 1978 season off in outstanding fashion, whipping Kansas, Boston College, Memphis State, and Texas Tech by a combined score of 170–21 to move to 4-0. Unfortunately, things quickly went awry, as we lost the next two games to Houston and Baylor, and our head coach, Emory Bellard, was essentially forced out of his job in mid-season.

That was terribly disappointing, and so was much of my senior year in '79. We lost a bunch of close games in my final season, and we went into the Texas game with a 5–5 record. We weren't going to make a bowl game for the first time in my A&M career, but we had one more chance to do something special against a Texas team that was coming into Kyle Field with a 9–1 record.

The night before that game our team gathered with 40,000 or more A&M students and former students for the burning of Aggie Bonfire. I'm normally a pretty laid-back guy, but something overcame me that night. When I was handed the microphone and given a chance to address the crowd, I said, "We're gonna kick their ass."

Looking back on it now, it probably wasn't a butt-kicking, but we did beat Texas 13–7 that next day and kept the Longhorns from winning a share of the SWC title. That was a great way to go out for me.

During my playing career in Aggieland, I was a two-year captain, a two-time All–Southwest Conference selection, and an All-America defensive end in 1979, the year I posted a school-record 20 sacks. I keep hoping that someone comes along and breaks that record, but at the time of this writing, I still hold it. I also still own school records for career fumbles caused [12] and most fumbles caused in a season [six in 1978].

But more than the records, I remember the guys I played with and the men who coached me. I truly enjoyed my time as a student-athlete at Texas A&M. To be honest, I'd say the best times of my life in football were in college.

I went on to become a first-round draft pick of the Seattle Seahawks in 1980, becoming an All-Pro and finishing my 12½-year NFL career with 116 quarterback sacks, which ranked fourth in AFC history at the time of my retirement. For all I accomplished at A&M and later in Seattle, however, I never won a championship. The Aggies went to three bowl games during my time at A&M, and the Seahawks made it as far as the AFC Championship Game in 1983.

Even at Kashmere High School, I was never part of a championship season. Twenty-one seasons at the high school, collegiate, and professional level, but no conference titles. So part of my incentive to return to Texas A&M is to complete some unfinished business. I want to do all I can from a fund-raising standpoint to help A&M win championships. The pieces are coming together for a very exciting future for Aggie athletics, and I want to play a part in that future by raising money, creating awareness, and doing whatever else I can to help.

I enjoy raising money for organizations that mean a great deal to me. Toward the end of my career with the Seahawks, I helped to organize the Jacob Green Charity Golf Classic, which benefits the Fred Hutchinson Cancer Research Center in Seattle. After losing my father to cancer in '83, I had a passion to do something to provide funding for cancer research. I teamed up with the Fred Hutchinson Center to host an annual golf tournament.

Hutchinson was one of Seattle's first sports heroes, starring as a pitcher for the Seattle Rainiers of the Pacific Coast League in the late 1930s and later earning national recognition as a player and a manager with the Detroit Tigers. Hutchinson died of lung cancer at the age of 45. My tournament attracted numerous athletes and celebrities, and it is still going strong today, enabling me to donate more than $1 million to the Fred Hutchinson Cancer Research Center over the last two decades and change.

After I retired from professional football, I returned to Houston to help Mom run the family landscaping business. My sister then persuaded me to help her open a home for teenaged kids in Houston.

My wife, Janet, and I bought a house and put 14 kids in it. That's how we started that particular foundation. We named it J.C.'s Children Center, after my dad. It's still going strong. I was kind of the director of operations there, and I did a lot of fund-raising for them. It is state-funded, but that will only go so far. The fund-raising was a necessity to put the kids in a position to succeed.

So I had some fund-raising background even before I came back to A&M. Once I got back here, I was reminded once again how special it is to be an

Aggie. All three of my daughters, Janelle, Jessica, and Jillian, have come through A&M, and they loved it as much as their dad. Janelle is now married to former A&M defensive lineman Red Bryant, who is—coincidentally—with the Seattle Seahawks.

Janet and I both love living in College Station and representing Texas A&M, which really gave me a shot at life. I probably could have gone somewhere else and maybe been successful, but one of the reasons that I am successful is because I went to school here.

84

Jacob Green was a two-year captain, a two-time All–Southwest Conference selection, and an All-America defensive end in 1979, the year he posted a school-record 20 sacks. He was a first-round draft pick of the Seattle Seahawks in 1980, becoming an All-Pro and finishing his 12½-year NFL career with 116 quarterback sacks, which ranked fourth in AFC history at the time of his retirement. Green and his wife, Janet, have three daughters—Janelle, Jessica, and Jillian—who have come through A&M. Janelle is now married to former A&M defensive lineman Red Bryant, who is with the Seattle Seahawks. Green is now a fund-raiser with the major gifts department of the 12th Man Foundation, Texas A&M athletics' fund-raising arm.

The
EIGHTIES

SCOTT POLK
LINEBACKER/DEFENSIVE END
1980–1984

M Y NAME IS SCOTT POLK…and I'm an Aggie legacy. My father was one, too. And I have been a fan my entire life. I will be until the day I die.

I'm proud of it. Outside of my faith and my family, it is one of the most prominent things that defines who I am, and I will forever be grateful to be associated with Texas A&M.

I will also be grateful that there are so many Aggie junkies out there just like me who still credit me—more than a quarter of a century later—for making one memorable play (actually, it may have been the only play I ever made).

But I will get to that later. Please allow me to start back at the beginning.

I grew up in Dallas loving Texas A&M and Aggie football. My dad, John, was class of '57. While I did not get to go to games when I was young, I remember pulling for the Aggies, with their old double-striped helmets throughout the 1970s. Guys who starred for the Aggies in that decade like Garth Ten Napel, Ed Simonini, George Woodard, and Bubba Bean were household names in my home.

As a kid, I often thought that if I was ever lucky enough to play college ball, A&M was the place for me. Fortunately, by the time I reached my senior year at W.T. White High School, A&M thought I was good enough to play.

My dad flew helicopters in the Army and then flew for American Airlines. He never pressured any of his kids regarding our college choices. My older brother, Johnny, ran track for TCU. My sister, Karen, was in a sorority at Baylor. So I was the last out of the nest.

My father was a very hard-working man who grew up dirt poor and made something out of his broken family. I believe one of the major influences of his life was what A&M taught him.

He received a degree from A&M in animal husbandry, and he served in the Army at Fort Sill. He passed away, but I still have his saber and senior boots from his days in the Corps of Cadets. I am sure seeing all that influenced me greatly, though unintentionally.

Even though I knew A&M was the place for me, I did what a lot of high school guys do, taking their little recruiting trips to see what's out there and to have some fun. I remember taking a recruiting trip out to Texas Tech, and they showed us some statue of a guy on a horse and they said his rear was pointed toward College Station. That actually made me kind of mad. They knew I wasn't headed to Lubbock.

I followed my heart and signed with Tom Wilson's Aggies in 1980. I played as a true freshman and even started a few games during the 1980 season. But the thing I remember the most about that first year was just thinking how big the campus was and how lucky we were to have the undying support of the 12th Man, the nationally famous Texas A&M student body.

87

We gave the students plenty of reasons to stay home on Saturday afternoons, but they kept coming out to support us. We only went to one bowl game in my five years as a letterman at A&M.

Yes, I said *five* years as a letterman. There's a great example of Aggie math. I endured a knee injury the spring after my freshman year. I tore an ACL and cartilage on the turf. That required the old-fashioned, full cast after opening the whole knee up for surgery, followed by six months of atrophy. That is the only thing I would change about my experience during my time at Texas A&M.

I was still not 100 percent the following fall. But I played enough as a sophomore to earn a letter in '81.

Then I severely tore my hamstring. So we decided to go ahead and get the medical hardship redshirt season. I then played the next three years, which technically made me a five-year letterman.

One of my favorite memories of my time in Aggieland was living as a team in Cain Hall. As the rock band Kiss so eloquently put it, "Those were crazy, crazy nights." At Cain Hall, I learned how to play backgammon, how to play

Pente, and how to hit a 2 iron down the third-floor hallway between pizza-man robberies and trash-can floodings in rooms.

I'm not exaggerating.

We never lived off campus, and I am glad we didn't. The food rocked at Cain Hall! And living with all my teammates and buddies meant often going duck or deer hunting with five minutes' notice, or road-tripping to some ridiculous destination, or country-and-western dancing to try to impress some teammate's date. We ate, drank, slept, worked out, studied, and did everything together.

My memories of practice are not so pleasant. There was a saying when players got tired and wanted to quit that, "Highway 6 runs both ways." That meant you could leave via Highway 6 just as easily as that highway delivered you to Aggieland.

Practice could make you want to leave. We practiced on the artificial turf at Kyle Field, and it was a beat-down during two-a-days. Offensive linemen would lose as much as 10 pounds of water weight in a single practice.

Even outside of two-a-days, practice generally stunk. Except that time when longtime A&M athletics department employee Billy Pickard came out for a November practice in nothing but a razorback hat and a jock strap in the freezing rain.

That was unforgettable...even though I have tried for many years to remove that image from my mind.

My favorite practices, by far, were on the Fridays before the games. We wore shorts and helmets, and it was all review. The highlight for the players was when the Aggie Band came out and played 10 feet from us. That was absolutely awesome! They took the field after our walk-through, and it was the coolest thing. It also created some mutual respect and admiration among the team and band members.

I often go back to that time in my memory, replaying *Patton*'s theme song in my mind. Although I never saw it as a player, I take pride in knowing that we never lost a halftime. And let me just say here that the "Aggie War Hymn" is, by far, the best fight song in the country.

Okay, now it is about time to address "the Play." I call it that not because it is dubbed so by anyone outside my immediate family, but because it is really the only play I ever made. But it's better to be a one-hit wonder than a none-hit wonder, right?

In the 1984 Texas game, Scott Polk picked up a blocked field goal and lumbered 76 yards to the Texas 7. The Aggies converted the block into an 18-yard Eric Franklin field goal and a 23–0 lead, which helped A&M to a 37–12 win. That game was a turning point in the A&M–Texas series.

Let's set the stage. It was in 1984 at Austin's Memorial Stadium (this was before the stadium and the field were named for 57 donors). We were leading the game, which was being broadcast nationally by an upstart sports cable network called ESPN.

But maybe I'm still getting a little ahead of myself. Let me rewind.

A year earlier, Texas A&M had taken a 13–0 lead over Texas as Kyle Field rocked and swayed like rarely before. Everybody inside the stadium and watching on television was wondering: *Could this be the year that the tide finally turned in A&M's favor?*

The answer was a definitive and authoritative *no*. The Longhorns stormed back from the early deficit in 1983 to score 45 unanswered points en route to a convincing 45–13 win. It was the 12th Texas victory in the last 16 meetings against the Aggies, and it was yet another painful reminder to A&M fans of the Horns' supremacy in the series.

So the following year, when we sprinted to a 20–0 halftime lead over the Longhorns in Austin, few A&M fans were breathing easily. And when Texas marched downfield early in the third quarter, there was a fear among many Aggies—probably even some on our sideline—of *Here we go again.*

Our luck against Texas hadn't been very good. Sometimes the ball bounces your way, sometimes it doesn't. Against Texas, it hadn't often bounced our way. But on this particular night it did. With the Longhorns at the A&M 10, Texas kicker Jeff Ward lined up for a 27-yard field-goal attempt that would have cut into our lead and given the Longhorns a major momentum boost.

Instead, Domingo Bryant—our great defensive back—swooped in from the right side to block the kick. I was lined up on the left side, and I picked up the loose ball and started running.

I made it 76 yards to the Texas 7. We then converted the block into an 18-yard Eric Franklin field goal and a 23–0 lead.

The fat lady began singing, while Texas fans began exiting. We went on to a 37–12 win, and I instantly became a folk hero of sorts. It was the type of play that had broken our hearts so many times in the past.

For whatever reason—namely Jackie Sherrill and the awesome athletes he was recruiting in those days—that win changed the series. Beginning with the '84 game, we rolled off six straight wins over Texas and won 10 of the next 11 against the Horns.

From my perspective, it is good to make one play because you automatically know which one it is if someone tells you they remember you when you played.

I would not want to have to recount game-changing play after game-changing play—like mid-1980s stars such as Kevin Murray, Johnny Holland, and so forth. That's too arduous.

Some people say I ran slowly because the place-kicker caught me, but that's nonsense. I think the name of the guy who caught me was Carl Lewis. Or maybe Usain Bolt. Not really, but I was actually trying to run the clock out because we had the lead. I had a lot of time to think during the run. Somewhere around midfield I began wondering what had happened to everyone.

Later in life, it became a watershed moment. If you graduated before 1970, you probably remember that I scored a touchdown. The later classes talk about monkeys and gorillas jumping on my back and other irrelevant topics. I stopped correcting the elders out of respect some time ago.

But believe it or not, neither that game nor that play—nor any other game—are my fondest memories of my time at Texas A&M. Oh, I loved the games, along with the trips to Georgia, California, Boston College, Mississippi, and all the conference games. And winning the bowl game was monumental in the annals of A&M history. Yes, we were undefeated in bowl games in my five years in maroon [1–0].

Who needs the Fiesta Bowl or the Rose Bowl? Who needs the bright lights of New Orleans or Miami? We went to Shreveport, baby, in 1981. And we whipped Oklahoma State, another agricultural school, in a bowl that was eventually sponsored by Poulan Weedeater.

How fitting.

My favorite memories at A&M were actually the relationships that I was blessed to have and that have endured over time. I had great influences, beginning with my roommates. I have no doubt today that a bond exists among my fellow Aggies that is similar to the Bible verse that states: "No greater love has any man than he would lay down his life for another." I have that kind of bond with so many of my former teammates, and I thank God for that.

Following my final season at A&M, I signed a free-agent contract with the Kansas City Chiefs. If only I had possessed a little more size and a lot more speed, I would have been a perfect fit in the NFL.

91

Instead, I was with the Chiefs for only a couple of months before coming back to Dallas to become involved in the family business. My grandfather started in the diamond business in the late 1940s, and today, I run a wholesale diamond jewelry company called Lyles-DeGrazier. God has also blessed me with a great family: my wife, Stephanie, my daughters, Shelbi and Becca, and my son, Cody.

My family life is wonderful, and my career is quite rewarding. It is enjoyable to work with something that is generally going to represent a good time in people's lives. Jewelry is usually a symbol of someone's love for another person, and it's nice to think that what we are producing could become an heirloom and something that they are excited to receive. It beats selling caskets.

Speaking of which, I hope part of my legacy always involves Texas A&M. I was never a great player, but I feel very blessed to have played college football and to have been at A&M.

I had to have a knee operation, and my wife once asked me, "Knowing all you know now with your knee, would you do it over again?"

I told her I would absolutely do it again. I feel blessed that God provided some unbelievable relationships for me and some real growth in my life when I was at A&M. I was blessed to have been involved in a great church down there, Grace Bible Church. The friends that I made and just the experiences I had while I was at A&M have meant so much to my development physically, mentally, and spiritually. I wouldn't change a thing if I had it to do all over again.

I even made a play that some people still remember.

Some reporter once wrote that that was the play that changed A&M football. I don't know about that, but it was certainly the start of a lot of years of success against Texas. We went to one bowl in the five years while I was there, but it did seem like we were building up under Jackie Sherrill. The year after I left, the Aggies went to three straight Cotton Bowls. So, depending on one's view of life, you could say I was either part of the dead wood or part of building something special. Selfishly, I like to think I was part of the latter.

Scott Polk forever etched a place in Aggie lore when he picked up a blocked field-goal attempt against Texas in 1984 and returned it 76 yards to the Texas 7. That helped A&M build a 23–0 lead en route to a 37–12 win. After signing a free-agent contract with the Kansas City Chiefs, he returned to his hometown of Dallas to become involved in the family business. Today he runs a wholesale diamond jewelry company called Lyles-DeGrazier. He and his wife, Stephanie, have three children—daughters Shelbi and Becca and son Cody.

TOM ARTHUR

12th MAN KICKOFF TEAM

1983–1984

As a walk-on at Texas A&M in the early 1980s, I once thought that the proudest maroon moment of my life would be when I suited up for the Aggies and ran onto Kyle Field. While that was certainly an unforgettable time in my life and one of the great milestones of my early twenties, it actually pales in comparison to what I experienced many years later when I watched my oldest suit up in his Aggie uniform.

My chest really swelled with maroon pride during the 2009 baseball season, as I watched Scott trot onto Olsen Field and fulfill his lifelong dreams of representing the Aggies.

I thought back to the years of sacrifice he had made, along with thousands of batting practice pitches I'd thrown to him and the thousands of miles we had traveled en route to tournaments. Blood, sweat, and tears. Bruised arms and egos. Torn batting gloves and tough-love talks. It was all worth it.

The first time I saw him take the field in his Aggie uniform, I just about fell over. That was the coolest thing for my wife, Lynn, and me to be able to see our son in his A&M uniform. I can't paint a better picture. My mind also went back to when he was four years old, sitting on my shoulders, at an A&M football game.

He's known that he wanted to be an A&M student-athlete for a long time, so it was so nice to see him on that field. Who knows what his future holds?

Tom Arthur transferred from Stephen F. Austin State University, where he was a scholarship player, to walk on for Jackie Sherrill's 12th Man Kickoff Team.

But no matter what happens, I'll always remember that first time I saw him in that uniform.

Suiting up in a Texas A&M uniform has become quite a tradition in our family. I vividly recall the first time I slipped into mine in 1983. I was originally a scholarship football player at Stephen F. Austin State University, but I transferred to A&M and decided to walk on in an attempt to become one of the original members of Jackie Sherrill's 12th Man Kickoff Team. The following year, I was the captain of the 12th Man Kickoff Team.

Two years later, my younger brother, Mike, arrived in Aggieland. By the time he was done at A&M in 1990, Mike was a first-team All-America center. He would go on to play six seasons in the NFL.

And before either Mike or I came to A&M, our older brother, Bob, came for two years before transferring out. That's what kind of got A&M in my mind back in the mid-to-late 1970s. I used to watch the Aggies and soak in the atmosphere. That's where the family tradition first began for our family.

I also remember one year when I was in high school, and the Aggies were playing Texas at home. A friend and I drove to College Station, even though the game was sold out and we couldn't get a ticket. So we climbed an oak tree on the south end of the stadium—long before there was a Bright Football Complex—and watched the game from that tree with all the black birds. That was the greatest athletic spectacle I had ever seen.

But what's interesting is that the A&M baseball coaches had no idea about our family background when they were recruiting Scott. They liked his speed and his hustle, and they said he was the kind of player they look for in recruiting.

95

It wasn't until after Scott had committed to A&M that the coaches learned about his family background. And it wasn't until a barbecue in the fall of 2008 when head baseball coach Rob Childress came up to me and said, "I didn't realize that you and your brother were football guys here." I told him that my brother was a very good player at A&M, but that it was pretty easy to overlook me.

I was a pretty decent high school athlete who could cover 40 yards in 4.5 seconds. At 6'1", 200 pounds, I was also fairly attractive to smaller schools like Stephen F. Austin. I possibly could have been a three-year starter at SFA, but in the back of my mind, thoughts of Aggieland continued to rise. And when a beautiful young woman I had met at SFA decided she was transferring to A&M, I decided it was time for me to transfer, as well.

It was a smart move on several fronts. I continued dating the woman when we moved to A&M, and 27 years later, Lynn and I are still happily married.

I also found a way to get on the field in Aggieland. I arrived at A&M in the fall of 1982, and although I was ineligible my first year because of transferring, I moved up the depth chart in the spring of '83. Up until I was injured in the Varsity–Former Students Game, I had been competing for the backup free safety position.

But I hurt my knee in the alumni scrimmage, and I got it scoped, which was a pretty new technique back then. It took me forever to come back from that, and it derailed me heading into the fall. Besides, a guy named Domingo Bryant was just coming into his own, and—as just about every Aggie knows—he turned out to be pretty special.

I got pushed aside as the backup at safety, but the 12th Man Kickoff Team was just being introduced by head coach Jackie Sherrill, so that's where three or four of us walk-ons who had been position players ended up. That's where I kind of found a home, and it turned out for the best. It was a lot of fun being part of those first 12th Man Kickoff Teams.

Those early kickoff teams attracted national attention to Texas A&M and energized the student body. I also knew right away that Coach Sherrill's experiment would provide me with an opportunity to earn playing time.

In the 1983 victory over Arkansas—one of the most significant wins of the season—I recovered a fumble by James Shibest that proved to be a big play. I played well enough on the kickoff team that I earned the chance to play on most of the other special teams. I even got a chance to travel to some road games.

I lettered in 1983 and 1984, and I have a lot of great memories from that time. I was a part of the victory over Texas in Austin at the end of the '84 season, and I also got to play in the game before that when we beat a very good TCU team coached by Jim Wacker and led by Kenneth Davis. A good friend of mine played at UT, and we ended up matching up on kickoffs and punt coverages. Playing one-on-one against each other was something I will never forget.

Just being part of that tradition was very special, too. I think Coach Sherrill's 12th Man idea was really cool. I don't know if I would've made it on a regular kickoff team or not, but it opened a door for me, and I will always be grateful for the opportunity. Coach Sherrill and I weren't especially close, but he got on my butt from day one, which showed me that he cared. I also developed a good relationship with former defensive backs coach Curly Hallman, who gave me every opportunity to do something as a regular player, not just a walk-on.

After playing for two years, I graduated in 1985 with a degree in industrial distribution, and I took a job in Houston's chemical industry out of college.

I spent five years in that role and then became a marketing manager for one of the oil refineries for the next six years. Roughly a decade ago, I partnered with a gentleman, and we started our own business in the chemical- and fuel-trading industry.

My football background at Texas A&M prepared me for the risks that must be taken in opening a business.

After all, I threw away a scholarship to walk on at Texas A&M, which was a major risk. Mom and Dad supported it, but the bottom line is that it taught me to take a gamble a little bit to advance in my life. Giving up a full ride at SFA and then walking on at A&M turned out to be one of the best things I ever did. I really grew to love that school and appreciate what it meant to be an Aggie.

I shared that love for A&M with my younger brother and my oldest son. And my other two kids, as well.

My middle child, Travis, is also a promising baseball prospect who would love to play at A&M one day. And it probably wouldn't be too surprising if our youngest child, 13-year-old daughter Morgan, finds her way to Aggieland one day, as well.

I can't predict what Travis or Morgan will do, but it will be fun to watch how Scott develops at A&M and to see what the other kids decide to do. Regardless of what happens in the future, however, it's a major understatement to say that Lynn and I are awfully glad we decided many years ago to transfer to A&M.

Texas A&M provided us with much more than an education. It taught us to stretch to be the best that we could be, and it made us a part of a great extended family—the Aggie family.

Originally a scholarship football player at Stephen F. Austin State University, Tom Arthur transferred to A&M and decided to walk on in an attempt to become one of the original members of Jackie Sherrill's 12th Man Kickoff Team. The following year he was the captain of the 12th Man Kickoff Team. Two years later Arthur's younger brother, Mike, arrived in Aggieland, where he would eventually become a first-team All-America center. Tom and his wife, Lynn, have three children—sons Scott and Travis and daughter Morgan. In 2009 Scott made his debut in an Aggie baseball uniform, and he was a starting outfielder and leadoff hitter for the 2010 team.

LOUIS CHEEK

OFFENSIVE LINEMAN

1984–1987

I<small>T'S BEEN AN AWFULLY LONG TIME</small> since I visited Baylor on a fall afternoon in 1982. But time has not diminished my crystal-clear memory of that day or the chance meeting that occurred in the underbelly of what is now Floyd Casey Stadium.

Today, I look back on that trip to Waco and laugh. But it was not the least bit humorous then.

I felt exposed and guilty. Like I had been caught red-handed. Adrenaline surged through my body. The sweat glands began kicking into high gear. In reality, I'd done absolutely nothing wrong. But I didn't feel that way after bumping into Texas A&M head coach Jackie Sherrill. I remember being pretty panicked at the time, hoping I hadn't blown it with Coach Sherrill and the Aggies' scholarship offer.

At the time, I was senior at Fairfield High School, and I had committed to Sherrill and the Aggies as soon as they had started displaying interest in me. Growing up in Fairfield, a community of about 3,000 people located along I-45 in Freestone County, I had attended a couple of A&M games in College Station. On those trips, I recall feeling an instant attraction to Aggieland.

In addition to playing offensive guard and defensive end at Fairfield, I also worked on the family farm. I enjoyed ranching, roping, and rodeos, and I was an active member of the Future Farmers of America. So, when I first heard

Louis Cheek's trip to the 1986 Cotton Bowl turned out to be more than merely a reward for a great season in 1985. It was on that trip to Dallas that Cheek met his wife, Suzanne, a Dallas native who was home for the holidays from Texas Tech.

the masses at Kyle Field yelling, "Farmers Fight!" I figured I was in the right place.

I had no connections to A&M growing up other than the fact that my father had some friends who lived in the area and invited me to come to a couple of games. When I finished my junior football season, I started getting letters from schools in the spring. I got a letter from A&M assistant coach Curley Hallman. Right away, I knew what I really wanted to do.

All the other schools in the conference, except for Texas and Arkansas, recruited me. Baylor tried really hard, and I loved former Baylor head coach Grant Teaff. He was a hero of mine. I was very interested in Baylor until A&M started to recruit me. When A&M showed interest in me, I committed to Coach Sherrill.

Nevertheless, Baylor did not give up hope. Coach Teaff and his staff stayed in touch with me, and they invited me to attend the Baylor-Arkansas game in Waco. I somewhat reluctantly agreed after Teaff encouraged me to just come watch the game. I told Coach Teaff I was sold on A&M; Teaff told me to come anyway.

So I went, and Baylor won the game to mess up Arkansas' season. After the game, the Baylor recruiting coordinator brought us to the locker room.

I was standing outside the door waiting for Coach Teaff to take us in the locker room. All of the sudden, Jackie Sherrill walked up in a coat and tie. He'd been in the press box scouting the game because A&M was off. He came down to see Coach Teaff after the game.

Jackie saw me, smiled, and said, "Louis, what are you doing here?" He was smiling, but he scared me to death. I though I was done. I said, "Coach, I promise I am not changing my mind." About that time the door opened, and Coach Teaff pulled me in and shut the door on Jackie.

But Coach Teaff was not able to change my mind about my collegiate destination. I arrived at A&M in the summer of 1983, and after redshirting that first season, I started the next four years. I was so blessed to be blocking for teams that won three consecutive Southwest Conference titles from 1985 to 1987.

I had great coaches and teammates. Even that redshirt year was tremendous for me. My line coach was Pat Ruel, our strength coach was Bert Hill, and our scout team coach was Paul Register. We worked our tails off, we trained, we matured, and we shaped up.

I ate it up right from the start—quite literally. I arrived in College Station as a skinny, 237-pound prospect. By the time I went home for Christmas at the end of the fall semester, I had ballooned to 282 pounds, thanks in large part to the training table at Cain Hall.

As I bulked up, so did my teammates. I moved into the starting lineup during the fall of '84 after an injury to Ken Reeves. Before I fractured my lower leg late in the season against Rice, I showed some potential for a brighter future.

Ditto for our '84 team. We ended the 1984 season with program-altering, back-to-back victories over TCU and Texas. Up until those two monumental wins, Coach Sherrill was under fire because he had a 14–16–1 record in his first 31 games in Aggieland. But those two wins set the tone for the next three years of domination in College Station.

My personal life benefited from those Cotton Bowl appearances, as well. During the first trip to Dallas in December 1985, I met my future wife, Suzanne, a Dallas native who was home for the holidays from Texas Tech.

Meeting Suzanne was the key to my future success. And in recalling those times, I think the key to Coach Sherrill's future success, in general, was his ability to motivate us and to increase our power of belief.

Coach Sherrill spent a lot of time with us, building us up. He'd bring in motivational speakers and successful businessmen like Clayton Williams to talk to the team. We would have goal-setting sessions, and he did everything he could to give us a competitive advantage.

He also filled the team with good character guys, hard-working guys. He combined his motivational techniques with a solid coaching staff, and then he put great players in place. It was a recipe for success. Hopefully, it's the same recipe Mike Sherman is putting in place nowadays. I am very encouraged by what Coach Sherman is doing now. Hopefully, we're about to turn things around under Coach Sherman like we did with Coach Sherrill. It would be great to see us back in the national spotlight.

After I played for the Aggies in the mid-1980s, I earned a chance to play in the National Football League. I was chosen in the eighth round of the 1988 NFL Draft by the Miami Dolphins, where I spent two seasons. My four-year NFL career also included stops in Dallas, Philadelphia, and Green Bay. Our first child, Emily, was born in Dallas.

I possibly could have landed another shot in the NFL, but after a knee injury and some disappointments regarding the business end of the NFL, I decided to take a position with a commercial truck tire company in Greensboro, North Carolina, where Suzanne's parents lived at the time.

101

It seemed like a temporary role of sorts, where we could live in the guesthouse on Suzanne's parents' property. But then our second child, Joseph, was born in Greensboro. At that point, I became seriously involved in the company and spent the next 12 years working for the family-owned business in Houston, Athens (Georgia), and back in Houston. Then in 2005 I landed with Columbia, Missouri–based Southern Tire Mart, where I manage their business in San Antonio.

Throughout my numerous travels, I've always kept tabs on the Aggies, and I have always attempted to bring my family back to Aggieland at least once or twice a year. That's not always been easy, especially when our family lived in Athens. It's also been difficult in recent years as our children have gotten older and become involved in their own activities.

Our daughter, Emily, earned a volleyball scholarship at Loyola Marymount University in 2008. I was so proud of Emily when she earned that scholarship that I could practically feel my chest burst with pride. I never thought anything could match that feeling until Joseph committed to play football at

Texas A&M. [As this book goes to press, he is scheduled to sign his national letter of intent with A&M in February 2011.] Not only was that an unforgettable moment to experience as a father, but my maroon pride spilled over in ways I could have never imagined. It is going to be so much fun to see Joseph in an Aggie uniform.

It's also fun watching our younger kids grow and develop their own interests. God has blessed us with four great children, and I am equally as proud of Abby, our 10-year-old daughter, and our six-year-old son, Henry.

All four of our kids are all very active and personable. And it's very rewarding for me, as a former athlete, to see them have success on the fields and courts as they pursue their own dreams.

Being part of a team can teach you so much about life, setting goals, stretching to achieve those goals, bouncing back from adversity, and so many other lessons. I have so many good memories of my time as an athlete. And I am so grateful that I know the pride associated with being an Aggie.

Louis Cheek was a two-time All-SWC offensive lineman for the Aggies in 1986 and 1987. He was chosen in the eighth round of the 1988 NFL Draft by the Miami Dolphins, where he spent two seasons. His four-year NFL career also included stops in Dallas, Philadelphia, and Green Bay. Cheek and his wife, Suzanne, have four children: daughter Emily, who earned a volleyball scholarship at Loyola Marymount University in 2008; son Joseph, who is committed to play football at Texas A&M beginning in 2011; 10-year-old daughter Abby; and six-year-old son Henry. Cheek manages the San Antonio division of Southern Tire Mart.

DAVID COOLIDGE

12th MAN KICKOFF TEAM

1985–1987

As an all-district and all-city safety at Houston's Westbury High School, I probably could have taken an easier route. I could have accepted the financial aid offers from several small colleges and potentially been a star. I could have gone the Division I-AA route and eventually worked into the playing rotation.

I could have been a Bearkat, a Bobcat, a Buffalo, or a Bulldog. But, quite frankly, I was born to be an Aggie. My father, John, was Class of 1952. My sister, Sally Coolidge-Cheadle, was a 1982 graduate. And my older brothers, Danny and Andy, were both attending Texas A&M when I was coming out of high school.

So, while I could have possibly been a big fish in a number of small ponds, I decided I would rather pursue my lifelong dream, sinking or swimming as a walk-on at A&M.

Fortunately for me—all 5′11″ and 180 pounds of me at the time—I arrived at A&M at just the right time for a walk-on. The full 12th Man Kickoff Team was just getting started under Jackie Sherrill. I still had some aspirations of playing defensive back, but I figured that the only way I was going to get on the field was by trying out for the 12th Man.

I never became a big star in Aggieland. But my childhood fantasies eventually became a reality, as I covered kicks during one of the most successful eras in Texas A&M history.

After failing to make the 12th Man Kickoff Team in 1984, David Coolidge (7) made the squad in 1985 and recorded a tackle on the first play of the first game he ever played in an A&M uniform.

It wasn't easy. I was cut from the team on my first tryout, battered and bullied from time to time in practices as a scout teamer, and my last season ended prematurely with a torn ACL. But the pains I endured were well worth it. I followed my dreams. And the memories I possess today of running onto Kyle Field in front of 70,000 fans, including my beaming, maroon-blooded family members, still brings me a tremendous sense of pride.

I don't know if I have one single greatest memory of my career at A&M. Playing in the Cotton Bowl was a highlight, and I also got to play at Memorial Stadium against Texas because we had an extended travel roster for the last away game. I also made a few tackles along the way and was voted as the special-teams player of the week once.

Earning that special-teams award may have been more humorous than anything else. We were playing Southern Mississippi in 1986, and it was a tight game in the fourth quarter at Kyle Field. We entered that game at 1–1 after opening the year with a loss at LSU and beating North Texas State in the second game. But Southern Miss was playing an exceptional game, and we had just scored to take a 16–7 lead in the fourth quarter.

We could not afford to give up a big play on special teams, although the Eagles had an outstanding kickoff-return team. We kicked off, and I was running down the right side of the field. The Southern Miss returner was coming on the left side of the field, but I was staying in my lane—as I had been taught to do.

Then, in an instant, the returner cut, and I was one-on-one with him. No one else touched him. I had to make the tackle or he might have gone for a touchdown. I dove into him and made the tackle at the Southern Miss 25. When I came to the sideline, the guys were saying that if I had not tackled him, he would have scored.

The next day Coach Sherrill handed out the offensive and defensive players of the game awards and then he began talking about the special-teams player of the week. He said, "If this guy had not made a tackle in the fourth quarter, Southern Miss would have scored, and the game could have been much different." He said a few other things and then said, "David College, come on up here and receive your award."

As I walked to the podium to shake his hand, a lot of the guys had their hands over their faces trying not to laugh too loud. Coach Sherrill didn't know the difference between David Coolidge and David College, but at least he remembered that somebody named David made a play.

I have many great memories from playing in specific games, but the biggest highlight is just the fact that I had dreamed of playing football for A&M all of my life. That thought pretty much consumed me. And the first time I ran onto that field was the fulfillment of my dream. For a kid who had come to Kyle Field all his life, to be in that uniform on that field, it couldn't get much better than that.

But it did take some perseverance. I first arrived at A&M in 1983 and then tried out for the 12th Man Kickoff Team in the spring of '84. But I didn't make it. When I got cut, they said there were a lot of seniors on the current 12th Man Team and told me not get discouraged. So I made a vow to come back the following year. In those days, we had 200 guys trying out for the team, and there were some really fast, strong guys.

In 1985 when I tried out again, they narrowed it down to 40 guys pretty much on just physical appearance alone, and I made that cut. It was amazing when we got out there. Basically, the guys who made it were the ones who played in high school and knew how to play football a little bit. It was a big deal to make that squad.

The '85 team opened the season on the road at Alabama and did not take the 10 walk-ons from the 12th Man Kickoff Team. But on the first kickoff of the first home game against Northeast Louisiana, I lined up to fulfill the chance of a lifetime. I then proceeded to make the first tackle of my collegiate career on my first play.

That was a pretty good way to start. I think my family was pretty proud of me. One of the really interesting things to me was that we didn't feel like outsiders on that team, and we didn't spend a lot of time just thinking about how great it was to be on the team. When you're in there and competing on the kickoff team, you feel like you have a job to do.

We didn't feel out of place around guys like Kevin Murray and Johnny Holland, who were not only great college players, but were going to be great pro players. While it was awesome in some ways, at the same time, covering kickoffs was my job, and I wanted to make sure that I did it successfully. I took that role very seriously.

I lettered in 1986, and I almost received an opportunity to play defensive back during our 74–10 win over TCU late in that season. In fact, defensive assistant coach Curly Hallman told me and a fellow 12th Man Kickoff Team member late in that game that we were going into the contest at cornerback as soon as TCU took possession. But just as Sean Page and I were stretching on the sideline, the Horned Frogs roughed the punter. Our offense received a fresh set of downs and ran out the clock.

That was a little disappointing, but the biggest disappointment of my collegiate football career came the summer afterward while we were preparing for the 1987 season-opener against LSU. In a full-speed drill, the 12th Man Kickoff Team did an outstanding job bottling up Rod Harris and the first-team kickoff-return squad, drawing the ire of Coach Sherrill.

Coach demanded that the return team try again, and on the second kick, I tore my ACL while trying to avoid a blocker. Teammates said they heard such a loud pop that it sounded like a gun had gone off.

That injury ended my career and opened the door for Warren Barhorst to assume my spot on the kickoff team. Barhorst would later become a part of Aggie lore in the Cotton Bowl when he stole Tim Brown's towel, enraging the Heisman Trophy winner. I still joke with Warren that he owes me for my bit of bad luck.

But, in all honesty, I'm the lucky one. While going to school at A&M, I met my wife, Ashley Bell-Coolidge, and earned my degree in industrial distribution. That degree provided me with a great foundation for future success.

After graduating from A&M in 1988, I first took a job in California for one year and then returned to Texas, where I began a career in the oil and gas industry. I then began a pretty successful career in trading natural gas commodities, which has allowed me, among other things, to make sure that our four kids—Catherine, Maddie, Will, and Cole—will have the opportunity to one day attend A&M, as well.

I am very proud to be an Aggie and delighted that my role as a manager for a natural gas fund has allowed me to give back to my university.

The grass practice fields just south of Kyle Field are now named in honor of my wife and me. I was initially reluctant to donate so that our family name could be on something at Texas A&M. That seemed somewhat self-serving.

But, after a while and after being encouraged by others, I finally realized that the donation was not about me or a naming opportunity; it was about giving current and future Aggies the best facilities to follow their dreams— just like I had many years ago.

The dedication of those practice fields was an emotional event. My wife and I were overwhelmed, overjoyed, and honored to see our names on the entrance of those fields. We didn't do it for our personal recognition; we did it because we believe in Texas A&M.

But I admit that I was relieved to see that they got our name right. It was spelled "C-O-O-L-I-D-G-E," not "C-O-L-L-E-G-E."

David Coolidge followed his father, sister, and two older brothers to Texas A&M, where he became part of the full 12th Man Kickoff Team under Jackie Sherrill. In 1985 he proceeded to make the first tackle of his collegiate career on his first play. While at A&M, he met his wife, Ashley Bell-Coolidge, and earned his degree in industrial distribution. After graduating from A&M in 1988, he eventually began an extremely successful career in the oil and gas industry. Coolidge has made numerous major gifts to the 12th Man Foundation, and the grass practice fields just south of Kyle Field are named in honor of Coolidge and his wife. The couple has four children—Catherine, Maddie, Will, and Cole.

AARON WALLACE

LINEBACKER

1986–1989

Admission time: coming out of Dallas' Roosevelt High School in the mid-1980s, I initially was leaning strongly toward attending SMU. The Mustangs had won 10 games or more in each of their seasons from 1981 to 1984, and I thought it might be nice to stay close to home.

Besides, my official recruiting visit to Texas A&M was not a particularly good one, which made me lean even further toward SMU. Fortunately for me, though, the Aggies' defensive coordinator at that time, R.C. Slocum, was a relentless recruiter who showed a strong interest in me as a person—and not just as a football player. Coach Slocum and my dad, A.J., developed a particularly strong bond during the recruitment process. And both my dad and my mom, Marilyn, encouraged me to get away from Dallas.

I was an inner-city kid, and they knew that a lot of the potential pitfalls of the inner city would follow me to SMU if I stayed in Dallas. Thanks in large part to Coach Slocum and my parents' influence, I finally decided to go to Texas A&M.

What a great decision that was for me. By going to Texas A&M, I had a chance to play on two Southwest Conference–championship teams and be a part of three title teams, including my redshirt year in '85. I was a two-time All-SWC pick and, along with John Roper, I became recognized as one of the Wrecking Crew's Blitz Brothers. I finished my career as the Aggies' all-time career sack leader.

Once I arrived in College Station, I also met guys like Chet Brooks, Kevin Murray, and so many others who all made me feel comfortable. It was an incredible time to be part of Texas A&M's football program, and I am so glad I didn't miss out on any of the fun.

I'm also glad I didn't end up at SMU. By 1987 I was winning a second straight SWC title in Aggieland. Meanwhile, SMU didn't even have a football team in '87 because of the NCAA's "death penalty." I suppose that's a great example of my father knowing what was best for me.

Looking back on my college days now, I feel so blessed to have been at A&M for so many reasons. I am now a physical education teacher and football coach at Conrad High School in Dallas, and my beliefs, strategies, and approaches to working with today's student-athletes were undoubtedly shaped by the time I spent with some tremendous coaches at A&M.

I played for some really good coaches. When I arrived at A&M, Bob Davie was my position coach, R.C. Slocum was my defensive coordinator, and Jackie Sherrill was my head coach. Those are three quality coaches, and I think I took a little from all of them in terms of my style and my way of communicating with kids.

Coach Sherrill was different from Coach Slocum, and Coach Slocum was different from Coach Davie, but they all provided me with a great foundation and were tremendous role models as coaches.

I remember that when I first came to A&M, I was scared to death, but Coach Sherrill and Coach Slocum made me feel comfortable throughout my redshirt season in '85. I hadn't been out of my neighborhood much, but they knew my family and background, and they brought out the best in me.

As a result, in the very first game I ever player at A&M, I sacked the quarterback on my first play. First game, first play, first collegiate sack. It was quite a way to begin my college career.

I collected 41 more sacks by the time my career at A&M was done, but the one most Aggies remember took place on October 14, 1989. That's the day the Houston Cougars, led by eventual Heisman Trophy winner Andre Ware, came to College Station with a No. 8 national ranking and the country's top offense. The Cougars entered that game averaging 60 points per contest. They left Aggieland bruised, bloodied, and beaten.

As a team, we intercepted three Ware passes and sacked him six times in a 17–13 win. But the image that so many people remember from that afternoon appeared in newspapers the next day and in *Sports Illustrated* later that week.

Above: Aaron Wallace (left) and fellow linebacker John Roper (right) were known throughout the region as the Aggies' Blitz Brothers. *Photo courtesy of Cathy Capps* *Lower left*: A promotional sheet from the Blitz Brothers' heyday. Wallace, a two-time All-SEC backer, established A&M's career sack record of 42 from 1986 to 1989.

It was of me, following a sack, holding Ware's helmet up, and it sent the crowd of 66,423 inside Kyle Field into a frenzy.

That may have been my proudest moment on the football field at A&M, but my proudest moment as an Aggie probably came 13 years later when I returned to A&M to finish my degree.

I considered not walking across the stage in August of 2002, but my mom was insistent. Now I'm really glad that I did. It was a proud moment for me, and earning that degree along with my Aggie Ring is a personal accomplishment that I take very seriously. After all, it wasn't easy to come back to college as a man in my thirties.

Following the '89 season, I was drafted by the Los Angeles Raiders in the second round. Playing in the NFL was the culmination of a lifetime of dreams. By even after I made it to the next level, I began thinking about coming back and finishing school and earning that degree in agricultural development. But I was living in California, playing with the Raiders, and I just never took the initiative. In fact, I would think of every excuse not to come back.

It wasn't until after I retired in 1998 that I started to get the itch to get back into football in some capacity. I wanted to either coach in high school or college. I started checking into it, and they told me that I had to have a degree. So I started checking into it and talking about it.

Some people were like, "Man, you don't need to do that." But my sister, Mitzi, went to school at A&M and went on to Pepperdine for law school. She thought I should come back, and my family in general was real supportive. So I just made the decision to do it.

It was weird coming back. I found myself sitting in classes sometimes, talking with a guy who was 18 or 19 and wondering, *What am I doing?* It was kind of uncomfortable, but I set my mind on what I wanted to do, and I was bound and determined to finish what I started.

Another part of my motivation to finish was to set a great example for my kids—16-year-old Aaron Jr., 13-year-old Alyes, and six-year-old Aiden. I'm divorced and living in Frisco, so I don't always get to see my kids as much as I would like. But I wanted to set a good example, and, of course, I would love to see them follow my footsteps one day by attending Texas A&M.

Being an Aggie means that you will forever be part of a great family of people who really care about you. It's been more than 20 years since I last suited up in an A&M uniform, but it never ceases to amaze me how many A&M former students still remember and care about me.

I can honestly say that being part of the Wrecking Crew was the highest point of my football career. I can walk around in Aggie gear today, and inevitably somebody will ask me my name. They may not know my face, but so many of them still know the name "Aaron Wallace" because of those days as a Wrecking Crew Blitz Brother.

What really gets me, though, is that I get these bearded, graying men coming up to me now and saying things like, "I was a kid in Kyle Field the day you held up Andre Ware's helmet."

That's a reminder to me that there's something really special about being an Aggie and that I'm getting really old.

Aaron Wallace was a two-time All-SWC linebacker at A&M in 1988 in 1989. Along with John Roper, he was part of the Wrecking Crew's Blitz Brothers. He finished his career as the Aggies' all-time sacks leader, with 42. He was drafted by the Los Angeles Raiders in the second round in 1990. After he retired in 1998, he returned to A&M to finish his degree. Wallace has three children—16-year-old Aaron Jr., 13-year-old Alyes, and six-year-old Aiden.

MICKEY WASHINGTON

DEFENSIVE BACK

1986–1989

WHEN I FIRST ARRIVED on the Texas A&M campus in the summer of 1986, I completed a short biography page for the sports information department. Along with basic information, I included my nickname—"Sticky Mickey"—as well as the reason for it.

At that time, I believed the nickname was applicable due to my hard-hitting nature on the field. Now, 25 years later, I hope the nickname still applies for different reasons, including sticking to my original goals and plans made many years ago.

As a child, I had three primary goals:

1. To play in the NFL—which I accomplished by playing eight seasons, making it to Super Bowl XXVIII as the starting cornerback for the Buffalo Bills.
2. To obtain a degree in accounting and to become an attorney—I fell short on the accounting goal, but I achieved the goal of becoming an attorney by earning a law degree in 2002 immediately following my NFL career.
3. To become a business owner—which I accomplished during my football career. Currently, I am a senior partner with Houston-based Washington & Ernster, LLC, which specializes in business law, labor, and employment.

One of the many things I learned from my parents, which was enhanced by playing football at Texas A&M under the direction of a goal-oriented man like Jackie Sherrill, was to never rest on your laurels and to never stop reevaluating your dreams.

While playing in the NFL and long afterward, I saw many guys—including me—who were taken advantage of by unscrupulous agents and business investors. At that time, I vowed to do whatever I could to prevent guys from being taken advantage of, which sparked my interest in becoming a sports agent. So, even after accomplishing the aforementioned goals, I have become a certified sports agent with the NFL in hopes of helping other athletes reach their long-term goals.

After my father passed away several years ago, my goals have been focused on helping people rather than attaining material things or monetary status. I continue to be blessed with a great stepfather, and my main priority now is to serve as a positive role model to my daughter, Eliana, as well as those closest to me. I want to be a role model for my daughter and other youngsters by helping them understand the importance of setting goals and maximizing educational opportunities. My life is a good example of what one can achieve by setting goals and working hard to achieve them.

I am a native of Port Arthur and Beaumont, Texas, and I discovered early in life that my work ethic and grades would lead to the opportunity to go to college. While rising to prominence at West Brook High School as a football player, I also made it a point to attend a university that would be more than just a stepping stone to the NFL. It was also important that it provide a strong academic program to continue fostering my intellectual capabilities and God-given talents.

I had several friends who went to school at A&M and did not play any sports. I had the opportunity to visit them on campus and learned more about the university before accepting a scholarship. I initially had a desire to follow defensive lineman Jerry Ball, a guy from my high school, to SMU. And I also considered following another buddy, wide receiver Daryl Owens, to LSU.

However, after visiting A&M, I thought, *Man, this is a big campus, but it also has a feeling like you are at home.* In addition, the school's academic reputation was outstanding, making my decision even easier. I felt at peace when I arrived on campus that first time, making it a perfect fit for me.

After determining where I would go, the next question to be answered was: where would I play? I played wide receiver and defensive back in high

After playing eight seasons in the NFL, Mickey Washington earned his law degree. Today he is a senior partner with Houston-based Washington & Ernster, LLC, which specializes in business law, labor, and employment.

school, and I initially began working as a running back at A&M. I also made an early impact on special teams as a return specialist.

Entering my sophomore season, I was switched to wide receiver due to an abundance of injuries and managed to work my way into the starting lineup as a wide receiver during the spring. But when I reported to two-a-days the following summer, the coaches had another move in mind, and I was switched to cornerback. As a result, I only had 10 or 11 days to move my way up the depth chart at cornerback.

Thanks to a lot of hard work, I became second string by the start of the season, and by the third game, I was starting. This really sticks out in my mind since we went on to play in the Cotton Bowl, where we beat Notre Dame. I had the awesome challenge of covering the Heisman Trophy winner that year, Tim Brown. I had a great game, which led to several honors.

I was named first-team All–Southwest Conference and an All-America honorable mention by the *Sporting News*. I also led the Aggies with four interceptions in '88.

More than the games or any of the football accomplishments, however, I vividly remember the camaraderie we had on those teams. Whether we were sitting on the back porch at Cain Hall or going to practice, we had a true family atmosphere, which is what being an Aggie was about. It was about togetherness and being bound to one another by a common belief that at Texas A&M, all things were possible. It was not just with the football players or athletes. There was a bond with all the students on campus.

While those are my fondest memories, I had a ton of great times on the football field, too. Although I was injured at the end of my senior season in 1989, I was still an eighth-round draft pick of the Phoenix Cardinals in '90, which is when my cross-country journeys began.

117

I was released by the Cardinals and played in New England, where I spent my first two NFL seasons (1990 and 1991) with the Patriots. I played the '92 season with the Redskins and then was part of two outstanding Buffalo teams in '93 and '94, playing in the Super Bowl as the starting cornerback in 1993. I finished my NFL career with a two-year stop in Jacksonville followed by a final season with the New Orleans Saints in '97.

In eight seasons, I played in 108 regular-season games, recording 326 tackles and 10 interceptions. I also began studying for the LSAT [Law School Admission Test] while still in the NFL.

While in New Orleans, a buddy and I started studying for the LSAT after practice. Although I felt like I did not accomplish much because I was so tired from football practice, I eventually took the LSAT.

When I did not receive a contract to play again in 1998, I applied for law school at the last minute, although I still thought I was going to go play football. I had been talking with other teams, and I figured I was going to sign with the Vikings or Raiders.

The day I received an acceptance letter to go to law school, I was scheduled to fly to L.A. to sign with the Raiders. But they called and postponed the appointment. To make a long story short, I entered law school instead of playing again.

During law school, I clerked with the Fort Bend District Attorney's Office the first summer and with a law firm called Taylor, Davis & Ernster the second year. The next summer, I went to D.C. and clerked at the NFL Players Association and returned for the last year of law school, clerking again at Taylor, Davis & Ernster. While preparing to sit for the bar, Cletus Ernster, who was the main partner I worked with, decided to leave the firm. Davis had left the firm prior to that. I chose to stay with Robert Taylor, and I worked at Taylor & Associates for a couple of years on cases with Cletus Ernster, who had gone out on his own.

A few years later, Cletus Ernster and I decided to form a partnership. We had a great relationship, and we complemented one another. I stayed extremely busy with the firm, while keeping a watchful eye on my alma mater.

I come back to campus from time to time and like to talk with the players on occasion. They are part of a different generation of players from when I played. They have so many more distractions. However, I like to emphasize how important it is to focus on finishing your education and establishing a foundation for the future.

In my opinion, A&M is one of the best places in the world to start a future since there is much more to life than football. Having a dream to play in the NFL is great, but it is extremely important to look beyond that and plan for the future.

Hopefully, I can serve as an example and role model for guys on the team, as well as students on campus. They are capable of achieving great things in their future if they work hard and stick to their goals. A&M was a special place for me while I was there, and I hope that others will have that same experience.

Mickey Washington was an All-SWC cornerback at A&M in 1988. He was an eighth-round draft pick of the Phoenix Cardinals in 1990, and he played eight NFL seasons, making it to Super Bowl XXVIII with the Buffalo Bills. Washington earned a law degree in 2002. Currently, he is a senior partner with Houston-based Washington & Ernster, LLC, which specializes in business law, labor, and employment. Washington has a daughter, Eliana.

RICHMOND WEBB

OFFENSIVE LINEMAN

1986–1989

As I look back on my four seasons at Texas A&M and my 13 seasons in the NFL, I can probably summarize all of my sentiments and memories with one word: blessed.

Including my redshirt season in 1985, I was part of three Southwest Conference championships at A&M and earned All-SWC and second-team All-America honors as a senior in '89. Most significant of all, I was chosen by my fellow teammates as the 1989 recipient of the prestigious Aggie Heart Award.

I was then selected in the first round of the 1990 NFL Draft by the Miami Dolphins, where I played in seven Pro Bowls. I became the first rookie offensive tackle to ever make the Pro Bowl, and I was the first player in Miami history to play in the Pro Bowl each of my first seven seasons. Considering all the great names in Miami history, that is truly humbling. And at one point in my career with the Dolphins, I was awarded a contract by Miami that made me the best-paid offensive lineman in the game.

The voters of the Pro Football Hall of Fame honored me by placing me on the NFL All-Decade team in the 1990s, and although I finished my career in Cincinnati for two seasons, Miami inducted me into the Dolphins Honor Roll on Christmas Day in 2006.

Like I said before, I have been seriously blessed as a football player...and in life. My wife, Chandra, and I have three wonderful daughters—Jasmine, Brianna, and Madison—and my success as an offensive lineman in the NFL enabled me to retire comfortably in Houston, where I now consider myself an investor.

To say that God blessed me beyond my wildest expectations would be a huge understatement. Growing up in Dallas and playing football and basketball at Roosevelt High School, I never would have even dreamed about playing such a long career as an offensive lineman—primarily because I didn't even play on the offensive line.

At Roosevelt, I was primarily a defensive lineman on the football field and a defensive specialist on the basketball court. One of my teammates at Roosevelt, future Aggie star linebacker Aaron Wallace, was also a high school basketball player with me. We both thought we had a little Michael Jordan in us, but there was one problem: neither one of us could score.

But not many guys wanted to come inside the paint against Aaron and me. While we didn't have much shooting touch, we were not afraid of contact. I remember one time when Coach Jackie Sherrill came to watch us play basketball. Aaron and I were both really nervous, hoping we would have great games.

We certainly wanted to make a great impression on Coach Sherrill. Little did I know then what a tremendously positive influence Coach Sherrill would have on my life. I find it fitting—and very rewarding—that Coach Sherrill and I were inducted into the Texas A&M Lettermen's Hall of Fame together.

He was certainly one of the primary reasons I chose to come to A&M. I didn't grow up with any ties to A&M. In fact, the only time I had been to campus previously was when I attended a Fellowship of Christian Athletes camp in College Station when I was in high school.

I liked the campus then, and I like the things the Coach Sherrill was saying when he recruited me.

He was a master motivator and a true players' coach. Coach Sherrill always had some sort of motivational technique going. And it was more than just words or a bunch of speeches. He'd always give us things to help us visualize his point. One year he gave us each a small piece of rope, and he told us about how we were a part of that rope. Such a small piece of rope wasn't much good for anything, but if we were all bound together, that rope could do amazing things. And none of us wanted to be part of the rope that broke.

I loved those kinds of things that helped to bond us together as a team. In fact, Coach Sherrill also provided me another visualization tool when he first

Richmond Webb, the 1989 recipient of the prestigious Aggie Heart Award, returned to A&M to earn his degree in industrial distribution in 1993.

recruited me. The first time we met, he sat down with me and talked about what he saw in my future. Then he pulled out his business card. Before he gave it to me, though, he wrote the words "Outland Trophy" on the back of his card. Then he told me to put the card in my wallet and that in four years from that point, he would go with me when I won the Outland Trophy.

At that time, I was energized about playing for Coach Sherrill. I honestly didn't know what the Outland Trophy—given annually to the nation's best interior lineman—was, but it sounded like something that would be nice to win. And it sounded like Coach Sherrill had the confidence in me to win it.

He might have given every lineman he recruited the same spiel about winning the Outland, but he made me feel special.

That warm and fuzzy feeling, however, quickly disappeared when I showed up on campus and realized just how far I had to go in order to be able to play. I showed up on the A&M campus weighing about 240 pounds, and I was overmatched by the offensive linemen I was going up against in practice.

That first redshirt season was pretty tough, and that second year [1986] was pretty forgettable from an individual standpoint, as well. I made one tackle as a freshman in '86. One.

That was 146 less than Johnny Holland, who led our defense that year. So, when the coaches suggested that I move to offensive line prior to my sophomore year, I was willing to give it a shot. Not surprisingly, none of the defensive coaches lost a lot of sleep over losing me to the other side of the ball.

During that sophomore season in '87, I backed up a great player, Louis Cheek, and I put on some weight from working out. I learned a lot from Louis and other guys on the offensive line like Jerry Fontenot. And then Joe Avezzano, who went on to have an outstanding career as a special-teams coach for the Dallas Cowboys, was the offensive line coach. He taught me a lot. But even with such great teaching, I knew I had a long way to go.

When Louis graduated following the '87 season, I knew I had to step it up in a hurry. I had a pretty good year as a junior in 1988, although that was a very disappointing and distracting season because it turned out to be Coach Sherrill's last in Aggieland.

But the next year Coach R.C. Slocum stepped in, and we didn't miss a beat. If not for two heartbreaking losses at Texas Tech and at home against Arkansas, we would have won the SWC in Coach Slocum's first year. Nevertheless, it was a good year overall, as we went 8–4 and played Pittsburgh in the John Hancock Bowl.

Even though I had improved quite a bit as a player and we played well as a team, in no way, shape, or form did I expect to be a first-round draft pick in the NFL. It caught me by surprise. Basically, I was going to school to get an education and play football for a university that I really loved. I didn't think much about the NFL when I was in college.

Once I got to the NFL and began playing at left tackle, I enjoyed it quite a bit. I loved playing for the Dolphins, and it was quite an honor to be playing with a quarterback like Dan Marino. Of course, I also felt a lot of pressure to perform, because I sure never wanted to be the one who allowed the great Dan Marino to get hurt.

Throughout my early years in the NFL, I also never forgot that I had some unfinished business back in College Station. Each off-season, I returned to A&M to go back to school, and in 1993, I graduated with a degree in industrial distribution.

I remember when I came back the first time and went back to classes with some of the guys. They would all ask, "If you're making all this money now, why are you coming back?" But that was the main thing I went to A&M for—to earn a degree. I was blessed to get a scholarship from A&M, and I always wanted to get a degree because of the strong alumni association and just the prestige of the degree. I also wanted to honor my mother and father, Bobbie and Richmond, who always stressed the importance of education.

Besides, A&M is one of the schools that is respected not only in the state of Texas, but in the United States, as well. The feeling of going across the stage to get my degree was hard to describe. But I advise all athletes to go back and get that. If they don't get it while they're playing, go back and get it. Of all my football memories at A&M, I am most proud that I returned to get my degree.

I am also proud that I have been able to give back to the university. I donated to the Championship Vision capital campaign, and I've been a part of the 12th Man Foundation, the fund-raising organization of A&M athletics.

A&M was so good for me that it would be impossible to ever repay the university for all it helped me to become. But I consider it an honor to be an Aggie graduate, and it was always an honor to represent A&M in college and in the pros.

Without a doubt, I was blessed.

Richmond Webb was part of three Southwest Conference championships at A&M and earned All-SWC and second-team All-America honors as a senior in 1989. He was also chosen as the 1989 recipient of the prestigious Aggie Heart Award. Webb was selected in the first round of the 1990 NFL Draft by the Miami Dolphins, where he became the first rookie offensive tackle to ever make the Pro Bowl, and he was the first player in Miami history to play in the Pro Bowl each of his first seven seasons. Webb and his wife, Chandra, have three daughters—Jasmine, Brianna, and Madison. He lives in Houston, where he works part-time as an investor.

WARREN BARHORST
12th MAN KICKOFF TEAM
1987

WHEN I FINISHED WRITING my first book in 2008—*Game Plan: The Definitive Playbook for Starting or Growing Your Business*—the opening paragraph in the preface was this:

> Let's get straight to the point right here on the first line of the first page of this book: you've got what it takes to succeed. There's no doubt in my mind about that. You are equipped to succeed in business. You have the genetic makeup to thrive as an entrepreneur. You have what it takes to make it on your own, to gain financial independence, to leave a legacy for your children. There it is, folks. There's your endorsement. There's your validation. There's the vote of confidence that so many people spend their entire working lives longing to hear.

I felt quite comfortable making that statement then—and now—for various reasons. I won't go into all of them here, but I believe I am living proof that ordinary men and women can accomplish extraordinary things in their lives if they learn how to train their minds and build on their successes.

Game Plan—and the accompanying website—is designed to provide entrepreneurs with a step-by-step blueprint to start or grow a business. It begins with the importance of dreams and walks readers through financing,

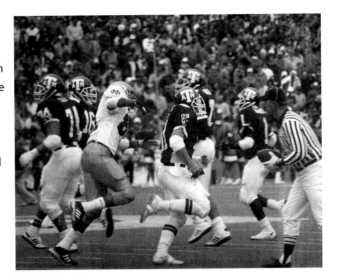

Before building a nationally respected insurance agency with offices across the state of Texas, Warren Barhorst earned national headlines in the 1988 Cotton Bowl for tackling and enraging Heisman Trophy winner Tim Brown.

business planning, marketing, technology, training, sales strategies, hiring, employee retention, and much more.

I felt qualified to write the book because of my own success in the insurance industry. I opened my first insurance office in 1993 with my wife, Lisa. We possessed major dreams and minimal capital. Today the Barhorst Insurance Group (BIG) is the No. 1 Nationwide Insurance agency in the United States, with more than 40 offices throughout Texas, 100 associates, and $50 million in sales in 2009. My goal is to have 500 offices and $1 billion in sales by 2020.

I really believe I will accomplish those goals because I know—like I stated in the opening paragraph of my book—that I have what it takes to succeed. And I first really started to believe that during my time as a walk-on football player at Texas A&M.

But let me backtrack first. My dream in life was never to be an insurance agent. The insurance industry, with its residual income and unlimited profit potential, simply provided me with the vehicle to reach my dream destination: financial independence.

Dating back to the time I first purchased my own bicycle, I've always wanted to be financially independent. As the youngest of six kids, I watched my father bust his butt throughout his entire professional career. He worked for a respected, nationally known company for 42 years. Day after day, week after week, and year after year, my father devoted his working life to collecting a paycheck while helping someone else get ahead. My father basically stayed on the corporate treadmill, sweating it out, but never really moving forward.

He never made more than a very modest income, and he was continuously passed over for virtually every promotion that he could have possibly received. As a result, my mother also worked the cafeteria line at my elementary school to help make ends meet. With six kids in the house, the ends rarely met.

I am extremely proud of my parents because they devoted their lives to developing their children. My five siblings and I have a total of six undergraduate degrees, two master's degrees, one PhD, two MDs, and a host of professional designations behind our names. My parents put their kids first, and we owe much of our success to them.

But despite all of that, money was a constant source of concern for my parents, and I decided at a fairly young age that I wanted to do something professionally that would allow me to earn a comfortable living. I didn't want to fret about money every day. I didn't want to live in fear of the car breaking down. So I went to college—first at Stephen F. Austin in Nacogdoches, Texas—and later earned a degree in industrial distribution from Texas A&M University in College Station.

126

It was in college where I began to realize the power of believing you can accomplish your dreams. I'd like to tell you that I learned this by breezing through my classes. But that would be a bald-faced lie. The truth is that I wanted to quit college two or three times. But my father, who was told numerous times that he never earned the promotions he wanted because he didn't own a college degree, wouldn't allow me to quit.

So I continued to persevere through my classes, scratching and clawing to grasp the concepts that seemed to come easily to many of the smarter students who shared those classrooms with me.

I earned the degree from A&M that hangs on my office wall in 1988. But the more valuable lessons I learned in college had nothing to do with actually making grades. The most masterful sales job I've ever pulled off came in college. I noticed Lisa Highsmith shortly after I transferred from Stephen F. Austin to A&M.

Like most beautiful women I've encountered throughout my life, she initially wanted absolutely nothing to do with me. But, after basically stalking her around campus for several months, she was left with two options: go out with me or solicit a court-ordered restraining order.

Fortunately, she chose to go out with me. She was out of my league in every sense, and I knew I was running a sizeable risk of being rejected. But despite what my inner voice was trying to tell me—like, *You don't have a chance*—I set my sights on winning Lisa's heart. With a little luck and a lot of begging, I did just that. Here's what I concluded from this courtship: if I could sell Lisa on spending the rest of her life with me, I figured I could sell just about anything else.

An equally significant realization for me that occurred in college came on the football field. I was a fairly decent prep fullback and linebacker at Jersey Village High School in the Houston area. But I was certainly not big-time college football material.

In fact, when I came out of high school, I weighed about 180 pounds, and I had convinced myself that my football career had come to an end. Truthfully, I was scared to even give it a shot at Division I-AA Stephen F. Austin. I had spent much of my life dreaming about playing college football, and I'd spent countless hours envisioning myself at Texas A&M.

I even had two older brothers and a sister who had preceded me at A&M. But fear stopped me in my tracks. In the pit of my stomach—although I never would have admitted it to anyone else—I didn't want to go to A&M because I wasn't sure I could cut it. And I didn't want to try out for the SFA football team because I didn't want to risk the chance of making a fool of myself.

After two years at SFA, however, I had gained about 30 pounds and—more significantly—a little courage. At the urging of my older brother, Alan, who had come back to A&M to work on his master's degree in mechanical engineering, I transferred to A&M and also decided to try out for the 12th Man Kickoff Team.

That team, consisting of 10 walk-on players and one scholarship kicker, had gained tremendous national recognition under head coach Jackie Sherrill, and approximately 350 A&M students tried out for it the same year I did [1986].

I made the squad, but I was unable to participate in any games because of the transfer rules. In 1987, however, I bulked up to 225 pounds, and I was a key contributor on the kickoff team. As A&M rolled toward a third consecutive Southwest Conference title, the 12th Man Kickoff Team continued to attract national attention.

And one of the interesting angles of the 1988 Cotton Bowl was the matchup between our 12th Man Kickoff Team and the Heisman Trophy winner. Tim Brown, the Oakland Raiders' all-time leading receiver, established a Notre Dame school record for the most career kickoff-return yards. It's a record that still stands and one that provided plenty of motivation for our kickoff unit. We certainly didn't want to let him beat us, and we looked at it as a real challenge to keep him under control.

Brown was one of the most gifted athletes I had ever seen. He was also from Dallas and had played high school ball against one of my teammates, defensive back Chet Brooks. Before the game, Brooks told the members of the 12th Man Kickoff Team that, if we had the opportunity, we should steal Brown's belt towel.

They had played each other in high school, and Brooks told the guys on the 12th Man Kickoff Team that stealing his towel would drive Tim crazy. Brooks was right. And after we had taken a 28–10 lead in the fourth quarter, I got my chance.

If you watch the film of that thing, I almost got beat. He was two steps away from going for six. But I made the tackle on him and acted on Chet's idea. Those guys had been stealing our towels all day, and I swiped it and started running off the field while trying to stuff the towel in my pants.

Before I made it to our bench, though, Brown jumped on my back, tackling me and grabbing his towel back. The infuriated Brown was flagged for a 15-yard, unsportsmanlike-conduct penalty, and we went on to win the game 35–10. On the following day, newspapers throughout the state of Texas and across the country featured pictures, headlines, and stories with my name prominently in print. And years later, in a survey conducted by the Texas A&M Lettermen's Association, my thievery of Brown's towel was voted the fifth-most memorable moment in Aggie sports history.

Here's the lesson to be learned from this story: stealing someone else's ideas and then implementing those strategies on your own can propel you into the spotlight beyond your wildest imagination. I'm living proof of that. And not just in the sports arena. I've been stealing ideas from other successful business people for many years, as I initially built my insurance agency from the ground up.

On average, I'd say that I still receive about four or five reminders per week that many Aggies still remember my taking Tim Brown's towel. In fact, in December 2009 Texas A&M graduate and Houston sports radio talk show host John Lopez had me on his show and—as a total surprise to me—he also had Tim Brown on the air.

It was a great interview, and Tim Brown was awesome. He's long forgiven me for taking that towel, and I hope that I can now consider him a friend. I've obviously received plenty of attention from that one play many years ago.

But I earned much more than my proverbial 15 minutes of fame while at Texas A&M. I found the love of my life while in Aggieland, and we have three wonderful children, including one who is now a student at A&M.

Because of all the doors A&M has opened for me, I have made it a point to give back to my university. I have been blessed with the opportunity to make some significant donations to the 12th Man Foundation—the fund-raising organization of A&M athletics—and I have played a role in Nationwide's sponsorships of A&M athletics.

I've also had the opportunity to come back to A&M to speak and to be a guest lecturer. I spoke to a class in industrial distribution about hiring and interviewing. I did a class for the students in Free Enterprise (SIFE) on my *Game Plan* book, and I have judged the MBA Tech Challenge several times. In my speaking engagements, I always share with the students this important lesson that I learned during my time at Texas A&M: in Aggieland, I discovered that even an anonymous walk-on like me has what it takes to bring down a Heisman Trophy winner.

Warren Barhorst is perhaps the most famous 12th Man Kickoff Team member in A&M history, as he drew national headlines for first tackling Heisman Trophy winner Tim Brown in the 1988 Cotton Bowl and then enraging Brown by stealing his belt towel. As Barhorst jogged toward the bench, Brown jumped on his back, tackling Barhorst and grabbing his towel back. The infuriated Brown was flagged for a 15-yard unsportsmanlike-conduct penalty, and the Aggies went on to win the game 35–10. Barhorst and his wife, Lisa, opened their first insurance office in 1993. Today the Barhorst Insurance Group (BIG) is the No. 1 Nationwide Insurance agency in the United States. In 2008 Barhorst authored his first business book, *Game Plan: The Definitive Playbook for Starting or Growing Your Business*. He and his wife have three children—son Spencer and daughters Shelby and Ashley.

BUCKY RICHARDSON

QUARTERBACK

1987–1991

GROWING UP IN BATON ROUGE, LOUISIANA, and attending Broadmoor High School, I was quite aware of the traditions, pride, passions, and pageantry associated with LSU football, especially in terms of night games at Tiger Stadium, affectionately known throughout Louisiana and the SEC as "Death Valley."

Throughout much of my life, I rooted for the hometown Tigers, and as I began to develop as college prospect at Broadmoor, I gave serious consideration to wearing the purple and gold and playing college ball in my own backyard. LSU was one of the final schools I considered as I narrowed down my list of possible collegiate destinations, and I probably could have been happy being a Tiger.

But deep down, I had a nagging feeling that LSU wasn't the right place for me. The Tigers' football team had been pretty good in the mid-1980s under Bill Arnsparger. LSU had been to the Sugar Bowl at the conclusion of the 1984 and 1986 seasons, and the Tigers played in the 1985 Liberty Bowl, as well.

Nevertheless, I didn't want to stay in Baton Rouge for the rest of my life. Nor was I that sold on the idea of staying in Louisiana. I wanted to go somewhere different; I wanted to experience new surroundings; and I wanted to expand my horizons. I'd always liked the state of Texas, even though I had only visited the Lone Star State a handful of times as a kid.

My visit to Texas A&M in 1986 was outstanding, as well. I was very impressed with the campus, and I remember being toured around by one of the great quarterbacks in the country at that time, Kevin Murray. I was a very different quarterback than Murray, who essentially rewrote all of the Aggies' passing records during his time in Aggieland.

I was more of a runner, to be sure. That was primarily a result of my background. I didn't even start playing quarterback until I was a 10th-grader at Broadmoor. My head coach in high school, Rusty Price, was a tremendous man who had been a war hero in Vietnam as a U.S. marine. Coach Price liked my rugged running style, and he moved me from running back to quarterback. But I still played the position like a running back. I wasn't one of those quarterbacks who slid before contact, and I didn't run out of bounds.

I played the game with passion, and I tried to run guys over who stood in my way. I became a pretty decent passer by my senior year, completing 42 of 98 passes for 699 yards, but I ran for nearly twice as many (1,277).

I also was a pretty decent baseball player in high school, earning all-state honors twice as a pitcher. The baseball diamond was where I first earned the nickname "Bucky." Up until my little league coach started calling me Bucky because I reminded him of former Chicago White Sox/New York Yankees/Texas Rangers shortstop Bucky Dent, everybody just called me John. But Bucky stuck, and I probably should have viewed it as an honor because Dent was considered as a scrappy, tough player who had a penchant for coming through in the clutch—like he did in the 1978 AL East playoff against Boston.

Anyhow, I was quite intrigued about the possibilities of attending Texas A&M. The Aggies had won back-to-back Southwest Conference championships in 1985 and 1986, and head coach Jackie Sherrill was putting together a monster 1987 recruiting class that included some sensational running backs like Darren Lewis, Randy Simmons, and Keith McAfee, as well as standouts at other positions like Chris Crooms, Larry Horton, Steve Lofton, Matt McCall, and William Thomas.

It seemed like an exciting time to be at Texas A&M, and I decided to leave my home state for Aggieland. That was not a very popular decision in south Louisiana. I announced I was choosing A&M over LSU on a local television station in Baton Rouge a few days prior to national letter-of-intent day. After my announcement, the station received a ton of angry phone calls, and my family began receiving our share of hate mail.

Bucky Richardson left his childhood hometown of Baton Rouge to become one of the most popular players in Texas A&M history. In the 1990 Holiday Bowl against heavily favored BYU, he passed for a touchdown, rushed for two TDs, and caught a scoring pass in A&M's blowout 65–14 victory.

But going to A&M was undoubtedly the right decision for me. I loved the friendliness of the campus, I developed a good relationship with my teammates and coaches, and I enjoyed a strong debut as a true freshman in '87.

Craig Stump was viewed as our primary passing quarterback, but I was able to start five games and eventually earned SWC Offensive Newcomer of the Year honors. I only completed 16 passes that whole season for 156 yards. But thanks to a great offensive line, I rushed for 102 yards, including an 82-yard run, in the first game I ever played against Southern Miss. About a month later, I rushed for 137 against Rice.

But my favorite memories from that first season involve the final two games. I didn't start the Texas game at Kyle Field, and when I first got into the game, it was pretty frustrating because the Longhorn defenders kept pulling off my shoe after they'd tackle me. I finally had to have our equipment manager, Billy Pickard, tape my shoes to my calves.

Late in the game, with the score tied at 13, the SWC title on the line, and our fans whipped into a feverish pitch, I kept the ball on a speed option play to the right and scored on a seven-yard run that helped us secure a 20–13 win. It was A&M's fourth win in a row over Texas, and it gave us a third consecutive conference title. It also sent us to the Cotton Bowl, where we squared off against Heisman Trophy winner Tim Brown and the Notre Dame Fighting Irish.

On a chilly Friday afternoon in Dallas, we thoroughly whipped Notre Dame 35–10. The Irish scored first to take a 7–0 lead, but we took control in the second half. Darren Lewis hit Tony Thompson for a 24-yard TD on a halfback pass to get us rolling, and we never looked back. I was fortunate to earn MVP honors after rushing for 96 yards and two scores.

As smoothly as '87 went, I had huge plans for the next couple of years. But '88 started as a bit of a disappointment, and it finished in bitter fashion. We lost our first three games of the season against Nebraska, LSU, and Oklahoma State. I blew my knee out in the Texas game, and we finished 7–5. Coach Sherrill resigned under pressure at the end of the year, and I missed the entire 1989 season as I rehabilitated from major knee surgery.

In 1990 I made it back onto the field, splitting time early in the season with Lance Pavlas. By the end of the year, I had worked my way back into the starter's role and finished that season with what was probably the greatest game of my collegiate career—the 1990 Holiday Bowl in San Diego.

From a team standpoint, it was as close to the perfect game as I've ever been a part of in my life.

It was an old-fashioned, behind-the-woodshed whipping, which ended with BYU head coach LaVell Edwards first confronting our offensive coordinator, Bob Toledo, and then refusing to shake anyone's hand. Edwards and the rest of the BYU contingent were convinced that we had run up the score. Perhaps the Cougars should have considered that possibility when they were so busy running their mouths prior to the game.

The 1990 Cougars had climbed to as high as No. 2 in the national polls. Then, following a late-September loss at Oregon, BYU began running up the scores on opponents to move back into the national title picture and tried to run up the numbers for Heisman Trophy candidate Ty Detmer. But on December 1 BYU blew its national title aspirations when Hawaii crushed the Cougars 59–28. The loss sent BYU to the Holiday Bowl, and the Cougars were extremely disappointed about the matchup against an unranked, 8–3–1 A&M team.

Our team, on the other hand, looked forward to the bowl and had a great time. We visited SeaWorld and experienced the sights and sounds of San Diego. But once practices began, we were all business. We practiced at a junior college in San Diego, and we got after it. We knew BYU was a very good opponent, and everybody knew that Detmer was a great quarterback who had just won the Heisman. We felt like we had our work cut out for us.

Once the game started, we took the opening kickoff and marched 80 yards for a touchdown, but BYU quickly answered with a seven-play, 65-yard drive to knot the score at 7. After that initial exchange of touchdowns, I remember going up to Coach R.C. Slocum and telling him that this was going to be a shootout. Instead, it turned into a blowout. William Thomas intercepted Detmer on BYU's next possession, and the rout was on. We outscored BYU 58–7 the rest of the way. I rushed for my first touchdown early in the second quarter, caught a touchdown pass from Darren Lewis later in the second quarter, and then threw my first touchdown pass of the night just before halftime.

When it was finally over, we had won 65–14. We rolled up 680 yards of total offense and limited the BYU passing attack to 197 net yards. And the Wrecking Crew, led by Thomas and Quentin Coryatt, held BYU to minus-12 yards rushing.

I am regularly reminded of that game, as A&M fans have consistently talked to me through the years about it. I was inducted into the Holiday Bowl Hall of Fame with Detmer in 2001, which was quite an experience.

As good as the Holiday Bowl was, though, the following year was even better because we won the SWC title again for the first time since my freshman year in '87. We opened the season by trouncing LSU 45–7 and finished the regular season by pounding Texas 31–14.

After that season, I was drafted by the Houston Oilers in the eighth round. I spent the next three years playing with the Oilers and continued to be amazed by the Aggie network. I loved the A&M fans and former students when I was in school, but I really began to appreciate the Aggie family even more when I moved to Houston. The Aggies were so supportive of me, regardless of whether we were playing in Houston or anywhere on the road.

Following three years with the Oilers, I had short stints with the New England Patriots, Dallas Cowboys, and Kansas City Chiefs. I then considered pursuing a career in the Canadian Football League, and I even met with the Montreal Alouettes.

But ultimately, I decided to enter private business, and that's when I really began to understand the power of the Aggie network. Way back when I was a sophomore at A&M, Coach Sherrill had introduced me to Charlie Milstead, who had been a quarterback for the Aggies in the late 1950s. During school, I became good friends with Mr. Milstead's son, Lyle, who was also a student at A&M.

When I left football for good following the 1996 training camp, I asked Mr. Milstead to introduce me to some businesspeople in Houston in hopes that I might land a job. Soon thereafter, Mr. Milstead offered me a sales job with his company, Environmental Improvements, Inc. (EI²), a company that works with cities throughout Texas and Oklahoma on installing and integrating new water treatment and waste treatment systems.

I have been with the company ever since, and I am now a partner with EI², along with Lyle Milstead and former A&M linebacker Larry Kelm. And with each passing year, the power, reach, and sincerity of the Aggie network never ceases to amaze me.

Other than my decision to ask the love of my life, the former Tracey Turner, to marry me in 1997, my decision to choose Texas A&M over LSU is probably the best one I have ever made. Being an Aggie involves so much

more than going to school at a place for four or five years or merely returning to campus for a few football games each year.

Being an Aggie means you are part of a family that is always looking out
for each other for the rest of your life. I hope our own kids—daughters Jordan and Jenna, and our son, John Paul—get to experience the unique family
atmosphere of being an Aggie one day for themselves.

I have made sure that I have constantly exposed them to Aggie football,
Aggie basketball, and so many other events through the years, as we regularly make the trip from our home in Missouri City to College Station. If
they do attend A&M one day, they will not need to ask me for directions.
They have that trek memorized by now.

Bucky Richardson is one of the most popular players in Texas A&M history. In
addition to earning SWC Offensive Newcomer of the Year honors in 1987, Richardson was also named as the MVP of the Aggies' 35–10 win over Notre Dame
in the 1988 Cotton Bowl, after rushing for 96 yards and two scores. He blew
out his knee in the 1988 Texas game and missed the 1989 season. He returned
in 1990 and led the Aggies to a historic 65–14 win over BYU in the Holiday
Bowl. In that game Richardson rushed for two touchdowns, caught a touchdown pass, and threw a touchdown, earning Offensive MVP honors. Then in
1991 Richardson again led the Aggies to an SWC title. He was drafted by the
Houston Oilers in the eighth round in 1992 and spent the next three years
playing with the Oilers. He also had short stints with the New England Patriots, Dallas Cowboys, and Kansas City Chiefs. Richardson is now a partner with
Houston-based EI^2. He and his wife, Tracey, have three kids—daughters Jordan and Jenna, and son John Paul.

KEVIN SMITH

DEFENSIVE BACK

1988–1991

BEFORE I WAS BORN, my family, which included three older brothers and two sisters, had a family dog that was named "Pup." Everybody loved the dog, especially my two sisters. Sadly, I never got a chance to meet the dog. My sisters were told that the dog must have run away, although I later heard other stories. For the twins' sake, however, I'll stick with the runaway story.

Anyway, my sisters were still very upset when my mother went to the hospital to give birth to me. One of my brothers, in an attempt to cheer them up, told the twins that our mom would be bringing Pup home from the hospital.

You can imagine their excitement…and then their disappointment when Mom brought me home instead. From that point forward, though, I was known as "Pup."

Many years later when I came to Texas A&M in 1988, I thought the nickname might fade away. But I was so baby-faced, so thin, and so small, my teammates and coaches at A&M continued referring to me as Pup.

I looked as much like a puppy as Reveille, the school's canine mascot, ever did. One of our strength and conditioning coaches at A&M, Allen Kinley, acknowledges that when he first saw me he figured I had to be somebody's younger brother. And then when he found out I was actually one of the

Aggies' recruits, Kinley—who is still at A&M—predicted that I was too thin and fragile-looking to ever play.

Of course, it should also be noted that Kinley said the same thing about Dat Nguyen a few years later because Dat was so overweight. Fortunately for Dat and me, Kinley's first impressions weren't accurate ones. Dat went on to become the leading tackler in the history of Texas A&M, and I became the Aggies' career leader in interceptions.

But I can hardly blame Coach Kinley for thinking that about me. Even when I flip through the pages of some of the old media guides, I am amazed at how young I look. I was part of the same recruiting class as Quentin Coryatt, fullback Robert Wilson, offensive lineman John Ellisor, and many others. But those guys looked like young men in their freshmen pictures, while I was looking quite boyish.

That used to kind of bother me back then. Now, more than 20 years later, I only feel young at heart. I no longer look that way.

But whenever I think back to those great times I had at Texas A&M, I do feel rejuvenated. I was part of some great teams in Aggieland, including the team that gave R.C. Slocum his first championship as a head coach in 1991.

Coach Slocum was my defensive coordinator during my first year at A&M, and he was also from my hometown, Orange. He had been a really good player at West Orange–Stark High School in the early 1960s, earning all-district honors on a team that reached the state semifinals.

But I always joked with Coach Slocum about the difference between our high school days at Stark. I liked to remind him that, while he made it to the state semifinals, I was part of two state championship teams in 1986 and 1987.

It was all in good fun, though. I always felt like I had a real bond with Coach Slocum because of our similar backgrounds.

When I arrived at A&M in the summer of 1988, my goal was to find a way to earn playing time. That was going to be a difficult challenge, because we had some outstanding defensive backs, including Mickey Washington, Gary Jones, Alex Morris, and others. But I worked very hard, and I learned as much as I could from our coaches and my teammates. And as a true freshman, I ended up playing quite a bit. In fact, I broke up five passes and intercepted two, including one that I returned 52 yards against Baylor.

While I played pretty well as a freshman, my sophomore season—Coach Slocum's first as head coach—was my real breakout year. We opened the 1989

Cornerback Kevin Smith earned All-America honors in 1991 and finished his career as the all-time leader in school history with 20 interceptions.

season at home against No. 7 LSU, and Larry Horton returned the opening kickoff 92 yards for a touchdown. Later in the game, we were up 21–10 when LSU quarterback Tommy Hodson tried to make something big happen.

Instead, I intercepted Hodson's pass and took it back 40 yards for a touchdown. I guess that was a sign of things to come.

Throughout the rest of the year, opposing quarterbacks kept challenging me, and I kept intercepting passes, especially at home. I intercepted at least one pass in every home game we played and finished the year with nine picks.

In 1990 I added seven more interceptions. In 1991 I guess opposing coaches and quarterbacks finally decided to quit trying to pick on the "little guy" (I was about 5'11", 175 pounds). They didn't throw too many passes in my direction during my senior year. I intercepted two passes in '91 to finish my collegiate career with a total of 20.

I ended up making 38 consecutive starts in college. I earned consensus All-America honors in 1991, and I was an All-SWC selection for three straight years. I also had a lot of fun returning punts in college.

But, honestly, it's not the specific games or numbers that first come to mind when I recall my time in Aggieland. When I look back on my college career, I think about Cain Hall, walking through the crowd while the band was playing and walking into that stadium. The feeling of Kyle Field shaking as the crowd built up and then running onto that field are what I remember the most.

I remember some of the games and some of the scores, but what I really remember is the pregame and game-day atmosphere. I have brought friends down to A&M games over the years with no ties to A&M. They go in as a Grambling State Tiger or a Sam Houston State Bearkat, but they leave as Aggies once they experience one game day at Kyle Field.

I've played in stadiums of all sizes across the country, but there is just no other place like Kyle Field. I am so grateful that I played my collegiate career at a place like A&M. I also feel so fortunate that I was able to continue playing in my home state after I completed my career at A&M.

140

I was the No. 1 draft pick of the Dallas Cowboys in 1992, and I broke into the starting lineup as a rookie cornerback. I was the youngest player on the Cowboys' roster when we won Super Bowl XXVII. And I was a part of three Super Bowl titles in my eight-year NFL career.

To play high school football in Texas, then to go to A&M and then be drafted by the Cowboys—America's Team—and to win three Super Bowls was a dream come true for me. Playing my entire career—all three levels—in Texas was really an unbelievably positive experience.

I didn't escape without my share of bumps and bruises, however. I tore my Achilles in 1995 against the New York Giants, jeopardizing my career. But one of my proudest professional accomplishments is that I was able to come back from the injury and once again perform at a top level.

The Achilles injury wasn't as painful as I thought it might be, but the rehab was really tough. And I thought one of my best years as a pro was the year after the Achilles tear—thanks to one of the world's best strength coaches, Mike Woicik. What some people forget is that it was really my back that forced me out of the game.

Back problems forced me to miss eight games in 1999, and although I was in training camp in 2000, I never returned to the playing field again. Two years later, however, I did return to A&M to serve as the color analyst of the Aggie Radio Network's broadcasts. I enjoyed the experience, but I quickly realized I wasn't cut out for broadcasting.

The thing that hurt me as a broadcaster was that I was too much a fan of the game. At times during the game, I got caught up being a fan when I actually should have been announcing the game. But I was thankful for the opportunity.

I was also thankful for numerous business opportunities following my retirement from the Cowboys. I was involved with a newspaper called *DFW Sports*; I was the chairman of an information technologies company in Dallas; and I was the vice president of business development for a financial company. After the hustle and bustle of the mortgage world, I have decided to get back to my roots. I've started Sportzdreamz.com. Sportzdreamz events and products have been designed to help promote and assist charities, booster clubs, youth leagues, at-risk kids programs, and other organizations with fund-raising needs around the country. Our goal is to help raise funds to supplement the organizations' budgets by using my large contact list of former professional athletes to provide motivational speaking, autograph signings, etc.

After I walked away from the game, I decided to give back by sharing my knowledge of the game. I also train young defensive backs in Lewisville. My agent had been trying to get me back into the game for years. He would always say, "Look at your résumé."

I am proud of that résumé, which includes recent honors, such as being selected as a member of Dave Campbell's Texas Football 50th Anniversary All-Time High School and College Team, along with being named to the Texas All-Century High School Team. I have been blessed, and it's an honor to give back.

But my primary interests are my kids—my son, Kevaughn, and my daughter, Elizabeth. I live in Plano, and I thank God daily for my kids, my numerous blessings, and the fact that I had the opportunity to attend school and play football at a place like A&M.

Texas A&M opened so many doors for me and provided me with a tremendous foundation for success. I always felt like my time and experiences at A&M provided me with an edge as a pro football player and as an entrepreneur.

And because of the confidence and skills I developed in Aggieland, this "Pup" always believed he could emerge as the leader of the pack.

Kevin Smith earned first-team All-America honors at cornerback in 1991. Smith made 38 consecutive starts, and he was an All-SWC selection for three straight years. Smith is the all-time interceptions leader in A&M history with 20. He was the No. 1 draft pick of the Dallas Cowboys in 1992, and he broke into the starting lineup as a rookie. He was the youngest player on the Cowboys' roster when Dallas won Super Bowl XXVII. He was a part of three Super Bowl titles in his eight-year NFL career. Smith is a successful businessman in the Dallas area, and he has two kids—son Kevaughn and daughter Elizabeth.

The NINETIES

DERRICK FRAZIER

CORNERBACK

1989–1992

WHENEVER I MEET NEW PEOPLE and they discover that I played collegiately at Texas A&M and played professional football with the Philadelphia Eagles and Indianapolis Colts, I am often asked about the most intense, physical, and difficult games of my career.

I certainly played in some games on the collegiate and professional level that would fall into that category. But in all honesty, most all of the games I played in were easy compared to the practices we endured at Texas A&M.

When I arrived at A&M in 1988, I tipped the scales at a whopping 155 pounds. It was obvious that I needed to redshirt in order to add some weight and develop some strength. During that redshirt season, I had the opportunity to play on the scout team against the likes of tailback Darren Lewis, fullback Robert Wilson, and wide receiver Rod Harris. It was brutal, to say the least.

During that season and subsequent ones, I specifically remember how remarkably intense the individual battle between Wilson and linebacker Quentin Coryatt would be, setting the tone for the rest of the team. Wilson, who would go on to be a third-round NFL draft pick in '91, and Coryatt, a first-round pick in '92, would hit each other so hard that their face masks would end up turned toward the side of their heads.

The sound of the hits would reverberate throughout Kyle Field or across the practice fields. I can still hear some of those crushing hits when I think

Derrick Frazier established the all-time school record for career passes broken up, with 36 from 1989 to 1992.

145

back to those days. And they didn't just happen occasionally; those kinds of hits happened play after play.

Our offense ran a lot of option plays in those days, and we always felt that, if we could stop quarterback Bucky Richardson, contain Lewis—who would go on to become the leading rusher in Southwest Conference history—and handle the blocking of Wilson, we could stop anybody we played in the SWC.

We competed so hard against each other that I am really serious when I say that most of our practices were more demanding and difficult than the games. That's why we won so many games and two SWC championships during my time at Texas A&M. It's also how we led the nation in total defense and passing defense in '91.

I'm so proud of the numerous things we were able to achieve as a team during my career at A&M. And I am so pleased that I originally chose to go to A&M. I didn't have any ties to A&M, but my high school football coach at Clemmons, Bob Boyd, did talk to me about A&M from time to time, beginning in my sophomore year. That's when I started following A&M and really started watching their defense.

I immediately loved the way the Aggies played defense and the overall style and swagger of the Wrecking Crew. I remember watching guys like Chet Brooks, John Roper, Aaron Wallace, Mickey Washington, Gary Jones, and so forth. I actually followed Roper for years, as he attended the high school where my mom taught. All of those individuals caught my attention, as did the coaching styles of head coach R.C. Slocum and defensive coordinator Bob Davie.

All of those factors helped me to narrow my decision down to A&M and Colorado. I had met both Kevin Smith and Robert Wilson on my recruiting trip, and we all ended up choosing A&M.

Once I got to A&M, my first impression—as a city boy from Houston—was culture shock. But I did have a good time, and I loved the closeness and the camaraderie of the team, especially when we all lived together in Cain Hall. We were so tight, and our chemistry was so strong back then. I think that really helped us as a team once we stepped on the field. When we came out of the locker room, it was obvious that we were a close-knit team. We developed that bond at Cain Hall.

146

I vividly recall that we had all night domino games and card parties. Playing card games into the wee hours of the morning tends to bond you together. You get to know each other as much more than just football players; you get to know all about each other as young men.

I think that's something that's really missing in today's college sports now that there are no more athletic dorms. We all eventually moved off campus, but initially, it was good that we all lived together. Especially as freshmen, we had just moved away from home. We all still missed our parents, and living in the dorm together taught you the value of friendships and brotherhood.

Without that family atmosphere of the dorm nowadays, it seems like the student-athletes are more on their own. You practice together and then go your own way. That's almost like the situation at the professional level. So I'm really glad that I got a chance to play at A&M when I did.

Most of all, though, I'm just glad that I played at A&M, where I set the all-time school record for the most career passes broken up with 36 from 1989 to 1992. Today I have a maroon room in my house, which serves as my office.

I also tell my five children on a regular basis what a great place Texas A&M is to go to school.

I don't think I'll ever really force A&M on my kids. But I did tell my oldest daughter that she could go to any college, but if it's not A&M, she will have to pay for it herself. So I guess I'm already recruiting my kids to A&M.

I like to tell them about Aggie values and the great atmosphere A&M has to offer. My kids are like, "Well, A&M's not that good anymore." But I tell them everything goes in a cycle, and our time is coming back. We had a good run in the early 1980s and all the way into the late 1990s. We've been down a little bit, but I think we're back on the way to rebuilding the program.

I've always thought that if we could get it rolling again—with the great facilities we now have on campus—there would be no stopping A&M, because there is just no other place like Kyle Field to play.

Philadelphia is a wild place to play, and I have played in Arrowhead Stadium and other so-called great stadiums in the NFL. I have also played at LSU and other big-time college stadiums. But to me, there is no place like Kyle. I have always said that whenever I come back, I enjoy it so much because the atmosphere is so different than any place I have ever played.

When I think back on my time at A&M, I just remember looking up in the stands and seeing everybody rocking and swaying from side to side, yelling their lungs out. You are not going to get that anywhere else in the country. I don't care where you go. You can go to Michigan, where they have 100,000 people, and you won't ever see it. You can go to the Super Bowl, and you won't see it. A&M is just a special place in my heart and my memories. To me, it doesn't get any better than A&M, no matter what level you're talking about.

I was proud that I got a chance to play in the NFL, though. I had always dreamed of playing at the next level. Once I got there, however, it almost turned into a nightmare. In the first NFL preseason game I ever played, I picked off a pass on the game's second play. But just as I was proving I belonged, I suffered a serious knee injury, tearing my ACL in the first quarter of that first game.

I missed my entire rookie season in 1993, while the Eagles' executives and coaching staff wondered if I was damaged goods. I eased those concerns the following season, rehabilitating my knee and returning to action. Overall, I played five seasons in the NFL—three with the Eagles and two with the Colts.

To come back from an ACL injury, especially playing my position where it is based on speed and quickness, and to get five years in the NFL, is something I look back on with pride. It was hard initially to come back from the injury because my game was always based on confidence and speed. When I came back from the ACL, I didn't think I was as fast as I used to be so I didn't have a lot of confidence. I had to get mentally strong again, and I eventually returned to be almost the same player that I once was.

While playing with the Colts, I was reunited with my former A&M teammate, Quentin Coryatt. And after our playing days came to an end, we formed another team.

In 1998 Coryatt and I began discussing the possibility of producing a magazine together. Originally, we envisioned a publication primarily focused on the Houston market. But the regional concept evolved into a national publication.

Controversy magazine was designed "for the man on the go and in the know." It was a mixture of fashion, finance, fitness, entertainment, and sports, often taking the controversial slant on its topics. And it was heavily weighted toward the all-time favorite male spectator sport: female watching.

While the magazine produced modest profits for us, we sold it and turned our attention to other interests. Quentin and I currently have a company called Perfectjumper.com, which helps athletes improve their vertical jump and overall lower body strength. I also have a couple of irons in the fire where I'm working toward putting a sports complex together right now.

I've done a lot of entrepreneurial things since my football career, including writing a book called *Find Your Game: Play Like the Pros.* My original vision was to publish the book in typical print form, but I decided to produce an interactive CD, which was targeted for youths who are seeking an edge for their game.

The interactive CD features plenty of printed tips and pointers. But it also includes video clips and interviews from former NFL players such as Marshall Faulk, Keenan McCardell, and Alfred Williams, as well as former A&M stars like Aaron Glenn, Richmond Webb, and Coryatt.

Most of my business ventures have addressed two primary objectives: helping others and challenging myself to continually strive to be the best I can be.

Just because I have left the game doesn't mean that my competitiveness has decreased any. God has blessed me with some abilities and contacts, and I want to use those things to the best of my ability. I think I have developed a good business sense, and I know I still love to compete and take on challenges—just like I did when I was back at A&M.

After a relatively slow start to his A&M career, Derrick Frazier blossomed into an outstanding coverage cornerback. Frazier still holds the all-time school record for the most career passes broken up, with 36 from 1989 to 1992. Frazier, who intercepted eight passes at A&M, was a third-round draft pick of the Philadelphia Eagles in 1993. He played five seasons in the NFL—three with the Eagles and two with the Indianapolis Colts.

QUENTIN CORYATT

LINEBACKER

1990–1991

Texas A&M fans and former students never cease to amaze me. It's been a long time since I last suited up in my Aggie uniform, but I am often stunned to discover how many Aggies still remember specific games and plays I made while playing middle linebacker in 1991–1992.

In fact, what's more stunning to me now is that there are Aggie students and fans who were not even born when I first arrived at A&M who can vividly describe certain plays I made. I guess I should thank the Internet age. Or a specific online site like YouTube. Or the Texas A&M video staff. Or all of the above.

They have all played a role in keeping one of my big hits in the forefront of fans' minds. On November 7, 1991, in the midst of a 44–7 victory over TCU in Fort Worth, I was in the right place at the right time to make a play on a receiver coming across the middle. TCU's receiver, Kyle McPherson, was looking back toward the quarterback as the ball arrived, and I hit him. Unfortunately, it ended up shattering McPherson's jaw in three spots. I never intended to injure him, but I always played the game at full speed.

I knew at the time it would probably make the highlights on ESPN *Sports-Center*, especially since we were playing on a Thursday night on ESPN. But I could have never imagined that it would still be replayed, relived, and recited by A&M fans. I'll be at an airport or the grocery store or some place like that, and people will say, "Hey, you're a pretty good-sized guy. Did you play football?" I'll tell them I used to play at A&M, and I tell them who I am. What usually comes up first is that TCU game. They'll say, "I remember that." They go on and on from there. It may have been years ago, but a lot of people haven't forgotten that one.

From my perspective, there are several ironic things about that hit. First of all, it's really not the first thing that comes to mind when I recall that game. What I remember is how cold it was that night in Fort Worth. The wind chill was something like 13 degrees. I was born in the Virgin Islands and raised in Baytown. I wasn't accustomed to that kind of cold. I believe that was the first night I ever saw a snowflake, even though it didn't snow very hard.

Some of the younger A&M fans who have seen that one video clip over and over on their computer or on the Kyle Field video board before games probably think of me as a one-hit wonder. That's fine because I sincerely appreciate being remembered at all. But the reality is that I spent two very frustrating years at Texas A&M followed by two wonderful ones.

And I have a truckload of great memories that I play over and over again in my mind…not just one play.

I didn't have any prior connections to A&M, but I had heard about the school from a high school teammate, Chris Crooms. Everything he said about A&M helped to lure me to College Station, as well as the fact that I remember watching the Aggies whip Notre Dame in the 1988 Cotton Bowl, which was when I was still a senior at Baytown Lee.

I remember being so impressed by watching players like John Roper and Dana Batiste, and the mystique of the Wrecking Crew was very attractive to me. Those guys were so relentless and played their style of defense, making plays and big hits from sideline to sideline. I could tell it was really a family atmosphere on the defensive side of the ball, and I wanted to be a part of that.

My older brother, Patrick, played football at Baylor, and he later encouraged me to look seriously at A&M. He talked about the university and the strength of the program. Playing against the Aggies, he experienced the tenacity of the defense, and he thought I would fit in in Aggieland.

A&M was also close to home, so it was easy for my parents to come to my games. It was only about two and a half hours from Baytown to College Station, so that was another big factor in my coming to A&M.

I remember arriving at A&M and being shocked by the strength and knowledge of the upperclassmen. It was an adjustment just to be able to deal with the tempo of practice. It was intense and extremely hard-hitting.

152

Quentin Coryatt earned Southwest Conference Newcomer of the Year honors in 1990. As a senior in 1991, he played on the nation's No. 1 defense and was selected as the SWC's Defensive Player of the Year.

When I got to A&M, I was practicing with guys like John Roper, Dana Batiste, Brent Smith, Alex Morris, Terry Jones, William Thomas, and other very seasoned guys. Those guys made an impression on me, and it also impressed me to see how the coaches always prepared us to be successful. Looking back, I truly admire the coaches' time and effort in always doing what was needed to have us prepared. Their dedication to winning and their love for the game made such a difference in our success.

I spent a short time with Jackie Sherrill, but the majority of my time at A&M was spent under the direction of Coach R.C. Slocum. I appreciate Coach Slocum much more today than I did in my youth. He instilled values in you as a player that can be applied to every aspect of life. He taught us to be accountable for our actions on and off the field; he stressed education so that we could have a solid future; and he touched on skills and values that carry you through a lifetime of difficulties and hardships.

He talked about intensity and being a person who can be trusted. He would always tell us, "If you lie to me, you'll steal from me." That still sticks with me. He just wanted you to hold on to the morals that every young man should have at that stage in his life.

Coach Kirk Doll, our linebackers coach, was a major influence in my life. He always stressed education. School, school, school. He always reminded me to make sure to get my education. He also encouraged me to continually strive to be the best I could be—even in the face of adversity.

Those lessons from Coach Slocum and Coach Doll were especially valuable to me in 1988 and 1989—my first two years at A&M. While so many of the guys I came in with were playing and contributing to the team, I was unable to play those first two years because of Proposition 48. It was very frustrating, and I felt like transferring a time or two.

But my coaches and my teammates helped me through the hard times. We were required to live in Cain Hall our first three years, and then we were able to move off campus our senior year. I have many memories of Cain Hall. Imagine the testosterone level with more than 60 crazy males in one place. It was like having a bunch of crazed wildebeests caged up in one pen.

But living in Cain Hall was very good for us personally and as a team. We were a family. We all hung out together—white guys, black guys, it didn't matter. You had urban guys; you had country guys; you had inner-city guys. You had guys with money and guys with no money, all under one roof. We were a family and we stuck together through thick and thin.

We didn't always get along, but we always found a way to get through it together. If you had a disagreement, you would apologize or find a way to resolve it like a family. But we always stuck together. We were all of one accord because we lived together.

Those first two years also made me extremely anxious about finally getting on the field, which I did in 1990. I broke onto the A&M scene in a good way, earning Southwest Conference Newcomer of the Year honors. And as a senior in 1991, I played on the nation's No. 1 defense and was selected as the SWC's Defensive Player of the Year.

I registered 92 tackles, 4½ sacks, and six tackles for losses despite missing one game with an injury. My favorite game of that season was the one after the TCU game. We were playing Arkansas at Kyle Field on November 16, 1991. We were 7–1 and were playing exceptionally well.

Arkansas came out in the wishbone in an attempt to confuse us. But I really believe they didn't think they could throw against our secondary that included Crooms, Kevin Smith, Patrick Bates, and Derrick Frazier.

Arkansas only tried three passes that day, and the Hogs did not complete a single one. Meanwhile, I had 20 tackles, and we held Arkansas to 121 yards of total offense in a 13–3 win.

Overall, I had a great senior year, and it was rumored that I could be the No. 1 pick in the 1992 NFL Draft. Leading up to the draft was the first time I truly began to understand the politics of pro football. It was so surreal. I couldn't believe this was happening to me. All the hard work I had put in was paying off. It was a dream, and that's the honest truth.

The Indianapolis Colts had the first two picks of the '92 draft, and right before the draft started—around 5:30 or 6:00 in the morning—they called me and told me that Steve Emtman, a defensive tackle out of Washington, did not want to be the second pick in the draft. He was highly sought-after that year, too. He wanted to be the No. 1 pick.

My agent called me that morning, and I told him I just wanted to play football. I wasn't all caught up in going first, second, or third. I just wanted to get drafted, play football, and have fun doing it. So the Colts took me second. While there were some memorable moments in the NFL, nothing in the pros came close to matching the exhilaration of playing at A&M.

Professional ball is nothing like college ball. It's business, it's work. It's like work in corporate America. Playing college ball is more exciting, especially coming from A&M. The synergy and the camaraderie we had at A&M were unlike anything I had ever experienced.

Playing with guys like Bucky Richardson, Kevin Smith, Patrick Bates, Derrick Frazier, and so forth was so much fun. I still stay in touch with those guys. That's the type of relationship that was built while I was at A&M. We were just really blessed with the group of guys who not only played well together, but became great friends.

I played eight years in the league and maybe stay in touch with five guys. I stay in touch with about 10 or 15 guys whom I played with in college. That goes to show that we had something special. A&M is a great place to play football, a great university. If I could do it all over again, I would still come here.

In retrospect, I wouldn't do it any differently. I miss playing the game. But I've moved on, and I take the competitive nature I had on the field into the business world.

I am now in marketing, sales, and promotions. I have a product for basketball that increases player accuracy called Perfect Jumper. I also import coffee to the U.S., and I train kids who are psychologically challenged, whether they have bipolar disorder or ADD or what have you. It's a big challenge to work with them, but I serve them as a personal trainer.

155

Whether I work with kids or in expanding business, I always refer to my times at Texas A&M. I learned so much in Aggieland, including the real meaning of brotherhood beyond your blood relatives. I also have a wonderful brother, Sean, who played at A&M and wore No. 44.

But beyond my biological brothers, I have many more extended brothers from my time at A&M. The members of the Aggie family truly care about one another. Knowing there are people out there who are truly interested in your success and are willing to help you along the way is priceless. That's what makes me the proudest to be an Aggie.

Quentin Coryatt broke onto the A&M scene in a big way, earning Southwest Conference Newcomer of the Year honors in 1990. As a senior in 1991, he played on the nation's No. 1 defense and was selected as the SWC's Defensive Player of the Year. He was the No. 2 overall pick in the 1992 NFL Draft (Indianapolis Colts), and he played eight years in the league. Coryatt now works in marketing, sales, and promotions.

MARCUS BUCKLEY
OUTSIDE LINEBACKER
1990–1992

I'VE HAD SOME VERY DIFFICULT assignments in my life. As an outside line-backer at Texas A&M and then for eight years in the NFL, I often had difficult jobs within a game plan, whether it involved taking on a tough individual blocker or keeping containment on a speedy running back.

I also had my share of challenging coursework in the classrooms. In fact, tough academic assignments are fresh on my mind because I am currently working toward finishing what I started many years ago at Texas A&M. I want to finish my degree, and there is a bit of a family race going on right now.

My oldest daughter, Raven, is a junior psychology major at Texas A&M, so I better hurry if I want to graduate before her.

I still have to take some tough courses before I'm finished. But of all the difficult assignments I have ever had, this one right here is one of the most challenging.

Describing what it means to be an Aggie is nearly impossible because it is so all-encompassing and truly amazing on so many levels. I also find it really hard to put into words how much fun it was to represent Texas A&M back in the heyday of the Wrecking Crew or to even try to describe the unbelievable feeling we had when we ran onto a sold-out Kyle Field.

But please allow me to try to paint a picture for you by taking you back to November 28, 1991. We came into the Thanksgiving Day showdown against

One of the highlights of Marcus Buckley's (9) collegiate career came on Thanksgiving night in 1991 when he stepped in front of a Peter Gardere pass on Texas' first offensive play of the game, picked it off, and raced 19 yards for a touchdown.

the Texas Longhorns ranked No. 9 nationally and leading the nation in total defense.

We were a supremely confident defense that carried the Wrecking Crew reputation with great pride. We swarmed opponents with a bunch of ball-hawking, hard-hitting assassins. Guys like Quentin Coryatt, Patrick Bates, Chris Crooms, Mark Wheeler, Eric England, Sam Adams, Kevin Smith, and Derrick Frazier would go on to play a long time in the NFL. And they were downright dominating in college.

So Texas came into our house on Thanksgiving night in 1991 with a 5–5 record and a 4–3 mark in Southwest Conference play. If the Longhorns beat us that night, they could possibly get to a bowl game. But there was no way in hell they were going to beat us.

One year earlier, Texas had beaten us 28–27 in Austin to secure an unbeaten SWC record and a berth in the Cotton Bowl.

We were determined that '91 was going to be much different. More than 76,000 fans were piled into Kyle Field that night, and I still remember the energy of that stadium. It was supercharged. Just thinking about it now causes goose bumps to form on my arms.

We didn't want to just beat Texas; we wanted to destroy them. Right after the coin toss, we kicked it off to them, and they started at their 20. I'll never forget that right before we ran onto the field, our defensive coordinator, Coach Bob Davie, told us, "Go set the tone right away. Somebody do something big!"

I was practically foaming at the mouth in anticipation when the Horns came to the line of scrimmage. Their quarterback, Peter Gardere, dropped back to pass on the first play from scrimmage. They tried to run a swing pass, and Gardere never saw me. He tossed the ball toward the running back, and I stepped in front of it and raced 19 yards for a touchdown.

More than 59 minutes were still left to be played, but for all intents and purposes, it was over right then.

Kyle Field was deafening. It was rocking and rolling, and we kept the Longhorns reeling. We cruised to a 31–14 victory and held Texas' offense to just 165 total yards. It was total beat down, and our passionate fans loved every second of it.

158

I have a lot of great memories of my time at Kyle Field. But that game was really special. That's the one I think of whenever anyone asks me about my favorite games during my time in Aggieland. I've been in a lot of great stadiums since that game on the collegiate and professional level, but no atmosphere has ever surpassed that one.

That's the game I have so often told my kids about. And that's the one that was truly symbolic of the unique relationship we had with our fans. Virtually every team has an advantage when it plays at home, but our fans were worth a touchdown or more. They were every bit as intimidating to opposing offenses as our defense. And our fans knew the game. They knew when to get loud and when to turn it up another octave or two.

I am so glad that I ended up at Texas A&M in the first place. Coming out of Fort Worth Eastern Hills, I had essentially narrowed my collegiate choices to Texas Tech and A&M. I liked my visit to Lubbock, and I thoroughly enjoyed Spike Dykes. I had been a running back at Eastern Hills, and I might have played tailback if I had gone to Tech.

But I was intrigued about what Texas A&M was doing with its defense. Coach R.C. Slocum told me about how they had turned William Thomas from a high school quarterback into a great rush linebacker, and he believed I had that kind of potential, as well.

I visited A&M on February 3, 1989—just a few days before National Signing Day. It was raining and sleeting, and we got stuck at the Hilton Hotel on University Drive. I got to view the campus a little bit, but the students were gone because of the weather. We did get to see Kyle Field, which was impressive, but it was hardly the greatest visit ever.

Nevertheless, I liked the campus, I loved what A&M was doing on the field at the time, and I felt comfortable around the players, as we just sat around and talked to the guys at Cain Hall because the weather was so bad. So I decided to sign with A&M, which turned out to be one of the best decisions of my life.

When I came to A&M as a freshman in 1989, I had to sit out the season due to Proposition 48. So I couldn't participate with the team yet. I lived in Cain Hall with Jason Medlock, another Prop 48 player, we became pretty close as friends because we worked out together and studied together. O'Neill Gilbert was a former player who worked in academic services at the time. He made sure we were taking care of business—going to class and staying eligible.

My sophomore year, once I started playing, was when I truly felt a part of the Aggie family. I worked my way into the starting lineup as a sophomore in '90, and our linebacking corps was nothing short of sensational. As a sophomore, I started alongside Thomas, Coryatt, and Anthony Williams. We had a solid season in 1990 and ended up destroying BYU 65–14 in the Holiday Bowl.

But we were far from satisfied. We worked extremely hard in the offseason and came back stronger than ever. Coryatt and I returned as starting linebackers, and Jason Atkinson and Otis Nealy replaced Thomas and Williams. We blitzed and bullied opponents all over the field.

We went 10–2 in my junior year and then 12–1 in my senior year. In my three years of playing, we went 31–6–1 and never lost a game at Kyle Field. We also won two SWC championships and did not lose a league game in my final two years.

As a result of all of our team accomplishments and Texas A&M's tremendous defensive reputation, I was selected as the SWC Defensive Player of the

Year in 1992 and was also chosen as a first-team All-American. I am proud of those individual accomplishments, but I am even prouder that I carried on the great defensive reputation that started with guys like John Roper, Aaron Wallace, and William Thomas before me and continued with guys like Antonio Armstrong and Keith Mitchell after me.

I really loved my time at A&M for so many reasons. The camaraderie we developed at Cain Hall and in practices was incredible. Living in Cain Hall together made us a stronger team. It's a shame there are no more athletic dorms, because you really get to know each other better by living in a place like Cain Hall. You can't help but see each other every day.

Football is only played very hard for three or four months a year, but living together allowed us to develop relationships that will last a lifetime.

Of course, enduring the incredible heat of the artificial turf at Kyle Field during practices was a bonding time, as well. Beginning with practices in the summer and continuing late into the year, it always seemed hot on Kyle Field. I remember September games when we came out of the weight room at the south end of the field, and you could literally see the heat waves rising from the field.

Because we practiced on that field daily, we were accustomed to the heat. But that intense heat wilted some of our opponents even before we turned up the defensive heat after kickoff.

Our practices were tough for other reasons, too. We had great talent, and practices really were harder than many games. I remember our fullback, Robert Wilson, who was nicknamed "Bull" because of his running style. Covering him, taking on his blocks, and tackling him were some of the toughest assignments I ever encountered. And it was certainly no picnic when we broke into positions. In our linebacker drills, I went against some of the premier athletes in the state on a daily basis—guys like Coryatt, Thomas, Steve Solari, Atkinson, Nealy, Reggie Graham, Larry Jackson, and Antonio Armstrong.

Going against those guys shaped me into a great player and prepared me for a future in the NFL. Playing in the NFL was an honor, but it was nothing compared to my time at A&M.

I loved playing for the fans at A&M. I felt their passion and their intensity every time I stepped onto Kyle Field. It was hardly like that in the NFL, which is a business. We had a lot of great crowds at Giants Stadium when I was with New York, but you knew the crowd could turn on you in an instant.

I remember a playoff game against Minnesota when we were booed and actually had snow balls and ice balls thrown at us on the field. By the end of the game, the fans were throwing ice balls at Minnesota, as well. Something like that would have never happened at A&M—and not just because it never snowed in Aggieland. One thing we could always count on was the 12th man standing behind us.

Even though it has been an awful long time since I last suited up in an A&M uniform, I still feel that support from fellow Aggies whenever I meet them. Lots of schools support their athletes when they are playing, but A&M makes you feel like a part of the family long after you have played your last down.

That family atmosphere and togetherness that A&M creates is unlike anything else I have ever experienced. And it's not just the athletes who experience it—it's all the students. My daughter, Raven, is experiencing it now. And I sincerely hope that my other kids—my son, Marcus Wayne (10), and my daughter, Madison Imari (six)—will have the opportunity to experience what it means to be an Aggie for themselves, as well.

Fortunately, my wife, Tamika, and I have been able to take our kids to games so that they can be captivated by the same indescribable spirit of Aggieland that lured me in many years ago. I tried to describe it to them—like I've tried to do for you—but some things are better experienced for yourself.

Being an Aggie is one of those things.

Marcus Buckley was a consensus All-American as a senior in 1992 and was a semifinalist for the Butkus Award. He was also the SWC Defensive Player of the Year in 1992 when he recorded 70 tackles, caused three fumbles, recovered four fumbles, and had 12 sacks. Buckley was a third-round draft pick of the New York Giants in 1993. He spent eight years in the NFL. His oldest daughter, Raven, is currently at Texas A&M. He also has a son, Marcus Wayne, and another daughter, Madison Imari.

GREG HILL
RUNNING BACK
1991–1993

During the course of my football career at Dallas Carter High School, Texas A&M University, and in the National Football League with the Kansas City Chiefs, St. Louis Rams, and Detroit Lions, I was extremely blessed to receive numerous honors and awards.

When I hung up my cleats and shoulder pads for the final time in 2000, I sincerely thanked God for all that he allowed me to accomplish as a player. While I had my share of injuries and obstacles that cut my career short, I was still able to experience numerous personal highlights, and I attained many of the lifelong goals that I had set for myself.

I left the game feeling fortunate and extremely blessed. And I didn't really think that any honor I received in my post-playing career would ever be able to match the personal satisfaction I so often experienced as a player.

But my mind was changed in the fall of 2009 when I was humbled on a whole new level. In the summer of '09, I was notified that I had been chosen to be inducted into the Texas A&M Athletic Hall of Fame, sponsored by the Texas A&M Lettermen's Association.

It was extremely gratifying to be selected by my peers into such a prestigious group. But, even though I was thrilled upon my notification, I could not have envisioned just how meaningful it would be to me when I was officially inducted at the Burgess Banquet.

Part of the reason the induction ceremony was so special to me was because my kids—daughter Jordan and son Jayden, who goes by the nickname "G2"—were there to share the honor with me. And during that weekend, I was able to tour my kids around campus, showing my daughter the vet school and my son Olsen Field, among many other campus landmarks. We also went to Midnight Yell Practice together—something I was never able to do as a player at A&M.

As I spent time with my kids and other family members during the weekend festivities, all of the emotions came rushing back to me. For so many reasons, I am extremely proud to be an Aggie. I love the values that Texas A&M represents, I love the passion of Aggie fans, and I cannot even put into words how much being an Aggie means to me.

My time at Texas A&M shaped me and helped to turn me into the man I am today. I was challenged physically and mentally at Texas A&M, where I also grew spiritually. One of the best decisions I ever made was to attend A&M, and it is one of my fondest wishes that my own kids will eventually experience what it means to be an Aggie.

I have so many great memories of my time at A&M, dating back to the first game I ever played in an Aggie uniform. Just a few days prior to the 1991 season-opener against LSU, seniors Keith McAfee and Randy Simmons went down with injuries. I knew I needed to step up in a big way, and I'm proud to say that is exactly what I did. I set an NCAA freshman record by rushing for 212 yards against the Tigers as we crushed LSU 45–7.

I went on to rush for at least 100 yards five times during my freshman season, and I ended the year with 1,216 yards. I was able to carry the ball so many times during my freshman season as we ran out the clock in victories, that fans, teammates, and even media members began referring to the fourth quarter as "GHT," signifying that it was "Greg Hill Time."

I was selected as the SWC Offensive Newcomer of the Year in 1991, and I was a first-team All-SWC running back, as well. More important than any of those honors or numbers, though, was the fact that we won the league championship in '91 for the first time since 1987.

The following year, we won a second consecutive SWC title, and I rushed for 1,339 yards to become the fastest player in SWC history to reach the 2,000-yard rushing plateau. I also finished fifth in the nation in scoring in 1992, averaging 8.5 points per game.

My first three seasons at A&M (including my redshirt year in '90) were absolutely sensational. My one regret from my college days is that I was cited, along with six other A&M players, in an NCAA investigation that involved donor payments for work not performed. If I could do it all over again, I obviously wouldn't be involved in that. But I also learned a lot as a young man in my early twenties in the aftermath of that event.

I quickly stepped forward to acknowledge my mistake, and I vowed to my coaches and teammates to atone for my involvement. But because of A&M's past track record involving rules violations, the NCAA did not show any mercy. I was first suspended the week before the 1993 Cotton Bowl and then was forced to sit out of the first four games of the 1993 season.

It was a very frustrating and difficult time for me, and some people turned their backs on me. But not my teammates. Not my coaches, either. And not many of the great Aggie fans.

Here's what I remember most about that whole ordeal. When I returned to the field in the fifth game of the '93 season, I received a standing ovation from the Kyle Field crowd. That's one of the things that still makes me so proud about being an Aggie. They recognized that I had made a mistake and then they forgave me.

After that ovation, I tried to show my thanks for the fans' support. I rushed for 707 yards in the final seven games and played a major role in leading our team to a third straight Cotton Bowl. When I finished my career at A&M, I was the only running back in school history to average more than 100 yards per game in three consecutive seasons.

Following the 1993 season, I was a first-round draft pick of the Kansas City Chiefs. I spent four very productive seasons with the Chiefs before signing a free-agent contract to become the featured back for the Rams prior to the 1998 season. I was leading the league in rushing and scoring through the first two games of the '98 season before I broke my leg in the third game. It was the first significant injury of my entire football career, and it put my future in jeopardy.

But I tried to never allow adversity to derail me, and this time was no different. I battled through a painful rehabilitation process and actually gained some speed. The Rams traded me to Detroit, where I started eight games in 1999 and rushed for 542 yards and two touchdowns in my final NFL season.

In perhaps the most memorable game of my final season, I starred in the Lions' Thanksgiving Day win over the Bears and was awarded John

Greg Hill burst onto the A&M scene in a big way by setting an NCAA freshman record by rushing for 212 yards in his first game, as the Aggies whipped LSU 45–7 in the 1991 opener at Kyle Field.

Madden's famed "Turkey Leg Award," which the TV commentator annually provided to the Thanksgiving MVP. On national television, I thanked Madden and dedicated the game to the 12 Aggies who died and the many others who were injured in the Bonfire collapse one week earlier.

I considered it a real blessing to be able to stand before America and bring attention to one of the true loves of my life: Texas A&M. God leads my life, and I am so thankful he led me to Texas A&M. What I learned from my time at A&M—on the fields and in the classrooms—also contributed tremendously to the success of my various business endeavors in the Dallas area.

Even before I left the NFL for good in 2000, I became the co-owner of an audio-video business in Dallas that did very well, and then I began a financing company in 2004. In 2007 I used my experience as an entrepreneur and a father to open a by-the-hour childcare center called "Child-N-Play" that provided constant camera surveillance, tutoring, high-end playground gear, Xboxes for live Internet games, and so forth. The high-end daycare center was tailored for kids ranging from six weeks to 12 years old, and it was very successful.

In the midst of opening businesses, I joined FOX Sports Southwest's college football team as a studio analyst in 2003, and I played a role in the network winning a Katie Award from the Press Club of Dallas. I have continued to stay active in broadcasting through the years, and as anyone who listens to KRLD-FM (105.3 "The Fan") in Dallas knows, I am one of the few voices representing Texas A&M's interests in the Dallas–Fort Worth market.

But I do more than just talk a big game when it comes to A&M. I've also put my money where my mouth is. When the 12th Man Foundation unveiled the initial phase of the Championship Vision capital campaign on March 24, 2000, I attended the ceremony at the Zone Club at Kyle Field and was one of the first two former A&M athletes—along with Dat Nguyen—to pledge my financial support to the project.

Nine years later, I was back in that same facility being inducted into the Texas A&M Athletic Hall of Fame. That night, as I thought back on everything A&M has done for me and how I have always tried to represent the school in the most positive light possible, my emotions really began to overcome me.

166

It was a proud moment that I will never forget, and one that will be nearly impossible to ever top. Of course, I've learned to never say "never," especially since I have already begun to ponder how proud I would be if my kids one day walk across the stage as A&M graduates.

In 1991 Greg Hill set an NCAA freshman record by rushing for 212 yards against LSU in his first game as an Aggie. He was selected as the SWC Offensive Newcomer of the Year in 1991 and was a first-team All-SWC running back. In 1992, as the Aggies won a second consecutive SWC title, Hill rushed for 1,339 yards to become the fastest player in SWC history to reach the 2,000-yard rushing plateau. Following the 1993 season, he was a first-round draft pick of the Kansas City Chiefs, where he spent four productive seasons before signing a free-agent contract with the St. Louis Rams prior to the 1998 season. Hill finished his NFL career with Detroit in 2000 and then began an extremely successful business career in Dallas. Hill was inducted into the Texas A&M Athletic Hall of Fame in 2009. He has two children, daughter Jordan and son Jayden.

ANTONIO ARMSTRONG

OUTSIDE LINEBACKER

1991–1994

O F ALL THE TITLES I've ever held in my life—ranging from All-America football player at Texas A&M to my current position as the owner of 1st Class Personal Training Studios in the Bellaire and Galleria areas of Houston—the ones I take most seriously are "husband" and "father."

I was born to a 15-year-old mother and fathered by a 16-year-old boy. My dad had good intentions, but he was unequipped, unprepared, and unable to provide for a child when he was essentially a boy himself. My father dropped out of high school to find a job when I was born, and, when money became scarce, he turned to the streets.

The next thing you know, he became involved in drugs, and the streets consumed him. He died the month before I came to Texas A&M, and I never really knew him. That's a big reason why I take being a father to my three kids—Joshua, Antonio Jr., and Kayra—so seriously. Being a father is one of my primary purposes in life. I cherish that role, and I don't want to see my kids struggle like I struggled growing up. My mother didn't have the ability to give me a home like my kids have now.

Likewise, one of my top goals each day is to be the best husband I can be to my wonderful and beautiful wife, Dawn Whitely Armstrong. God has blessed me with a soulmate in Dawn, who is my best friend, my partner, and the absolute love of my life.

Antonio Armstrong overcame a life-threatening medical condition before he arrived at Texas A&M and went on to become a first-team All-America linebacker in 1994.

I try to honor God each day by leading my family in a manner that reflects His glory. We first serve the Lord in our house, and everything else falls into place. We attempt to instill biblical values, and we are determined to raise our kids to become men and a woman of character and integrity. We want them to be beacons of God's light at school, just as we—as their parents—attempt to be the same in the workplace, in our community, and beyond.

In today's world, that can be very challenging. Fortunately, God has prepared me for the challenges ahead of me by testing me, molding me, and strengthening me in the past. I know my kids will face many obstacles and adversities as they continue through school. But I will be able to help guide them through those difficulties by simply citing some examples from my own past.

My life is a testament to the fact that faith can move mountains and that the best way to start attacking any problems is through prayer. I've been through a lot, and I now can clearly see that God used those struggles and hardships to develop my character, my resolve, and my faith.

The fact that I ever became a first-team All-SWC linebacker in 1993 or an All-American in 1994 is pretty miraculous, considering I had a brain aneurysm in high school that put my life in jeopardy.

Without a father figure and with my mother, Kay Shorter Specks, working around the clock to do what she could to provide for us, I was fortunate as a kid to turn to sports instead of gangs or the streets to find a place where I belonged. By the time I got to Houston's Kashmere High School, I had visions of becoming the next Lawrence Taylor. I found refuge on the football field and emerged as a fairly recognizable name among the high school players in the Houston area. But just as I began to rise to new heights, my health sunk to the lowest of depths. As a senior at Kashmere, I was diagnosed with a brain aneurysm.

The doctors didn't know if I was going to live or die. They said that if I did come out of it, I would never play football again. Thankfully, I had a praying mother, and she wouldn't stop praying.

With the aneurysm, I would come in and out of consciousness. Days would pass, and I would not know where I was. The medical staff administering to me kept me sedated to prevent me from having seizures. I didn't eat, and I lost tons of weight.

At that time in my life, I knew of God, but I didn't know Jesus Christ as my personal savior. But about two or three weeks after I was released from the hospital, the doctors ran a CAT scan and told me I would have scar tissue and would have severe headaches for the rest of my life. That diagnosis devastated me.

To make a long story short, though, I went to a church service and met a man who asked the congregation if anybody had physical ailments. I raised my hand, stepped forward, and went up to the front of the church. I was certainly skeptical about miracle healings because I know there are some crooked people in the pulpit who prey on believers through fake healings.

I can't speak for everyone else, but I can tell you what happened to me. This man prayed for me, asking God to heal me. I went back to the doctor, and he said there were no traces of scar tissue, and he released me to play football. It was nothing short of a miracle from God.

But even after my recovery, most of the schools that had shown interest in me before the brain aneurysm—Oklahoma, Colorado, and UCLA, to name a few—no longer wanted me. But A&M continued to express interest, so I signed with the Aggies in 1991.

After losing so much weight, however, I was in for a rude awakening when I arrived on campus. I was so undersized during the early part of my freshman season that the A&M video staff—at the direction of defensive coordinator Bob Davie—made me the star of a mock "crash dummy" tape, showing footage of tight ends like Greg Schorp, James McKeehan, and Jason Matthews driving me 10 to 20 yards off the line of scrimmage.

That's one prominent memory I have of those early practices. Another is the extreme heat. When we got to College Station to start two-a-days, the artificial turf was so hot that the bottoms of my feet were burning through my shoes. Not only that, it was so hot that it heated my shoes so much that the top of my feet were burning, too.

I wasn't even 200 pounds as a true freshman. I was probably closer to 190 on the day I first stepped foot on campus. But I familiarized myself with the weight room and worked hard. I was always asking our strength and conditioning coach, Mike Clark, "What do you want me to do next? I'll do anything, Coach, just tell me what to do."

I primarily played on special teams as a freshman, but I worked so hard in the off-season and increased my strength so dramatically that Coach Clark had me tested for steroids. But I was as clean as a G-rated movie.

I then took a summer job moving furniture and practically lived in the weight room. As a sophomore in 1992, I improved quite a bit. I still didn't play a whole lot because I was backing up the great Marcus Buckley at outside line-backer as we won our second straight Southwest Conference championship.

By 1993 I weighed 225 pounds and finally broke into the starting lineup, earning All-SWC honors with 73 tackles and 8½ sacks. We also won our third straight conference championship in '93.

Prior to my senior year, I decided to honor the father I never really knew by changing my last name from "Shorter" to "Armstrong." That really allowed me to gain a sense of peace regarding his shortcomings and his death. I also dedicated my senior year to my father.

It was a memorable season, to say the least. Our defensive unit finished fourth nationally in scoring defense [13.4 points per game] and fifth in total defense. As a team, we completed just the ninth unbeaten season in Texas A&M history [10–0–1] and the first since 1956.

I recorded 62 tackles in 1994, including 17 behind the line of scrimmage to earn All-America honors. And my three sacks against Notre Dame in the 1994 Cotton Bowl—going against All-American Aaron Taylor—helped me earn defensive MVP honors in that game.

171

What makes me most proud of my accomplishments as a senior was that I did those things with a debilitating injury. Prior to the season, I was diagnosed with a rare and painful condition called osteitis pubis, in which I was constantly tearing my abdominal muscles from my pelvic bone. Today it would be called a sports hernia. I struggled with pain every day, but I battled through it because I wanted to be part of that unbeaten year.

Even though I made All-American as a senior, I didn't play as well as I could have because of the physical limitations. I lost a step or two in my quickness, and it really bothered me. The injury didn't allow me to run for all the scouts, either. I was labeled as "damaged goods" by the NFL, and that's why I slipped into the sixth round before the San Francisco 49ers took me.

I literally cried on draft day. But things quickly began working out in San Francisco. With the injury finally behind me, I played well in training camp and moved to second team on the depth chart. But then I fractured my right leg, and on my 22nd birthday, the 49ers released me.

The Dolphins picked me up the next day, and I spent the rest of the 1995 season in Miami. But after Jimmy Johnson became the head coach, I was told I didn't fit into Johnson's system. Then it was on to St. Louis, where I was later released by the Rams. I sat out the entire 1996 season and then gave the Canadian Football League a shot in 1997 at Toronto.

The scenario north of the border was basically the same. I actually made the team, but I was released three days into the season. That was a devastating blow followed by an all-time low.

After being released by Toronto, I found myself at the lowest point in my life. At first, I was making $10,000 to $12,000 every two weeks, and I was living in the fast lane. I wasn't ever really bad and into hardcore drugs or anything like that, but from a biblical standpoint, I wasn't living a holy life. Then my cars were repossessed; I lost my home and found myself with absolutely nothing. I was in my mother's house at rock bottom. I can remember it was November 10 or 11 in 1997, and I went to church and gave my life to Christ. I was tired of living the way I was living.

From that point, my outlook began to improve. In 1998 Toronto traded my rights to the British Columbia Lions, and I was married to Dawn later that same year. She and I figured the CFL deserved one more shot, and it turned out to be the shot in the arm we needed.

Dawn and I packed our oldest son, Joshua, into a little Beretta with about $900 to our names and drove from Houston to Vancouver, British Columbia. Everything we owned was inside that little blue Beretta.

We went up there with our faith in God, and I believed that he was going to make a way for us. Either that, or my football career was going to be over. Things worked out, and before the season was over, I moved to middle linebacker. One week I was the CFL Defensive Player of the Week, and my career began to take off from there.

Things were going exceptionally well in 1999 after I was traded to Winnipeg. I was having a career season in 2000 until I broke my leg again on October 15—my birthday. My leg didn't heal correctly, but when the cast came off, I returned to action and helped lead the Blue Bombers to the Grey Cup game on a bad leg. I then returned to College Station for another surgery, and up until the summer of 2002, I was hoping for one more shot at the NFL.

The call from the NFL never came, and I began pouring more time and effort into a nutritional sales company, my personal training, and of course, my family. Business is going exceptionally well, and my family is thriving. But I know that life is filled with peaks and valleys. And whenever I'm thrown another curve, I'm prepared to handle it.

Part of the reason I now feel equipped to handle any adversity and to also handle prosperity without allowing it to go to my head is because of the time

I spent at Texas A&M. I grew up so much in Aggieland—physically, mentally, emotionally, and spiritually. I also learned so much from coaches like R.C. Slocum, Shawn Slocum, Kirk Doll, Bob Davie, and Mike Clark, as well as from teammates like Quentin Coryatt, Marcus Buckley, Kevin Smith, Aaron Glenn, Steve Solari, Otis Nealy, Wilbert Biggens, Clif Groce…and the list goes on and on.

The greatest decision I ever made was to accept Jesus Christ as my savior. Second best was choosing Dawn as my wife. But third on my personal list was choosing to attend Texas A&M. It helped to shape me as a person, a husband, a father, and a man.

What does it me to be an Aggie? To me, it has meant more than I could have ever imagined.

Antonio Armstrong recorded 62 tackles in 1994, including 17 behind the line of scrimmage to earn All-America honors. His three sacks against Notre Dame in the 1994 Cotton Bowl—going against All-American Aaron Taylor—helped him earn defensive MVP honors in that game. Armstrong and his wife, Dawn, have three kids—Joshua, Kayra, and Antonio Jr. Armstrong, who was an All-SWC linebacker in 1993 when he went by the last name of Shorter, has built a thriving business in Houston in the fitness industry.

CHRIS RUHMAN
OFFENSIVE LINEMAN
1994–1997

Through the years, various people have asked me if I have any regrets about playing football at Texas A&M University. They've set up different hypothetical scenarios, challenging me to go back to my high school days at Aldine Nimitz, and asked me—knowing now what I didn't know then—if I would have done things differently.

There was a time in my life when my answer might have been, "Yes, I'd do things differently." But now, without a doubt, my answer is not only, "No," but, "Hell no."

Now I truly understand what it means to be an Aggie and understand the awesome power of the Aggie network. Now I clearly see how my decision to attend Texas A&M was one of the best moves of my life.

It's too bad I didn't realize it sooner. My college experience might have been even more personally rewarding and satisfying if I had fully realized how great I had it in Aggieland.

But before I get to that, let me take you back, way back to when I first fell in love with Texas A&M. Growing up in the Houston area, I obviously had some familiarity with A&M. I was born in 1974—the year former A&M head coach Emory Bellard began turning things around in College Station. And as I began playing youth sports in the mid-1980s, the Aggies, under the direction of then–head coach Jackie Sherrill, were kings of the Southwest Conference.

Then in the late 1980s, I attended my first A&M game with my dad and the pastor of my church. A&M was matched up against LSU in the home-and season-opener. It was all new to me, as I had no idea what was going on. I didn't know any of the yells, the A&M traditions, or anything of the sort. I just remember the energy in the stands and that A&M beat the hell out of LSU. It wasn't even a game; it was like boys against men.

At that point, I decided Texas A&M was where I want to go to school, and I wanted to play football for the Aggies while pursuing my education, if afforded the opportunity. I obviously didn't understand the depth of the A&M family or the strength of the Aggie network at that point, but I could sense there was something special about being an Aggie.

Years later, I developed into a pretty good offensive line prospect at Nimitz, where I earned multiple All-America accolades. Numerous schools began recruiting me, but I turned down schools like Notre Dame and Tennessee, staying true to my original plan to attend Texas A&M.

I showed up in Aggieland in 1993 looking like a man on the outside, but like most freshmen, I was still immature mentally and did not realize what it took to compete for a starting job for the Aggies. One of the blessings in disguise in '93 was that I injured my shoulder early in the year and was forced to redshirt. I played in a couple of games early in that '93 season, but I really needed the extra year to mature both mentally and physically.

If some of my former teammates are reading this, they are probably laughing right now. The word *mature* was not often associated with me in college.

In 1994—my redshirt freshman season—I developed enough as an offensive lineman that I split time at right tackle with Hunter Goodwin, making five starts. The following year, I started all 12 games at left tackle—a feat I duplicated in 1996. And even though I missed a few starts as a senior in 1997 because of a knee injury, I finished my collegiate career with 38 starts.

By the time I finished at A&M, I was a pretty solid offensive tackle. I credit former A&M offensive line coach Mike Sherman—the Aggies' current head coach as I write this chapter—for keeping me focused during my early years at Texas A&M. I am forever grateful that Sherman and others on the A&M coaching staff didn't give up on me when I was sowing some of my wilder oats.

Despite the efforts of Sherman and others, I was more rebellious than responsible throughout most of my collegiate career. My wild streak was matched only by my mean streak. And in my personal road map of life, I once lacked direction.

Fortunately for me, football was always a constant that kept me from making too many wrong turns. I am so thankful for so many former teammates and coaches who kept me from completely going off the deep end. I made some off-the-field decisions that I wish I could erase, but know now that those experiences have helped mold me into the Aggie I am today.

But along with some of the mistakes I made, I also have plenty of positive memories. As a redshirt freshman in 1994, I was part of an undefeated team, although we were on probation and ineligible to go to a bowl game. And even though we had a disappointing season in 1995 [9–3 overall] and a very disappointing season in 1996 [6–6], we righted the ship in 1997.

In 1996—the first year of the Big 12 Conference—the critics wondered aloud if A&M could compete with the upper echelon teams of the new league. We quickly put an end to that kind of talk the next year.

I remember my senior season in '97 like it was yesterday, especially the way we ended the year with a 27–16 win over Texas at Kyle Field. The game was played in a torrential downpour that was so bad the network broadcast was knocked out. And when you picked up your helmet after standing on the sideline, a bucket of water would fall out.

Even though the score was relatively close, we physically whipped their asses. That was one of my favorite memories. Ricky Williams had a couple big plays against us, but they didn't result in many points. The footing was bad, and it made it a lineman's game. Beating them was a great feeling since we had lost the previous two years to them.

The one sour taste in my mouth from 1997 was Nebraska in the Big 12 Championship Game, a 54–15 loss. Other than that, as seniors, we felt like we did all we could, and we left the program in good hands. That was just an embarrassing campaign in 1996. I'm really glad I didn't have to leave A&M on that kind of note.

In 1997 we had a veteran offensive line. We had three seniors in Steve McKinney, Koby Hackradt, and me. Rex Tucker, Cameron Spikes, and Semisi Heimuli had been playing, and I just think we were all determined not to go through another season like 1996. So I think 1997 was a good year and a good springboard for team leaders like Dan Campbell, Dat Nguyen, Rich Coady, and Rex Tucker to take it all the way to the Big 12 Championship in 1998. I felt good about leaving on a positive note.

Chris Ruhman was a powerful force for the Texas A&M offensive line before becoming an attorney with Cokinos, Bosien & Young in the Houston area.

I continued to feel good the following spring when I was the first Aggie to be selected in the 1998 NFL Draft. I was a third-round draft pick of the San Francisco 49ers, fulfilling a dream of making it into the NFL. I was ecstatic to be taken on the first day. Not only was it a step in the NFL, but it cleaned up a lot of the stuff from my college years. I kind of went cuckoo there for a little while and alienated myself from a lot of people at A&M. Going into the NFL kind of gave those people an opportunity to look at me in a different light. It really helped out. I couldn't have been happier going to a team like the 49ers and playing with guys like Jerry Rice and Steve Young.

But the most important person on the 49ers roster to my future would turn out to be Marc Edwards. I first met Edwards on a recruiting trip to Notre Dame. Edwards played for the Irish and was drafted by the 49ers the year before San Francisco selected me.

We rekindled our friendship in San Francisco, and Edwards introduced me to a former Notre Dame cheerleader named Sondra, who would soon become my wife.

I always jokingly say she was cruising the parking lot for ballplayers. But Sondra was already out in San Jose where our training facilities were located. She was working for Motorola at the time. Whenever the team traveled, Marc's wife would stay with Sondra, because the team stayed in a hotel. One time after a game, we all went to dinner, and Sondra and I hit it off. I saw her and knew I was going to marry that girl. We met on September 27 and were engaged a week before Thanksgiving. I was like, *Boy, I can't mess this one up.* So I brought my A game. She's been my rock, especially during some difficult times.

My NFL career ended much sooner than I anticipated. After spending one season in San Francisco, I was traded to the Cleveland Browns. I suffered the first knee injury of my NFL career during my second season with the Browns. The next season, I signed with Denver. Unfortunately, I reinjured my knee during camp with the Broncos. Although I rehabbed, I failed my physical with the Raiders, and at 26, my NFL career was over.

That's when Sondra was especially influential in helping me look toward the future. I owe her a lot. She's a one-in-a-million woman. She's a former Notre Dame cheerleader who is also an aerospace engineer. I think that combination says something about what a rare kind of person she is. She also has a great perspective on life, and she helped me to realize I needed a new direction in life.

After my NFL career ended, I had gone on a couple interviews for sales positions, but I knew I really didn't want to be in sales. My wife and I were sitting around one day, wondering what I should do next. I went through A&M, I got my degree in agricultural development, but I still didn't know exactly what I wanted to do.

My wife asked me, "Why don't you go to law school?" My first thought was that I didn't have any background in that. But I went and started looking into it. To make a long story short, I got everything done that I needed to do. I interned at the Brazos Valley's DA office, took my classes for the LSAT, and passed the test.

When we met and married, Sondra and I had agreed that she would follow me wherever my football career took us. And once football was done, I would follow her wherever her career took us. Her sales position took us to Chicago, and that's how I ended up going to law school at Valparaiso, which is about halfway between South Bend, Indiana, and Chicago.

During my second year in law school, I truly began to understand what I had never fully comprehended about being in the Aggie family. At that point in my life, I liked my affiliation with A&M. But I soon loved my connection with A&M.

I had been giving some money back to the 12th Man Foundation, the fund-raising organization behind A&M athletics, and I had joined the 12th Man's Advisory Board. As part of that organization, I had met a Houston-based lawyer named Gregory Cokinos, the managing partner of the Cokinos, Bosien & Young law firm. We had met at a Texas A&M baseball game, and Cokinos told me to give him a call if I ever needed anything.

179

As a second-year law student in need of a clerkship, I called Mr. Cokinos and point-blank asked him for a job. I reminded him that he had told me to call him if I needed anything, and he said that he had meant it. I sent him a résumé, and three or four days later, I received a phone call from one of the partners at the firm, offering me an interview.

To make a long story short, I have been with the Cokinos, Bosien & Young law firm since 2007 as an attorney, with a practice emphasis on construction law and commercial litigation. And I owe my job to my Aggie connections. Obviously, the firm didn't hire me solely because I was an Aggie. I had to earn the job through the interview process and my productivity. But I got my foot in the door because I was part of an amazing extended family that is the Aggie network.

I have been all over the world. I was in Tokyo, and I saw a guy with an Aggie Ring. I introduced myself as a fellow Aggie, and we instantly hit it off. There is an instant and everlasting connection with anyone who attended A&M. There's a bond among Aggies that is different than any other school I've ever seen.

Maturing and growing up has made me see A&M in a completely different light than when I was here as a student.

As recently as 2003 or 2004, I might have answered the hypothetical question—Would you still go to A&M if you could do it over again?—with a lukewarm response. Or maybe I would have said that I would have gone to Notre Dame or Tennessee.

But now I try to teach my son about the long-term values of attending school at an incredibly unique institution like Texas A&M. I hope he gets it long before his old man did.

When I was drafted, I could not wait to get out of College Station. Now I am trying to figure out ways to get back to Aggieland on a full-time basis. A&M feels like home. A&M feels like community. And it continues to build loyalty and camaraderie long after you have graduated.

So, what does it mean to be an Aggie?

To this one, in particular, it has meant more than I could have ever imagined, even when I was there as an undergraduate. I appreciated A&M somewhat back then, but it means the world to me today.

Chris Ruhman was a standout offensive lineman on the first A&M team to ever win a Big 12 South Division title (1997). Ruhman was the first Aggie to be selected in the 1998 NFL Draft (third round, San Francisco). Ruhman also played with the Cleveland Browns and Denver Broncos. After leaving the game, Ruhman earned his law degree. He is now an attorney with the Houston-based Cokinos, Bosien & Young law firm. Ruhman and his wife, Sondra, have one son, M.J.

KYLE BRYANT

KICKER

1994–1997

DESPITE A PRETTY GOOD KICKING CAREER at A&M Consolidated High School, I never needed to disconnect my telephone or move into a relative's home to escape the pursuit of college recruiters. Sure, I received my fair share of letters from universities, but I probably had more telemarketers calling my house in the early 1990s than recruiters. In fact, I only went on one official recruiting trip.

That trip—to Southwestern Louisiana, which is now known as the University of Louisiana-Lafayette—produced more misgivings than enjoyable memories. When the Cajuns called me for an answer to their scholarship offer, I tried to turn them down politely. But to this day, I will never forget the response I received from the USL special-teams coach.

I didn't feel right at USL, and I was more comfortable with the idea of staying close to home and walking on at Texas A&M. So I told the USL coach, "Thanks, but no thanks for the scholarship offer."

He said that he didn't understand my decision, especially since A&M already had two kickers on scholarship. I told him I realized that it may not make much sense, but I'd rather take my chances at A&M, where I had always dreamed about playing. Then, he got fired up and said, "Kyle, you can quote me on this: you will never start at Texas A&M."

That didn't sit well with me at the time, but ultimately it inspired me.

Not only did I end up starting at A&M, but I also earned All–Southwest Conference and All–Big 12 honors during my A&M career. I even set a few records at A&M for career points and field goals. Thanks for the motivational speech, Coach.

During my final two seasons in Aggieland, I connected on 80 percent of my field-goal attempts. And I am humbled by the fact that I earned Most Valuable Player honors in a bowl game, as I was blessed with the opportunity to kick five field goals in the 1995 Alamo Bowl against Michigan to earn the Offensive MVP trophy.

So I guess the USL coach was wrong…and I know that my decision to walk on at A&M was the right choice for me.

Going to A&M was one of the best things that ever happened to me. I loved my time as a student-athlete, and it really was a dream come true.

As far back as when I was an eighth-grader in College Station, I had stated that it was my goal to kick for the Aggies. While I was in middle school, a graduate student at Texas A&M named Russell Sweezy was assigned to do a profile on a male and female student for one of his classes. He chose me as his male profile and conducted an interview with me.

I told him that I would eventually like to be a kicker for Texas A&M and major in business. I had long since forgotten about that interview until I fulfilled that dream. Then I received a profile from the past.

When I received my scholarship, Russell sent me the profile he did on me in the eighth grade. It was interesting because everything about it was true except that I wasn't majoring in business; it was agriculture economics. That goes to show you that you should never underestimate the power of a dream.

Back then, the odds were probably a million-to-one that some little eighth-grader like me—who topped out at 5'7" and 160 pounds my senior year in high school—would be the kicker at a major university like Texas A&M.

Of course, no one—not even me—could have predicted my unlikely route to A&M. Among the records I was fortunate enough to establish at A&M, perhaps the most bizarre one is that I probably experienced the shortest walk-on tenure ever. I had committed to walking on at A&M prior to playing in the 1993 Texas High School Coaches Association All-Star Game. But I had a really good game that day, and I ended up attracting the attention from major universities that had shown no interest in me during the recruiting process.

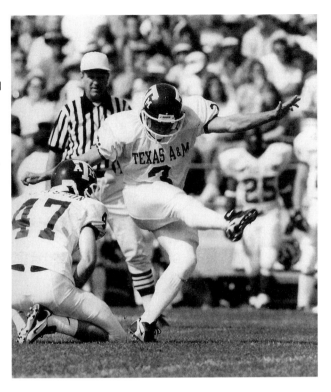

After enduring a very disappointing 1995 regular season, Kyle Bryant nailed five field goals in the 1995 Alamo Bowl against Michigan to earn the Offensive MVP trophy.

I hit a 55-yard field goal off the ground, which was my only attempt and a THSCA All-Star Game record, in that game, and Baylor and SMU offered me a scholarship following the game. Two days later I received a phone call from A&M associate athletics director Tim Cassidy, who informed me that head coach R.C. Slocum wanted to speak to me.

I was thinking, *I'm already committed as a walk-on. What more can happen here?* But I called Coach Slocum, who was in a hotel in Dallas at the time. He said, "Kyle, congratulations on the game. We're proud of you. I understand there are some other universities offering you scholarships." I told him yes, and that I was supposed to talk to them the next day.

He said, "If you'll give me a chance, if you'll not commit to anyone else, I'd really like to discuss something with you in person." I agreed and went to talk to him. We were probably 25 to 30 minutes into this conversation, and he was telling me about Tony Franklin and some other players. I wasn't sure where he was going with our meeting, then all of the sudden he told me he had never had three kickers on scholarship at the same time. But then he said he was willing to take a risk on me and said that he was going to offer me a scholarship. I almost fell out of my chair when he handed me a letter of intent. I think I signed it before it even hit the desk. I was so excited.

With Terry Venetoulias and Keith Waguespack already on scholarship, I was redshirted in 1993. But I got off to a good start in 1994, connecting on my first seven field-goal attempts. I finished my freshman season by hitting 17 of 25, including a freshman record 61-yarder. I thought it was too good to be true, and maybe it was.

My freshman season was so good that I probably took it for granted. I went into the next year overconfident, and I didn't work out as much as I should have the summer prior to my sophomore year. As a result, I paid the price.

I pulled my quadriceps muscle prior to the start of the season and had to miss most of two-a-day practices. During the early part of the season, I didn't handle the kickoff duties because I was trying to rehabilitate my quad. I was just handling field goals and extra points at the time, and I didn't do very well.

Looking back at it now, the '95 season was probably a great blessing in disguise because it taught me so many lessons about faith, family, and life in general. But at the time, it was a nightmare.

184

The 1995 season was supposed to be a great one for our team, as we started the year ranked No. 3 nationally in one poll. We had legitimate national championship aspirations, but instead of winning it all, we failed to even win the SWC.

We lost a big non-conference game against Colorado. Then we lost our first SWC game since 1990 when we went to Texas Tech. By the end of the year, our home winning streak also came to an end when we lost to Texas. It was a bitterly disappointing season for our team. And I could have been the poster boy of that season.

After my freshman year, I thought I was going to be in store for a super sophomore season. But I actually missed more field goals than I made in 1995.

I will never forget that in one of my lab classes, where there were only about 20 people, a guy was reading the school newspaper in the back of the room. All of a sudden he just shouts out loud, "Who is this Kyle Bryant guy? This guy sucks." He said we needed a new kicker, and then a girl right next to him told him to cut it out because I was in the front row of the class. Fortunately, I never felt that same sentiment from my teammates, despite the fact that I only hit 7 of 15 field-goal attempts.

I was roommates at the time with quarterback Branndon Stewart and tight end Matt Mahone. Those guys didn't talk about football much when I got home. We left my performances on the shelf and did not talk about it. We talked about everyday life. They were supportive of me, and I had other teammates like Brad Crowley and Hunter Goodwin, who were just as encouraging.

That's probably the time when I truly learned what it means to be an Aggie. The guy in my lab class was the minority opinion. My teammates and many of my other classmates were the majority. They encouraged me; they prayed for me; they stuck with me; and Coach Slocum continued to believe in me. When you have a culture like the one that exists at A&M, it makes it much easier to get through trying times. Other universities may have tradition, honor, and so forth, but no one has the resiliency, camaraderie, and togetherness of Texas A&M.

During that '95 season, my Christian faith was also strengthened. I realized very quickly that I could not rely on football for my identity. Dr. Rick Rigsby had a tremendous impact on my faith, and I began truly turning to the Lord for strength and guidance. And I believe God rewarded me for trusting in Him.

After a lousy regular season, my game was in sync for the 1995 Alamo Bowl against a very good Michigan team, which was headlined by players like Tim Biakabutuka, Amani Toomer, Charles Woodson, Brian Griese, and Jarrett Irons. Michigan head coach Lloyd Carr was quoted in the San Antonio newspaper the week of the game saying something to the effect of, "If the game comes down to A&M's special teams, we won't have anything to worry about."

As it turned out, special teams played a big role in the game. I had the opportunity to attempt six field goals and made five of them (27, 49, 47, 31, and 37 yards). Those five field goals and an extra-point accounted for 16 points in our 22–20 win.

From that point forward, I had a very strong finish to my A&M career and then gave professional football several serious shots. I tried the NFL and even landed a job with a start-up spring football league in Houston. Unfortunately, my teammates and I showed up to practice one day and discovered the league had folded.

With only part-time jobs and without a kicking future, I hopped into my car one day and remembered a business card I had placed in my glove compartment. I had met Richard Lamb, who was a walk-on at A&M in the early 1980s, while I was working part-time at the College Station Hilton in 1998.

Mr. Lamb wanted an autograph for his son, and we instantly hit it off. Mr. Lamb, the vice president of North American sales for the Hill-Rom Company, a medical device manufacturer, told me to give him a call whenever the NFL dream ended. And, with bills piling up and a league folding, I decided it was time to make the call.

He sent me some training tapes on two of their products and told me not to call him again until I knew them backward and forward. Not knowing much about health care at the time, I basically memorized the videotapes, word for word. For my interview I had to present two different beds for Mr. Lamb and two of our national marketing directors. During both demonstrations I didn't operate either bed at all, I just recited word for word what the training tapes said. I didn't pass it with flying colors, but they saw enough potential in me. So I entered training for that company in May 2000.

I was originally supposed to stay in College Station to cover the western U.S., but I moved from College Station to Indianapolis, then to Chicago. Then they moved me down to Raleigh, North Carolina, and on to a more permanent position in Albuquerque, New Mexico. I have been with the company ever since, and I still love my job.

The love of my life, however, is the former Yvette Okler, who was the first scholarship player in Texas A&M's women's soccer program. We were married in the summer of 2002, and in January of 2009, we had our first child. Our daughter's name is Emerson Rose Bryant, and with our backgrounds and genes, we figure that Emerson may have an edge in soccer-style kicking.

I just hope and pray that our daughter—as well as any other children we may have—is as fortunate as I was to live out my dream.

During his final two seasons at A&M, Kyle Bryant connected on 80 percent of his field-goal attempts. He also earned Most Valuable Player honors by kicking five field goals in the 1995 Alamo Bowl victory over Michigan. Bryant began a career in sales for a medical device manufacturer in 2000, which has taken him to College Station; Indianapolis; Chicago; Raleigh, North Carolina; and Albuquerque, New Mexico; where he is currently based. He and his wife, former A&M soccer player Yvette Okler, married in the summer of 2002. In January 2009 the couple had a daughter, Emerson Rose.

DAT NGUYEN

LINEBACKER

1995–1998

WHEN I LOOK BACK OVER MY LIFE, I am thankful for so many things. I am obviously thankful that my father, my pregnant mother, and my five older siblings escaped war-torn Vietnam on the night of April 28, 1975, made it to a Thailand port in late May, and arrived at a refugee camp at Fort Chaffee in Arkansas by the summer.

I'm thankful I was born in that refugee camp, where I received nutrient-rich baby formula from an early age—something my siblings never received. That might explain why I am nearly a foot taller and was nearly 100 pounds heavier at one point than what my father weighed during his twenties. I am also so thankful for my father's work ethic and the many blessings that God bestowed upon us as we made a new life in a new country. I'm grateful that we eventually landed in Rockport on the Texas coastline, where I met some wonderful friends and started learning how to play American football.

Also high on my list of things I regularly thank God for is Texas A&M. Becoming an Aggie was one of the most life-altering decisions I have ever made. I met my soulmate at Texas A&M—my wife, Becky. As a result, we have two wonderful daughters, Aubrey Mai and Remi Linh.

Texas A&M is also where I met so many lifelong friends and developed some of the most important relationships of my life. I earned my degree at A&M, giving me a foundation for future success. And, of course, I had the wonderful opportunity to play football at A&M. We won a pair of Big 12

Although he seriously thought of transferring from A&M in 1994, Dat Nguyen found his niche in Aggieland and became the all-time leading tackler in school history, with 517.

South championships and one conference title during my time in Aggieland. Playing for the Aggies also prepared me for a future in the NFL as a player and a coach. And now I am incredibly honored to return to Texas A&M as an assistant coach on Mike Sherman's outstanding staff.

I don't even like to imagine where I might be or how much different my life would look if I had not gone to A&M. So I am somewhat embarrassed to admit that I once seriously considered leaving A&M. After signing with A&M in February of 1994, I celebrated by eating. The recruiting services had written that I probably needed to be bigger to play inside linebacker at the Division I level. I used that as an excuse to stuff my face. Instead of getting bigger and adding on muscle, however, I just got fatter.

When we began practicing in the summer of 1994, I weighed almost 240 pounds. I looked around the practice field and evaluated the talent on the team. I quickly concluded that I might be the worst defensive player on the roster. Even many of the walk-ons were better than me. I wondered if I would *ever* play at A&M and if I had made a major mistake by coming to A&M in the first place.

The more I dwelled on my dilemma, the worse I felt about myself. I then decided I was going to teach A&M a lesson by either transferring to Michigan or quitting altogether. In reality, of course, it was I who needed to be taught a lesson. But it took me a while to come to that conclusion.

Of the five linebackers A&M signed in 1994—Trent Driver, Warrick Holdman, Quinton Brown, Phillip Meyers, and me—I was the worst player, by far. And I was the only one who didn't play in '94. At one point in the season, I think I was the No. 8 linebacker on the depth chart. I was seriously considering a transfer, although I didn't talk it over much with anybody, primarily because I was too embarrassed to admit how bad I was to any friends from home or my parents.

189

The only real talking I did was with God. I wasn't very spiritually mature, but I was asking God to give me a sign to show me what I needed to do. Sure enough, God provided that sign in the most unlikely of places—the sports section of the *Bryan–College Station Eagle*.

During two-a-days in 1994, a picture of me appeared on the sports section. I looked at it, studied it, and eventually understood what I needed to do about it. My arms were fat, my face was fat, and my gut was hanging out from my jersey and over the belt loop on my practice pants. The picture made me sick to my stomach.

It also became a lasting and motivating image to me. With that image as my motivation, I made a vow to myself that I would no longer be Fat Dat. I became very good friends with safety Rich Coady, and we worked our butts off throughout the '94 season and into the winter, spring, and summer months of '95. We immediately began bugging our strength and conditioning coach, Mike Clark, to provide us with extra workouts. Coach Clark obliged, and Rich and I pushed each other beyond what either of us thought possible.

By late in 1994, I was down to 215 pounds and moving even better than I had at Rockport-Fulton High School. And prior to spring practices in '95, I got the break I needed when head coach R.C. Slocum announced the hiring of Phil Bennett as the new defensive coordinator and linebackers coach. Bennett and I clicked immediately—unlike previous defensive coordinator, Tommy Tuberville, who couldn't stand me.

I went through spring practices in 1995 under Bennett, and he took notice. But even with as much progress as I made toward the end of 1994 and during the spring of 1995, I was still listed behind Trent Driver in the post-spring depth chart.

It was still that way on August 30—three days before the opener against LSU. We were running sprints to close the Wednesday practice when Trent suddenly went down on the grass practice fields. Trent possessed the muscular structure of a Rodin sculpture, but he apparently had ankles like the rest of us. Trent stepped in a hole while running sprints and turned his ankle. After he missed practices on Thursday and Friday, Coach Bennett informed me that I would be starting against LSU.

I played a pretty decent game, recording seven tackles in our 33–17 win. The rest, as they say, is history. I started the next 50 games in a row, establishing a school record with 51 career starts. I also set a school record with 517 career tackles. Following my senior year in 1998, I also won the Lombardi Award and the Chuck Bednarik Defensive Player of the Year Award.

And from a team perspective, I was able to play in three bowl games and two Big 12 Championship Games, including the 1998 game in St. Louis, where we won the Big 12 title by beating previously undefeated Kansas State.

Then, after all those accomplishments, I was able to play seven years with the Dallas Cowboys, and I even wrote a book in 2005 called *Dat: Tackling Life and the NFL*, which was published by Texas A&M University Press. In 2009 I finished up my third season with the Cowboys as an assistant linebackers/defensive quality control coach. I then had the chance to become the inside linebackers coach for A&M after being hired by Coach Sherman in February 2010. Returning to Aggieland, working on campus, and raising my family in this community are blessings from God.

I say all those things not to boast, but rather to point out all that I would have missed out on if I had decided in 1994 to go ahead and quit. I often thank God for providing me with just enough perseverance to endure that very frustrating start to my college career. I also thank God for giving me friends like Coady, Dan Campbell, Koby Hackradt, Toya Jones, and so many others who helped to shape me as a player and a man.

And, of course, I am most thankful that I met Becky. Our first meeting took place during the summer of 1995. We would have never met if I had left in 1994, and I can't imagine life without our two beautiful daughters.

I have so many great memories of my time at Texas A&M that it is difficult to know where to start. Our 1997 and 1998 teams had great chemistry, which allowed us to bounce back from the 6–6 season in 1996 to win back-to-back Big 12 South titles.

The 1998 team that won the league championship was especially close. My two favorite games from that season were the wins over Nebraska and Kansas State. On October 10, 1998, Nebraska came to Kyle Field on a picture-perfect day. I don't think I've ever been so excited for a game in my life.

But on the second play, I reached to make a tackle as a swarm of my teammates converged on the Nebraska ball carrier. As I was getting up, my right thumb suddenly began throbbing in pain. I have a pretty high pain tolerance, and I can usually shake things off quickly. Even as a four- or five-year-old kid, I remember helping my dad out along the docks of Rockport and trying to push the shrimp boat away from the dock. But I wasn't strong enough at the time, and the boat banged against the wooden pier, smashing my right thumb.

That hurt, but as I was walking back to the huddle for the third play of the Nebraska game, the throbbing went from bothersome to brutal. As I'd been trying to wrap up the ball carrier on the previous play, my teammate, Roylin Bradley flew in from the outside and smashed my right thumb between his helmet and the ball carrier's. As I looked down at my right hand and tried to shake it off, I noticed my thick glove filling with blood that was dripping onto my pants and onto the field. Coady looked at my bloody mitt and said, "Dat, get the hell outta here and get that fixed."

But it was third down, and I figured if we could stop Nebraska on third down, I could get to the sideline and get my thumb looked at without ever missing a play. Fortunately, that's what happened. If the Huskers had converted on third down, I might have passed out on the next series. Instead, I got to the sideline, and one of our trainers cut the glove off and saw that my thumb was broken and cut to the bone.

We ran under the tunnel on the west side of Kyle Field, and the trainers began stitching me up. Just as they were taping a pad on my thumb, I heard our crowd go nuts. Our quarterback, Randy McCown, had just hit Chris Taylor on an 81-yard touchdown pass.

For the next three and a half quarters, so many of our guys stepped up and played like champions as we built a 28–7 lead in the fourth quarter. Even when Nebraska came back to cut it to 28–21, another unsung hero, Sedrick Curry, stepped up with the game-saving interception to preserve our first victory over a top 5 team since 1975. The team that partied together in the summer now had a legitimate reason to celebrate together.

We had another great reason to celebrate two months later. After we dropped our regular-season finale against Texas, we fell to 10–2 overall. We then went to St. Louis on December 5 to face a Kansas State team with a 19-game winning streak. The Wildcats were ranked No. 1 in one of the national polls and needed to beat us and have Miami beat UCLA for a chance to play for the national championship in the Tostitos Fiesta Bowl.

K-State looked as if it was well on its way to playing for the national championship—and probably winning it—in the third quarter when the Wildcats went up 27–12, and the announcement was made that Miami had, indeed, beaten UCLA. The crowd at the Trans World Dome, which was filled mostly with K-State fans, went nuts. Even the Wildcats players burst into mini-celebrations on the field.

I heard several of them shout, "We're going to the Fiesta Bowl, we're going to play for the national title." But there was still a quarter to play, and we weren't about to quit.

Branndon Stewart, who was replacing the injured McCown, caught fire early in the fourth quarter, and he hit Leroy Hodge for a touchdown pass that cut the lead to 27–19. Later in the fourth quarter, K-State needed one first down to wrap up the game, but Warrick Holdman stripped quarterback Michael Bishop of the ball after Bishop had the necessary yardage for a first down, and Cornelius Anthony recovered it.

Stewart then hit Matt Bumgardner, who made an incredible catch, and later connected with Sirr Parker on a nine-yard touchdown pass with just over a minute left in the game. He then hit Parker again on a two-point conversion pass that tied it up at 27. Once we got it tied, we knew there was no way we were going to let it slip away. We traded field goals in the first overtime and then held K-State to another field goal in the second overtime. That's when Stewart, on third-and-17 at the K-State 32, hit Parker again on a quick slant. Parker hit the front pylon for a touchdown that gave us an amazing 36–33 win in double overtime.

As we piled on top of each other and celebrated one of the most improbable victories I've ever seen—let alone been a part of—we crumpled many of the huge tortilla chips that K-State fans had been throwing onto the field earlier in the game. Kansas State's players were so stunned that most of them couldn't even shake our hands.

Honestly, I can sympathize with K-State's dazed demeanor. To this day, it's still rather amazing to me that we won that game. So many things had to happen for us to win that game, and so many of our players had to come up with big plays. It would probably be easier to list the guys who didn't come up with a difference-making play than to attempt to recount all the ones who did.

The K-State game was yet another example of what can happen if you simply don't quit and keep on battling. I knew the value of not quitting before I came to A&M in 1994. But becoming an Aggie hammered it home for me. When I think about what it means to be an Aggie, that's what comes to mind: never quitting, never giving up, and never surrendering.

Dat Nguyen is the most decorated defender in Texas A&M history. In addition to earning All-America honors in 1998, he also won the Lombardi Award and the Chuck Bednarik National Defensive Player of the Year honor. Nguyen remains the leading tackler in A&M history, with 517 from 1995 to 1998. A three-time All–Big 12 selection, Nguyen was chosen in the third round of the 1999 NFL Draft by the Dallas Cowboys, where he spent seven seasons as a middle linebacker. After his playing career, Nguyen joined the Cowboys' coaching staff as an assistant, and in February 2010 he joined Mike Sherman's coaching staff at A&M as an inside linebackers coach. Nguyen and his wife, Becky, have two daughters—Aubrey Mai and Remi Linh.

RICH COADY

SAFETY

1995–1998

I'VE OFTEN SAID THAT, upon my death, the words on my tombstone will most likely read: "Here Lies Rich Coady, Former Walk-On." From the time I actually started playing at Texas A&M until my last game in the NFL, those words seemed to be attached to me like a body part.

Honestly, there was a time in my life when I was sick and tired of that label. But now, as I look back on my career, I do not mind that being a prominent part of my identity as a player. I am certainly honored that many walk-ons who followed me at Texas A&M through the years have drawn inspiration from what I was able to achieve.

I went from Mr. Anonymous to All–Big 12. And I managed to rise from nowhere on the two-deep collegiate chart to playing in two Super Bowls in the NFL. It was not an easy road, but it was quite rewarding.

My father, Richard, played for the Chicago Bears from 1968 to 1975. So, as a child growing up in the Dallas suburb of Richardson, I often envisioned following my dad's footsteps to the NFL. But, after a solid career at J.J. Pearce High School, none of the big-name colleges came calling. For some reason, most major-college programs weren't all that interested in a 170-pound linebacker who ran a 4.9 in the 40.

But I believed I could play at the next level, and I was determined to prove it at the premier college football program in the state of Texas in the early and mid-1990s—Texas A&M.

I actually chose A&M for three reasons: 1) it provided me with the opportunity to receive a quality education; 2) it allowed me to be part of a great university; and 3) it gave me the chance to walk on for a football program that had dominated the Southwest Conference during my high school days.

I didn't have any previous ties to A&M, as my mother was from Boston and my dad was from Chicago. But, while my parents didn't raise me on A&M traditions, they did instill in me the qualities that I needed to be successful at A&M, beginning with a tremendously strong work ethic.

I arrived at A&M in the summer of 1994 with big goals and plenty of confidence. But that self-assuredness was immediately tested once I looked at the athletes on the football team. Someone recently asked me if I was in awe of anybody when I first began practicing. Honestly, I was in awe of everybody.

Our athletes were amazing. I looked around the locker room and the practice field, and I just hoped that I could somehow get on the field as a 12th Man Kickoff Team member in my junior or senior years if I continued to work hard and got bigger and faster.

That first year was really tough. As a redshirt freshman walk-on, you often feel less valuable to the coaches than most of the equipment. I swear that most of our coaches didn't know my name throughout that 1994 season. My role was as a scout team tackling/blocking dummy, and my name was, "Hey, you."

After that first frustrating fall, I vowed to work harder than I ever had before and to make a name for myself in some way. My bed was at Cain Hall, but I practically lived in the weight room at Netum Steed. I became extremely close to head strength and conditioning coach Mike Clark, who provided me with the guidance and instruction to define and develop my body. I spent so much time in the weight room that Coach Clark became like a second father to me.

During that off-season, I also became very close to a chubby Vietnamese linebacker named Dat Nguyen, who had also endured a very frustrating '94 redshirt season. Dat had thought about transferring after that first fall, but together, we totally committed ourselves to reshaping our bodies and our images. Our philosophy each day was to be the first guys in the weight rooms and the last ones to leave.

By the next year, those countless hours in the weight room started to pay off for us, as Dat started the opening game of the 1995 season. And by the third game, we were both starting on the nationally recognized Wrecking

Crew defense. That third game of my redshirt freshman season remains a strong memory for me. Not only was it my first start and the first road game of my career, but it also involved two teams ranked in the top 10 in the polls.

We entered that game ranked No. 3 in one poll, while Colorado was No. 7. I started the game at strong safety, even though I had been listed sixth on the dept chart three weeks earlier and didn't even have a jersey number at that point.

By the time we played at CU, some of the coaches knew my name. Fittingly, though, they still weren't sure how to spell it. The name on the back of my jersey for that game read: "C-O-D-Y."

I played a pretty decent game that day, recording 10 tackles, but we made too many mistakes that afternoon to beat a great Colorado team. We lost the game 29–21, and we lost our shot at a national championship. In our next game, we also lost our 29-game SWC unbeaten streak when Texas Tech beat us 14–7 in Lubbock.

Overall, the 1995 season was a frustrating one, as we started the year with national title hopes and ended it with a 9–3 record overall and 5–2 mark in the SWC. But if '95 was disappointing, '96 was downright dismal.

In our first year in the Big 12 Conference, we opened the year by going to BYU for the Pigskin Classic. In that opener, Steve Sarkisian passed for 536 yards—a record against any Aggie defense—as the Cougars beat us 41–37. It was the first time in school history that A&M had scored as many as 37 points and lost a game. I also had my first college interception in that game, which incidentally, was the first interception in the history of the Big 12. Perhaps that would make a good—although rather meaningless—trivia question.

Our next game was even more embarrassing, as we lost to Southwestern Louisiana 29–22 in Lafayette. The Cajuns were a pretty good team, led by future NFL stars Jake Delhomme and Brandon Stokley. But the reason that we lost was because we turned the ball over eight times, including three that went for touchdowns.

We finally won a game against North Texas, 55–0, but then we opened up Big 12 play against Colorado. In the first Big 12 game ever played at Kyle Field, the Buffs jumped on us early en route to a 24–10 win. We never really recovered from that 1–3 start and finished the '96 season with a 6–6 record—the first non-winning season for Texas A&M since 1983.

During that season and immediately afterward, we heard the media saying that the Aggies couldn't compete in the Big 12; we heard fans speculating that

Rich Coady walked on at A&M in 1994, and in 1995 started his first game for the Aggies. Coady ended his collegiate career by winning a Big 12 championship and then began his NFL career by winning a Super Bowl title with the St. Louis Rams in 1999. *Photo courtesy of 12th Man Magazine*

the Wrecking Crew was dead; and we heard opponents mocking us, especially after we ended that year with a 51–15 loss at Texas.

Enduring all that outside negativity made the next two years even sweeter. In 1997 we won the Big 12 South title. One of the key victories in that championship run came at Colorado—a team that had derailed us the previous two years. Late in the game, with our team clinging to a 16–10 lead and Colorado deep in our territory, Buffs quarterback John Hessler threw a pass into the end zone. I picked it off, and we were able to hold on for a big win. That was sweet redemption, as was the 27–16 win over Texas in our season finale.

But the next year was even better. We opened the year with a 23–14 loss against No. 2 Florida State, but then we rolled to 10 straight wins to wrap up another Big 12 South title. We lost at Texas in the regular-season finale, when Ricky Williams had his record-setting day. But on December 5 in St. Louis, we shocked the college football world—but not ourselves—by upending No. 1 Kansas State 36–33 in double overtime.

The Wildcats were an unbelievably good team that probably would have won the 1998 national championship if they had gotten past us. But before 60,798 fans at the Trans World Dome, we rallied from a 15-point fourth-quarter deficit to tie the game in regulation. And we made just enough plays in the two overtimes to stun the Wildcats. For our seniors, 1998 was especially sweet since we had been part of such disappointing seasons in 1995 and 1996. We were proud to leave the program as Big 12 champions.

I had exceeded my original goals at A&M. I ended up leading our secondary in tackles three consecutive years. I finished my A&M career with 266 tackles and eight interceptions. And then I was selected in the third round of the NFL Draft.

On draft day, I was surrounded by family members and former A&M teammates Randy McCown, Matt Bumgardner, and Jason Bragg. When I was drafted by the St. Louis Rams, we all started jumping up and down in excitement. After we all quit jumping around and celebrating, however, I looked around the room and asked, "Who plays for the Rams?" We are all guys who follow football, and we could only come up with three or four guys who even played for the Rams.

The Rams had gone 9–23 in the previous two years and 45–99 in the decade of the '90s prior to the 1999 season. They had not just been bad. They had been horrible.

All the other A&M guys who got drafted that day were joking around with me, saying that the Rams were the worst team of the '90s. They were saying that we would be lucky to win two games in 1999.

They were wrong. By a long shot.

Along with former A&M teammate and fifth-round St. Louis draft pick Cameron Spikes, we were part of a turnaround that was truly magical. During that '99 season in St. Louis, we went 13–3 in the regular season and won the NFC West title, the franchise's first in 14 years. We also hosted a playoff game in St. Louis for the first time in the 32-year combined history of the Cardinals and Rams.

Rams fever spread in St. Louis with the same type of passion once reserved solely for Mark McGwire's assault on the home-run record. We beat Minnesota and Tampa Bay to reach Super Bowl XXXIV and then beat Tennessee in one of the greatest championship games in NFL history.

In back-to-back seasons, Cameron Spikes and I had won Big 12 Championship rings and Super Bowl rings. We had also gone undefeated in the Trans World Dome. After beating K-State in the 1998 Big 12 title game, we went 10–0 at home in our first year in St. Louis.

199

That first year in the NFL was great. Playing for head coach Dick Vermeil was awesome, and I played with eight Pro Bowlers—Kurt Warner, Marshall Faulk, Isaac Bruce, Orlando Pace, Kevin Carter, Todd Lyght, and D'Marco Farr. I ended up playing a total of seven years in the NFL with the Rams and Titans. I made it to two Super Bowls and vastly exceeded my most far-fetched football dreams.

But as much as I enjoyed the NFL, it also made me realize just how great we had it at Texas A&M. In college, you're in a situation where everybody on the team is pretty much the same age. You spend all day with your teammates, not only on the field but off the field, as well—from classes to working out, going out, and living together. In the NFL, it's more of a business. The camaraderie isn't the same. In college, we were playing for the love of the game and a love for Texas A&M.

I was very thankful to have the opportunity to play in the NFL, but there are times—even today—when I wish I could go back to A&M. The college days at A&M were the really fun times. Those are the times I'll never forget. I played on a lot of big stages in the NFL, but nothing compares to playing at Kyle Field in front of the famous 12th Man.

It probably wasn't until after I graduated that I really understood what it is to be an Aggie. When I was in the NFL, surrounded by guys from all the other schools, I realized that there really was something different about A&M. Most everyone feels a special bond to their university while they are in school, but Aggies are lucky enough to feel that bond for the rest of their lives. Earning that Aggie Ring is like receiving the keys to an amazing fraternity for the rest of my life.

Looking back, going to Texas A&M and deciding to walk on to the football team were the two of the greatest decisions of my life. Wherever I go in the future, I will continue to share my passion and my ever-growing appreciation for all that Texas A&M is and all that it represents.

Rich Coady was an All–Big 12 defensive back in 1998. He arrived at A&M as a walk-on in the summer of 1994 and broke into the starting lineup in 1995. Coady helped lead the Aggies to the Big 12 Championship in 1998, and he finished his A&M career with 266 tackles and eight interceptions. He was selected in the third round of the NFL Draft by the St. Louis Rams. Along with former A&M teammate and fifth-round St. Louis draft pick Cameron Spikes, Coady played on a 1999 Rams team that won the NFC West title and beat Tennessee in Super Bowl XXXIV. Coady played a total of seven years in the NFL with the Rams and Titans. He played in two Super Bowls.

RANDY McCOWN

QUARTERBACK

1996–1999

D URING MY TIME as a scholarship athlete at Texas A&M, I attempted to play quarterback with as much passion as humanly possible. My goal was never to be the prettiest quarterback in the land or to lead the Big 12 Conference in passing. I really didn't care how many yards we passed for in a game or a season.

I just wanted to win. I am certain my teammates knew that about me, and I am pretty sure that most A&M fans who watched me during that time period knew that winning was always my top priority. I'd sacrifice my body to gain an extra yard, and I was willing to pay whatever price was necessary for the greater good of the team.

I think I proved that in the 1998 Texas game in Austin. We had not played well for three quarters in that game, and we trailed 23–7 with 9:46 left in the fourth quarter. But then we rallied for 10 straight points to cut the lead to 23–17, and with a little over two minutes left in the game, we faced a fourth-and-goal at the Texas 1.

There was absolutely no way in hell that they were keeping us out of that end zone. We ran an option play, and I kept it. I was hit so hard that it broke my collar bone and forced me to miss the Big 12 Championship Game the next week against Kansas State. But…I got into the end zone.

Unfortunately, Texas rallied to win that game 26–24, which put a damper on our second straight Big 12 South title. But my point is this: I was going to

After breaking his collar bone in the 1998 game against Texas, Randy McCown helped to engineer one of the most meaningful victories in school history a year later when A&M upended Texas after the collapse of Bonfire.

do whatever it took to win the game. Throughout my career, I wasn't going to slide; I wasn't going to run out of bounds; and I wasn't interested in padding my statistics.

As I look back on my time in Aggieland, I am most proud of the fact that we won two South titles and one conference championship. We also recorded one of the most important victories in the history of the school in 1999 when we upset Texas in the tragic aftermath of the collapse of Bonfire.

I was able to throw the game-winning touchdown pass to my close friend, Matt Bumgardner, to help secure that victory. Matt is very proud of the story he wrote in this book about that game, so I will not steal his thunder.

I'll just stay that winning that game was one of my all-time proudest moments as an Aggie. And I'm very proud of the fact that we won at least nine games in each of my final three years at A&M. In my book, winning is the ultimate evaluator of a quarterback's success. So it doesn't matter to me that I only completed two passes in our 1998 win over Nebraska at Kyle Field—a victory that helped to propel us to the league championship.

What matters is that we won. Period.

With that said, many people have asked me over the last decade or so—knowing then what I know now—if I had regrets about coming to A&M. They have asked me point-blank: do you regret not going to a more quarterback-friendly offensive system?

My two younger brothers, Josh and Luke, have enjoyed lengthy NFL careers. Josh left Jacksonville High School and played at SMU for three years before transferring to Sam Houston State, where he passed for 3,481 yards.

In other words, he passed for almost as many yards in one season as I did in my entire career at A&M [4,187], and his 32 touchdown passes in 2001 represents 10 more than I passed for in four years at A&M. Josh was then drafted in the third round of the 2002 draft by Arizona.

My youngest brother, Luke, passed for more than 12,000 yards at Louisiana Tech, and he was then chosen by the Cleveland Browns. So with two brothers in the NFL, it has crossed my mind that if I had gone somewhere else, I might have had a chance, too.

When I was at A&M, we tried to stretch the field by running go routes and fly patterns. We had no short passes or crossing routes.

But my answer to the aforementioned question is: no. I would not trade my time at A&M for anything. I love being an Aggie. I love what Texas A&M represents.

I met the love of my life—my wife, Shellie—while at A&M, and we are currently raising four future Aggies—daughters Kylie and Laney, and sons Ryan and Brady—at our dream home outside of Jacksonville.

I love A&M, and when I am 50 years old, I will still be coming back to my school. Josh and Luke will never feel that strongly about their schools. But I will say that I am glad they didn't go to A&M. With A&M's past, I don't think they would have made it to the NFL at quarterback if they went to A&M.

But I can't help but be optimistic about the future because of Coach Mike Sherman and a quarterbacks coach like Tom Rossley. Those guys have been in the NFL. They know how to develop NFL talent at quarterback. When I see what Jerrod Johnson did in 2009 and how much he improved, I truly believe A&M is on the verge of producing some NFL quarterbacks.

If we can get over that hurdle, there's no limit to what we can accomplish as a football program. One of the reasons I believe A&M has struggled on the football field in recent years is because of the perception that it is not a place where you can go to develop as a pro prospect on the offensive side of the ball, especially in terms of the passing game.

But with Sherman turning things around offensively, I believe A&M will once again rise to the top of the national rankings. I have no doubt that we can regain our great defensive reputation, and maybe one of my boys—or both of them—can play quarterback for the Aggies in an era when A&M has become known as a national title contender.

Regardless, there's no other place I would want my kids to go than Texas A&M. To me, A&M is about so much more than football.

A&M is about loyalty, character, and integrity. Look at the military roots of the school, and you can understand why A&M is still one of the most patriotic, flag-waving, God-fearing schools in the country. I love the traditions of A&M, from Silver Taps to Muster.

I admire the friendliness of the campus and the conservative nature of so many of the students. Most of all, I love the fact that Aggies take care of one another and support each other long, long after they have graduated.

I was reminded of that wonderful trait regarding Aggieland not too long ago. On September 5, 2008, I left our house outside of Jacksonville early in the morning—a Saturday morning—to go to work.

204

God has blessed me with two businesses that have been a part of our family—Crosscut Hardwoods in Alto and M&H Crates in Jacksonville. As the owner of those businesses, I was up early on that particular Saturday morning to take care of some pressing details. Shellie called me at 7:05—a few minutes after I had left the house—and informed me that the fire alarm was going off. We initially thought that it was a false alarm, but it was not. In a matter of minutes, the house was ablaze. The fire had started in the boys' closet, but thanks to Shellie's quick response and God's guiding hand, my wife was able to remove all of the kids safely before the fire really took off.

We essentially lost everything in the house. We lost photos, furniture, and virtually everything else. Fortunately, my mother had some of my A&M memorabilia from my playing days, but I lost my Big 12 Championship ring in the fire, among other things. While sorting through the ashes, I did find my Aggie Ring, but it had been damaged by the fire.

Slowly, as word began to spread of our monetary losses, my former A&M teammates and our Aggie friends continually offered their time, money, and services to help us out. Our church family and our own families also went above and beyond the call of duty to help us in our time of need.

But Shellie and I were both reminded in the aftermath of that fire what a great university Texas A&M is, and what a typically wonderful kind of person chooses A&M.

Those memories and the friendships I made at Texas A&M mean more to me than even a national title or pro contract could have delivered me. A&M helped to prepare me to run my businesses and to raise my kids and to be the best husband I can be.

I had great coaches and mentors at A&M. I learned about dedication and sacrifice. And outside of my faith and family, attending A&M probably shaped me more than anything else in my life.

I actually once thought about transferring, but if I had gone to a place like Stephen F. Austin or Sam Houston, I would regret it today. I might have gotten a shot at the NFL, but then I wouldn't have the A&M connections that I have now.

I am not just blowing the old maroon-and-white horn, but I don't think transferring would have outweighed the friends and relationships that I made at A&M. I would do it all over again the same way.

In fact, I'm pretty sure that I am not even going to try to repair my Aggie Ring from the fire damage. I like it just the way it is, because it reminds me that it has been tested under fire—just like I was at Texas A&M.

Randy McCown finished his career as the fifth-leading passer in school history with 4,187 passing yards. McCown led the Aggies to the 1998 Big 12 South title, but he missed the 1998 championship game because of a broken collar bone. In 1999 McCown engineered one of the biggest wins in school history as the Aggies beat Texas in the aftermath of the tragic Bonfire collapse. McCown and his wife, Shellie, have four children—daughters Kylie and Laney, and sons Ryan and Brady. McCown oversees two businesses—Crosscut Hardwoods in Alto, Texas, and M&H Crates in Jacksonville, Texas.

MATT BUMGARDNER
WIDE RECEIVER
1996–1999

I KNEW TEXAS A&M was a special place when I signed a letter of intent in 1995. Besides having an outstanding football program, the university featured everything a person would want in a college: history, great facilities, and one of the largest student bodies in the nation. Plus, it was surrounded by a town built for college life. It really was an amazing place.

I grew up in a small town about 45 miles south of Austin called Luling, which had a population of 5,034 when I was in school. So the opportunity to play in front of 80,000 people at Kyle Field was awe-inspiring.

I could not have asked for a better college experience. I met lifelong friends; I met my future wife, Amy; and I played on some great Aggie football teams, including the 1998 squad that won the Big 12 title.

I was also in school in 1999 when Bonfire collapsed, killing 12 fellow Aggie students and alumni, and injuring at least 27 others. Bonfire fell on November 18, 1999, eight days before we played our annual rivalry game against Texas in my senior year. Watching Aggies everywhere rally for each other after the collapse changed my perception of the Aggie spirit and showed me what it truly means to be an Aggie.

My roommates and I lived about a mile from campus. The night of the collapse we were having a party at our house. Typical of our parties back then, the decibel level continued to rise throughout the night and into the wee hours of the morning. Sure enough, a police officer eventually arrived at our door, warning us about keeping the noise down. While he was talking to us, a dispatcher on his radio called for all units to respond to a campus emergency. Little did we know as he bolted out the door that he was headed to the most tragic accident in the history of Texas A&M University. We did not think anything of it, however, and soon shut things down and went to sleep.

I was awakened much later that morning by the sound of helicopters flying over our house. That was a very unusual thing for College Station, since we don't have traffic helicopters like Houston or Dallas. So I got out of bed to check out what was happening. Before I got to the door, my roommate, starting quarterback Randy McCown, stuck his head in the door, told me Bonfire had fallen, and—at that time—four students were confirmed dead.

I literally felt sick to my stomach. For the next couple of hours, we all sat glued in front of the television, watching in shock as news channels reported

Bonfire has not been built on campus since it collapsed during construction in 1999, although there is now an off-campus bonfire that is not sponsored by the university.

207

details about the accident. It seemed surreal watching the images and interviews of the students from the site of the collapse.

The descriptions students were giving about what had happened when it fell were alarming, to say the least. Dozens of students were anchored to the logs by cables at various places when the stack fell to one side. The students described the horrifying sounds when logs snapped and the stack collapsed. And there were even more sickening sounds later from those who had been trapped underneath.

The mere thought of a bunch of our fellow students trapped under a mountain of monstrous logs was difficult to accept. As the day wore on, no one really knew what to do. We did not know if we should go to class, go the fieldhouse, or stay put. I rode my bike to campus because I had a test that morning. As I walked into the room, the professor was already addressing the class. The students wore ghostly or expressionless looks on their faces as they listened to the professor fight back tears as he informed everyone that class would be canceled until further notice. He encouraged us to do whatever we could to help.

My roommates and I eventually headed up to the fieldhouse to find out what we were going to do about practice that Thursday afternoon…or if there was even still going to be a game. When we arrived at the locker room, all the other players were sitting around talking about what had happened and what—if anything—we could do to provide some kind of help.

It did not take long for us to conclude that our time would be best spent at the fallen stack where volunteers were moving massive logs one at a time. As a team, we loaded up in trucks and drove to the site.

The destruction we witnessed was worse than we had imagined. Even though it had collapsed, the massive pile of logs lay across the field about 30 or 40 feet high. There were several cranes moving logs on each side of the stack.

The redpots [Bonfire leaders] were also busy moving the giant tree trunks away from the site in groups of 20 and 30 people. We jumped in and began to assist in whatever way we could. Covered in filth and dirt, we laboriously moved the logs for the next four or five hours.

We were not the only ones helping, either. Looking around, I saw current students, former students, people from the community, and professors chipping in to help in various capacities. There were still students trapped underneath the logs. Some had already died, but everyone worked in the hope that some were alive and the rescue teams would reach them in time.

The next day we were notified by head football coach R.C. Slocum that, after meeting with the Texas coaches, the game would be played as scheduled. As players, we were relieved to return to the practice field even though our hearts were still heavy with the events of the previous day.

In a way, we players were lucky because we were able to immerse ourselves and occupy our thoughts and time while preparing for the game. Once we heard the decision was made to play the game, I remember how intense every player's focus was during practice. You could tell everyone from the scout team to the first team was preparing at a high level for the game.

I remember that Randy McCown—a passionate and emotional leader— told the media we were going to win the game for those affected by the collapse. While we all felt that way, it was a huge limb to climb out on. To essentially guarantee a win against a team ranked fifth in the nation took some serious courage. Especially since the year had not gone how we had planned up to that point. We had been upset early in the year at Texas Tech [21–19], blindsided at Oklahoma [51–6], and blanked at Nebraska [37–0].

We were coming off a 51–14 win at Missouri, but Texas represented a major hurdle for us, as the Longhorns had already wrapped up the South Division title when they came to play us. But Randy spoke his heart. That's the way he was, no matter the situation.

I do remember when Al Carter, who covered the team for the *Dallas Morning News*, and I were talking outside the media area about how risky it was to guarantee a victory in a game, especially a rivalry game like this one. Carter said, "I know you guys are emotional, but you just cannot say that." Normally, he would've been right, but this was bigger than a game to us, and losing was simply not an option.

The night before the game—Thanksgiving night—a candlelight vigil was held at Kyle Field in place of the Bonfire. The football team sat in some temporary bleachers on the south end of the stadium. Many students who were involved in the Bonfire construction and had been injured in the collapse gathered along the visitors' sideline. With all the lights off in the stadium, tens of thousands in attendance held up candles that had been passed out earlier that evening. We all sat in darkness, honoring those who had died only a week earlier. It felt like hours we all sat there staring into the night sky in silence, but in reality it was only 15 or 20 minutes spent in reflection of all that had happened. At the conclusion of the night, the team was led onto the field for a short Yell practice of sorts.

Matt Bumgardner caught the winning pass against Texas in 1999—a pass he says he momentarily lost in the shadows.

We immediately went to the students who had been working on the Bonfire. A few of them were in wheelchairs; some were bandaged; others wore casts on their limbs and abrasions on their faces. While we shook hands and hugged them, I recognized a fellow student from my major whom I remembered from some of my agriculture classes.

We knew each other casually from attending the same classes. Normally, he was a happy-go-lucky type of guy, but he wore a look of pain and distress. I am sure he was still struggling to cope with the tragedy. When he saw me, we embraced in a quick hug. Pulling back with his arms on my shoulders, he said something that is sure to stick with me for the rest of my life. His voice was shaky, but he said, "Catch a touchdown for my friend who died."

Chills went down my spine. As powerful as the whole evening was for me and my teammates, that moment was when the magnitude of the tragedy really hit home for me, personally. He may have just been encouraging me to do my best, but it reaffirmed that winning this game was something everyone needed. I didn't know how to respond except to say, "I will, man, I will." I remember getting into the van to go to the hotel later that night thinking how truly surreal all of this seemed to be.

When game day finally arrived, we were all excited to get back to playing football. As seniors, we knew this was our last game against our biggest rival, and it represented a chance to make our senior year very meaningful. We hadn't lost a game at Kyle Field in three years (18 straight games), and we were determined not to allow that streak to be broken.

After the most emotionally draining week many of us had ever been through, we were relieved it was time to play. Many of our players were paying tribute to those who had fallen by wearing something meaningful to them. Our starting tackle, Chris Valletta, had written the names of those who died on his undershirt. Others had scriptures and quotes written on taped ankles and wrists.

After warm-ups, there were several tributes. Four Air Force F-16s flew overhead in a missing-man formation; 12 white doves were released; and 20,000 maroon balloons filled the clear blue skies. We wore decals on our helmets featuring the outline of the Bonfire stack, as news media from across the country—and not just sports media—documented every move.

Every game against Texas is special. Each year, you sense the importance in the air, no matter the records of the two teams. The 1999 game was no different, except for the absence of trash talk. Texas' students, fans, players, and coaches were first-class in the aftermath of a highly emotional situation.

Once the whistle blew, it felt like a regular game. We took an early lead with a first-quarter touchdown, but at halftime, the Longhorns led 16–6. In the locker room, there was a strong sense of urgency with everyone, especially in the offensive meeting room. We all knew we had missed some scoring opportunities, which ate at us. Emotion was high as we discussed plays that would and wouldn't work in the second half.

One of our senior receivers, Chris Cole, had tears rolling down his face as he addressed the offense before we headed back out. He kept saying that it was our duty to make plays and win this game.

We arrived at the tunnel entrance of Kyle Field just in time to witness the Fightin' Texas Aggie band silently marching off the field in a T formation. Every fan—Aggie and Longhorn—was respectful of the moment. You could hear a pin drop, which was amazing considering there were 86,128 people in the stands.

Led by a strong defensive performance, a strong running game, and some big completions in the passing game, we closed the gap to 16–13 by the end of the third quarter following Ja'Mar Toombs' second touchdown run of the day. The fourth quarter seemed to play out like a game within the game, as we battled for field position and a chance to tie the game or take the lead.

The Wrecking Crew played exceptionally well and kept us in it. Early on, we had a 61-yard drive halted around Texas' 22-yard line when Randy fumbled a bad quarterback-center exchange. Our defense continued to hold strong, and we eventually got the ball back on Texas' 48 with about eight minutes left. After a huge fourth-down conversion, McCown hit Cole on a fade route for 24 yards at the Texas 13.

After a one-yard loss by Toombs on the next play, McCown got the play from the sideline and gave me a quick look before calling it out in huddle. As I jogged out to my position and set my feet, I had a feeling the ball was coming my way. Luckily, I didn't have much time to think about what that meant.

When the ball was snapped, I juked inside then pushed hard past Texas cornerback Ahmad Brooks. When I looked back toward McCown, I actually lost the ball for a second in the shadows the sun had cast across Kyle Field's west side. I just kept focused on where I thought the ball would reappear. Lucky for me, it popped out just in time for me to stop and leap up in front of Brooks.

Randy made a great throw to put it on my backside shoulder away from the defensive back, and I am just glad I located it before it bounced off my face mask. When I hit the ground and saw the umpire hold up the touchdown signal, I remember feeling almost numb with elation that I had scored and we had taken the lead. I immediately jumped into the arms of our offensive linemen and pointed up to the student section before heading to the sideline to celebrate with my teammates.

With a 20–16 lead and 5:02 left on the clock, though, we knew the game was far from over. Just a year before, we had celebrated a little early after a huge comeback in the fourth quarter in Austin, only to watch Texas kick the winning field goal with just seconds left on the clock.

Standing on the sideline, I knew today would be different, though. After we forced Texas to punt, their defense did the same to us. Fortunately, our All-America punter, Shane Lechler, pinned them down on their own 11 with a beautiful 54-yard punt. Texas moved to our 45 before defensive back Jay Brooks—coming on a blitz—blindsided quarterback Major Applewhite, causing the ball to jar free. After a chaotic scramble, linebacker Brian Gamble emerged from the pile with the ball.

The crowd went wild, as we went crazy on the sideline. I remember grabbing former athletics director Wally Groff and giving him a hug. The victory and celebration brought a sense of relief for Aggies everywhere—if only for a moment.

As fans ran onto the field, you could see many of them with tears of joy streaming down their faces. Many players had tears in their eyes, too, including McCown, who really put the game on his shoulders and left everything he had on the field. I didn't get emotional until later that day when, while at my house with my family, everything from the past week soaked in. It was just a game, but it was a good first step in the healing process for our great community of Aggies everywhere.

I believe things happen for a reason in this world. With all we had been through as a university, I can't help but think God had his hand in this victory. In my heart, I know He did.

Since that game in 1999, I can't count how many times I've been stopped or recognized by former students who want to talk about the Bonfire game. While it's the game and touchdown catch that spark the conversation, it never fails that we end up talking about our times at Texas A&M, what a great place it is, and how it has shaped me in so many ways.

Following that game, I chased some pro football dreams in the NFL and CFL for a couple years. But I hung up the cleats for good in 2001, and my wife, Amy, and I have settled down in The Woodlands, where she is a dermatologist and I work in the Special Education Department for Klein ISD. God has blessed us with two daughters, Brooklyn and Berkley. So my days as a football player at A&M sometimes seem like a lifetime ago.

But even though many years have passed, whenever Thanksgiving nears, I often catch myself daydreaming about that week in late November 1999 when, for a few days, we had to battle through a terrible tragedy and play the most important game of our lives. I hope those memories always remain to remind me of the strength of the Aggie spirit. To me, that time will always epitomize what being an Aggie is all about.

Despite battling through numerous injuries in his A&M career, Matt Bumgardner caught 37 passes for 582 yards and four touchdowns at A&M. He also caught one of the most important TD passes in A&M history—the game-winner against Texas eight days after the Bonfire fell on November 18, 1999. Following that game, Bumgardner pursued a career in the NFL and CFL after graduation before he and his wife, Amy, settled in The Woodlands, Texas, where she is a dermatologist and he works in the Special Education Department for Klein ISD. The couple has two daughters, Brooklyn and Berkley.

BRANNDON STEWART

QUARTERBACK

1996–1998

A T STEPHENVILLE HIGH SCHOOL in the early 1990s, I was extremely fortunate to play for some outstanding coaches—led by head coach Art Briles—and to play with some tremendously talented guys. We won the 1993 Class 4A state title, which brought a ton of attention to our team, our town, and me.

I received numerous scholarship offers as National Signing Day approached, and I ultimately decided to go to Tennessee. I considered myself an outdoorsman, and the mountains and mild climate of Tennessee really appealed to me. I also was pretty intrigued about going head-to-head for the starting quarterback position with a guy whose name some football fans might recognize: Peyton Manning.

I ended up playing in 11 of 12 games during my freshman year at Tennessee, and I felt like I played pretty well at times. But as that 1994 season progressed, it became pretty obvious to me that I might need to transfer to ever have a legitimate shot at the starter's role.

When I made the decision to transfer, Texas A&M was an easy choice. I had really liked head coach R.C. Slocum and his staff during the initial recruiting phase, and I felt like I could fit in at a friendly campus like A&M. When I enrolled at A&M in 1995, I was stunned by how big it was in terms of the campus and the total enrollment.

After transferring to A&M from Tennessee, Branndon Stewart etched his name permanently into A&M lore by leading the Aggies past No. 1 Kansas State in double overtime in the 1998 Big 12 Championship Game.

I thought Tennessee was big, but A&M had about three times as many students. That was kind of intimidating, but I was immediately impressed with the friendly nature of the campus. I also knew many of the players from high school ball. So from my first day on campus, it was a very welcoming environment, and it never really changed.

I had to sit out that first year because of my transfer. While I was initially disappointed about that, it turned out to be a blessing in disguise. I got to watch and practice with Corey Pullig, who was "merely" the winningest quarterback in Texas A&M history. Being able to spend even a little time with him was a huge help in my development. He was very calm, poised, and, above all, a winner.

Throughout my career at A&M, I was fortunate to play with some outstanding athletes like Dat Nguyen, who was always a positive influence. Dat always took care of his business. He didn't talk a lot; he stayed out of trouble, did his job, and was always nice to his teammates. He was obviously a tremendous player who earned all kinds of national honors, but he never let his success go to his head. He was always at practice, never skipped workouts, and those things add up. They make an impression on the rest of your team. If you get enough of those type of guys, you end up with a pretty special team.

217

We obviously had those kinds of players. After a pretty disappointing 1996 season, when we went 6–6 and did not make it to a bowl game, we turned things around in 1997. I remember some of the games in 1997, as we won the Big 12 South title and ended up meeting Nebraska in the league championship game in San Antonio. That was a *looong* afternoon, as Nebraska came out on a mission. The Cornhuskers pounded us 54–15 and went on to whip Tennessee in the Orange Bowl. Nebraska ended up sharing the national championship that year, and after playing against them, I concurred with that final ranking.

More than most of the games, however, I remember being with the guys and just the overall camaraderie that we had in those days. Practices were intense, but it was good to get out there on the field and unwind a bit after all the stresses of school.

The one thing I remember the most about practices were Coach Slocum's chats before we hit the locker room. He would go anywhere from five to 15 minutes—or even beyond—depending on what subject he was covering. Sometimes you were in for the long haul when he really got going.

Coach Slocum had a positive influence on me, and our quarterbacks coach, Ray Dorr, was probably the most influential coach in my life. He was a very methodical, technical coach. He didn't play a lot of head games, and he didn't get wrapped up in political issues. He was just a very good coach who prepared us for anything we might encounter on the field.

My favorite game memory was, without a doubt, the 1998 Big 12 Championship Game. Randy McCown and I had each played quite a bit at quarterback during the season, and Randy had led us on a great comeback against Texas in our regular-season finale. But in scoring the touchdown that put us ahead briefly against Texas, McCown broke his collarbone and was unavailable for the championship game against No. 1–ranked Kansas State.

It was a very unfortunate injury for Randy, but I just tried to make the most of the opportunity against a team I had not had much success against. I had completed just four passes for 32 yards the year before against K-State, as the Wildcats beat us 36–17 in Manhattan. And in 1996 at Kyle Field, I tossed two interceptions in a 23–20 loss to K-State.

Early in the '98 game against the Wildcats, I was tackled and heard a pop. I instantly felt shooting pain in my knee. I had never endured a debilitating knee injury, but as I lay on the artificial turf of the Trans World Dome in St. Louis, I initially figured I had torn a ligament. I thought my knee was gone. It felt bad enough to be very serious.

But as I lay there for a second, it popped again. I don't know what happened, but at that point, it started feeling better. I guess I just got lucky. When it popped, it started feeling better almost immediately. It still hurt, but I could bend it. It turned out to be hyperextended.

As the afternoon progressed, our defense did a great job of keeping us in the game. We trailed 27–12 one-third of the way through the fourth quarter when our offense really got rolling.

The fourth quarter was weird. It was like K-State was leaving guys open on purpose. And it just happened to be the guys I was looking at most of the time. I guess I was in a zone. I guess that's what it's like when you get into a zone. It seemed like they were going, "Okay, Branndon, we're just going to leave Derrick Spiller open on this one, so you might want to send him for 20 yards."

It was that easy. Then we had a couple of great catches. Leroy Hodge jumped up and caught it in the end zone, and Matt Bumgardner made a great diving catch. We were just clicking. Plus, we were throwing a lot, which is fun. When you do that to a defense—keep passing on them—they get frustrated and start making bad decisions, and you can just keep doing it over and over.

We ended up tying the game at 27–27 with 1:05 left in the fourth on a nine-yard TD pass to Sirr Parker. I also hit Parker on a two-point conversion pass. When we got a little momentum in the fourth quarter, there was a sense of calm on the sideline. Everyone knew we were going to win. I'd never been a part of anything like that before. Usually when you're down, some of the players start getting down, but none of the guys did that.

Then when we got it into overtime, we had all the momentum. They're frustrated on the other side of the field and don't know what's going on. I think they lost a little confidence at that point. People were smiling, having a good time on our sideline. We all knew that they were down on themselves, and all we had to do was go out and take care of business.

Despite the wave of confidence on our side of the field, we still appeared to be in trouble in the second overtime. We trailed 33–30 and faced a third-and-17 from the 32. When the play call came in from the sideline, I assumed we were simply setting up for a tying field goal.

We wanted to hit Sirr on the slant because that's a high-percentage pass, and you don't want to go for a bomb, miss it, and have a super long field goal. That's what I was trying to do, trying to get us in a position to be able to kick the football with a good throw and a good read.

But the short pass turned into a 32-yard run when Parker avoided a tackler and dove into the end zone to give us a 36–33 win. It took a few seconds to register. Then it clicked that they wouldn't get the ball back, and we'd just won the game. I don't remember much after that, but I do recall running around so fast, for so long, that I almost started hyperventilating. I thought I was going to pass out. I sprinted to the end zone and sprinted down K-State's sideline. I was just running around acting stupid, but it was a blast.

It's been a long time since that game, but I would say probably 90 percent of the Aggies I meet—they try to prevent it from being the first thing out of their mouth, but it's the second thing—say that was the best game they've ever seen. I guess when I'm 75, I'll be talking to people who are like, "Hey, great to meet you. A&M is a great school, and that was the greatest game I've ever seen."

But that is one of the great things about being an Aggie. Once you are a part of that family, fellow Aggies take you in and continually support you and remind you about what a unique culture and environment A&M possesses.

I live in Austin, where I am systems engineer for a high-technology company, so we Aggies have to meet in basements and back alleys. I'm joking…sort of.

But no doubt there is the Aggie family wherever you go. I speak at functions occasionally, and it always energizes you when you see the Aggie family at those events. I remember in San Francisco, I saw a guy from the Class of 1932, and that was really neat. There is a common thread with all former students. It's great how we are all linked together as Aggies. I never did get an Aggie Ring, but I have a Big 12 Championship ring, which I proudly wear.

My wife is a Texas graduate, and her dad, Bubba Thornton, is the head coach of the Texas men's track and field team, so we usually don't discuss the rivalry too much. But toward the end of 2009, we had twins, and I've already thought about when they get older and become curious about colleges. I'll start that conversation then, and it will be fun to tell them about some of the very memorable times their dad had when he was fortunate enough to wear the maroon and white.

After transferring to Texas A&M from Tennessee following the 1994 season, Branndon Stewart sat out the 1995 season before passing for 4,325 yards and 26 touchdowns from 1996 to 1998. But Stewart will probably forever be remembered in Aggieland for one game—the 1998 Big 12 Championship in St. Louis. Subbing for an injured Randy McCown, Stewart passed for 324 yards and three TDs as the Aggies shocked unbeaten Kansas State, 36–33 in double overtime. Stewart is now a systems engineer for a high-technology company in Austin. He and his wife had twins toward the end of 2009.

CHAD FRANTZEN

LINEBACKER

1996–1999

As I began pondering exactly what it means to be an Aggie, I initially focused on specific games, practices, interactions with particular teammates and coaches, and so forth. I was very fortunate in my time at Texas A&M to have played at the dawn of the Big 12 Conference and to be a part of multiple bowl games, as well as a couple of championship teams [two Big 12 South Division titles and one outright league championship]. And, of course, having a winning record again Texas helps with my personal memory book, too.

My first thought was to share a tale of all those stories, and I wrote down an extensive and detailed account of being a walk-on 12th Man Kickoff Team member and then becoming a scholarship linebacker on the Wrecking Crew. Those are terrific and cherished memories. I will always be thankful for the opportunity to become friends and to sweat it out alongside fellow linebackers like Dat Nguyen and Cornelius Anthony.

And—like so many others in this book—I absolutely love the many traditions that are so unique to Texas A&M University. I could fill these pages and many more with stories about Bonfire, the 12th Man, Silver Taps, Muster, Midnight Yell, the Aggie Ring, Reveille, Fish Camp, the Dixie Chicken, etc.

Many universities would love to have just one of these storied traditions as part of their legacy. We have so many that make me exceptionally proud.

But after much thought about the content of my chapter, I ultimately decided that I would like to share my story from a different perspective. So I will leave the details of the specific wins and losses, the championships, the battles against archrival Texas, and the meaningful traditions to my fellow lettermen in this book.

I believe there are times in life where you are absolutely certain that what you are doing at that very moment is transcendent. You almost feel like you need to pinch yourself to ensure you are not dreaming.

My time at A&M was like that. My experiences were shaping my life like clay in the potter's hands. And I was lucky enough to know that my life was being shaped during my collegiate days and to impact how it was all happening. To this day, I feel so lucky and blessed about my time in Aggieland.

Growing up, I had always dreamed of attending Texas A&M and playing sports for the Aggies. My father, Larry Frantzen, was Class of '67, and my uncle, Don Frantzen, was Class of '76. My sister, Lisa, would later go on to be Class of '97. So maroon was obviously in my blood.

But being an average and undersized athlete from a Class 2A high school [New Diana, enrollment 250] without a single academic or athletic scholarship offer from anyone, that dream seemed far-fetched, to say the least. Most of us have been told—at one time or another—that our dreams cannot be accomplished and that we shouldn't even waste our time trying.

Sadly, many people hear those words and accept them as statements of truth. But for me, those words are inspiring, driving me to set my sights on accomplishing what others say I can't because of a lack of talent, education, money, or connections. That was my motivation then…and now. And I am living proof that you can overcome great odds to achieve your dreams.

I feel quite fortunate that, in addition to being raised by caring parents and having a close spiritual walk with Jesus Christ, playing organized sports and being a part of the Texas A&M football program helped me develop into the man I am today.

I spent a good part of my career as a walk-on, wearing the No. 12 jersey on the kickoff team and representing the student body of Texas A&M. It is truly humbling to have 80,000 screaming fans looking directly at you and yelling specifically for you. And it is remarkable to experience the joy of those fans when you make a tackle on the kickoff.

Without a doubt, some of my most memorable game experiences were making unassisted tackles on kickoffs while wearing that No. 12 jersey and

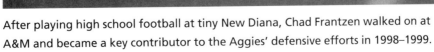

After playing high school football at tiny New Diana, Chad Frantzen walked on at A&M and became a key contributor to the Aggies' defensive efforts in 1998–1999.

representing the student body of Texas A&M. To me, the 12th Man tradition is symbolic of offering yourself and your strength to others. It shows that you are willing to give without expecting anything in return. Many of my walk-on teammates never played in a game, but they enjoyed being a part of the A&M football team and helping run the scout teams to help the scholarship guys prepare for that week's opponent.

It's not glorious to be a blocking or tackling dummy for some of the nation's elite athletes. But wearing the maroon and white made it all worthwhile. Even today, I stay in touch with some of these men, including fellow walk-on tight end Greg Knutson, who remains a very close friend.

Most young men age 18 to 22 tend to feel bulletproof. At that important stage of development, they seem quite cocky on the outside, but in reality, they are still so fragile and in need of fathering and guidance from others. I was like that at A&M, and I have a deep-seated respect for the college coaches who impacted my life, giving me the encouragement I needed.

I recall head coach R.C. Slocum saying repeatedly: "Character is what you do when no one is looking." That has stuck with me all these years.

Coach Ken Rucker, our running backs coach then, took the time to write me a personal note the summer after my first year to encourage me and let me know that the team needed me in the fall. I was a mere first-year walk-on, and I am sure that at least half the team didn't know me. But Rucker's words were truly impactful.

Linebackers coach Alan Weddell had the biggest role in my success in the program. He mentored and befriended me. He was a father figure who always looked out for me. Coach Weddell is a strong Christian man who modeled his faith to an impressionable young man.

Coach Mike Hankwitz, our defensive coordinator, trusted me to help run the Wrecking Crew and call the plays on game day. He guided me through learning our complex defensive schemes, and he taught me how to prepare each week for battle, even though I wasn't a blue-chip recruit.

And then there was quarterbacks coach Ray Dorr, a legend in the business, who never met a stranger. Coach Dorr was stricken with Lou Gehrig's disease (ALS) during my time at A&M, but he demonstrated how to overcome life's most difficult challenges, not yielding to that horrible disease until the very end. Coach continued to do what he loved—coaching quarterbacks—until the very end. We gave him a game ball toward the end of my senior year in recognition of the powerful life he had in what would be his last year coaching. I am still touched by the memory of someone who, in his dying days, could give so much of himself.

In this world, each of us faces our own mortality. We witness the loss of loved ones and friends who leave us suddenly and without warning. That's just part of life. It was also part of my time at A&M.

In addition to watching Coach Dorr battle ALS, I was deeply impacted as a senior in 1999 when Bonfire collapsed. I would have never dreamt that we would bury 12 Aggies in the prime of their youth as a result of that tragic accident. We ended up helping take the logs off the fallen stack as our fellow students were trapped and dying underneath. Gone was the normal excitement and build-up to our annual game against Texas.

There are bigger things in life than a football game. Life is so fragile, and that lesson was hammered home to even all of us football players, who often like to think we are bulletproof. But the sense of family and togetherness that was felt during this time of tragic loss of life illustrated just how good the human heart is and how remarkable the A&M community can be. I still remember the emotions of the candlelight vigil at Kyle Field on the night before the game, and I am still proud of the victory over the Longhorns the next day. It was just a game, but it helped us honor our fallen classmates.

Moments like those come but once a lifetime, and they are so very moving. That was the last game I played on Kyle Field.

As I watch college football games today, it is very clear to me that collegiate sports truly build and develop our country's next generation of leaders. Outside of the United States military, I cannot think of another organized institution that develops and produces future leaders, both men and women, consistently like collegiate athletics. And I believe Texas A&M is at the top in terms of developing those leaders with integrity and class.

I look around at my former teammates and see numerous accomplishments and various men living powerful lives. The guys I played with are teachers, coaches, professional athletes, businessman, lawyers, doctors, and police officers, to name a few professions that came from our roster. I am currently a Dallas-based certified financial planner and personal wealth coach with The Terrill Group, LLC. I have enjoyed career success, and I am so grateful to have been trained for life while in the A&M football program. Being part of those teams prepared me for success on so many levels.

Nowadays, as my wife, Kelli, and I raise our son, Tyler, I often spend time reflecting on my time at A&M. I was only there for a handful of years, but it had such a significant impact on the type of husband, father, and business owner that I am today.

A friend once asked me recently in a business discussion: "What would you do if you knew you could not fail?"

The question was so simple, yet so complex. As I began to ponder exactly what I wanted to do at this point in my life and what I want to do for my family and my business in the coming years, I thought about another time in my life when I answered this very question. Back then, I was an 18-year-old high school graduate from a sleepy East Texas town without a single scholarship offer or plan for what to do after high school.

Hey, kid, what would you do if you knew you could not fail?

In essence, without hesitation, I said back then: "I want to attend Texas A&M University and wear the No. 12 jersey for Aggies." And following the desire of my heart at that very moment to "bleed maroon" made all the difference in the world for me.

Attending Texas A&M, walking on, and eventually playing for the Aggies reaffirmed my belief in the power of dreams. I didn't listen to the doubters and the naysayers. I followed my heart and kept alive the dreams of my inner child. All my life I had dreamed about being an Aggie, but I never could have dreamt back then how playing at A&M would forever shape my future.

After initially walking on at A&M and serving as a 12th Man Kickoff Team member, Chad Frantzen earned a spot as a starting middle linebacker in 1999. Frantzen finished his career with 78 tackles. He is currently a Dallas-based certified financial planner and personal wealth coach with The Terrill Group, LLC. He and his wife, Kelli, have one son, Tyler.

CHRIS TAYLOR
WIDE RECEIVER/RETURNER
1997–2000

To be honest, I am still not exactly sure how I ended up as a wide receiver at Texas A&M. I played quarterback at Madisonville, a small Class 3A school, and we ran the triple option my senior year.

As a result, I wasn't highly recruited by the big programs. Madisonville is only 35 miles from College Station, so I had seen Kyle Field, and I most certainly knew about the atmosphere in Aggieland.

I have a few family ties to A&M. Not immediate family ties, but still family. My grandmother and cousin worked in environmental services at A&M, and another one of my cousins worked as a campus police officer.

I certainly enjoyed coming over to watch the Aggies' games, and I always admired the atmosphere generated by the famous Texas A&M student body, 12th Man.

During the whole recruiting process, however, Rice was the school I thought I would eventually attend because the Owls' staff showed the most interest. When I went on my recruiting trip to Texas A&M, I still thought I was destined for Rice. But to my surprise, A&M head coach R.C. Slocum sat me down in his office and offered me a scholarship. I was stunned. He told me I should cancel the rest of my visits, and, without hesitation, I agreed. I was an *Aggie*, and I was proud of it.

When I fist arrived on campus, I was very concerned that I was going to be overwhelmed. I was a kid who graduated from high school in a class of

100 people. But I was suddenly thrust into a major university with more than 43,000 students at that time.

Making the transition from high school football to college football was going to be the easy part. But I was truly nervous about fitting in elsewhere. I wondered how I would fare in the classroom. I had always been a pretty good student, but I was intimidated by the large classrooms and the collegiate curriculum.

When I was on the field, I was much more at home than I was in the classroom. I wasn't sure where I would play, as I had been recruited as an athlete. But I decided to stay on the offensive side of the ball, where I had played all my life. There was only one problem—we had also recruited Antoine Gandy, one of the best receivers in the state, and Dante Hall's cousin.

But I believed if I worked hard enough that I would somehow find a way to succeed. My parents, Earnest and Vernice Taylor, instilled that kind of work ethic in me, and they are the biggest reason for my success at Texas A&M. They worked extremely hard to make sure that my sister, my brother, and I understood the importance of hard work and that we always fought for what we believed in and what we wanted.

My dad worked as a correctional officer for over 20 years at the Texas Department of Criminal Justice. That was a maximum-security penitentiary. My mom also worked for TDC. Her job was not as extreme as my dad's, but she still had to deal with criminals on a daily basis.

When I wanted to go out and go to parties, they helped me to see further than the tip of my nose, and they made sure we stayed clear of trouble. They shared plenty of stories regarding the prisoners they worked around, and they made sure we understood the life-altering consequences of a bad decision here or there.

They had us focus on school, and they taught us to set career goals that are much higher than minimum-wage roles. My parents are the primary reason I was able to come to A&M and be successful.

There were times I would get mad at them about being overprotective and not allowing me to go to this party or that one. But when I look back at the trouble that I could have been involved in, I say thank you to both of them.

Fortunately, I met a lot of other players at A&M who had similar values to me. During my freshman year, I lived at Cain Hall and roomed with offensive lineman Tango McCauley. When I moved off campus my sophomore year, I roomed with fellow wide receiver Aaron Oliver.

In a key win over No. 2–ranked Nebraska in 1998, Chris Taylor took a short pass from quarterback Randy McCown and turned it into an 81-yard touchdown that electrified Kyle Field.

My final move during my time at A&M was to the Courtyard Apartments, where I roomed with linebacker Roylin Bradley. I may have had the most fun at the Courtyard. Teammates Jay Brooks, Sean Weston, Terrence Kiel, Amon Simon, Joe Weber, and Richard Whitaker also lived in the same complex, and we had numerous house parties, barbecues, and long conversations into the wee hours of the morning.

We covered some deep topics at the Courtyard. Far deeper than the ones we had on the field or in the locker room.

Practices were always competitive, and we made each other better. My favorite part of practice was one-on-one drills against the defensive backs. The trash talk that took place during those drills was unbelievable. Wide receiver Chris Cole was probably the leader of the trash talk, but the rest of the receivers would do their part to back it up.

That's how the receivers earned the nickname "the Guerillas." We prided ourselves on being guerilla-warfare tough, and we pushed each other to make the tough plays. Leroy Hodge, Matt Bumgardner, Cole, Darren Brinkley, Dwain Goynes, Bethel Johnson, founder Aaron Oliver, and I took pride in wearing T-shirts that read "Guerillas" under our pads.

You had to have thick skin in the locker room. Nothing was off-limits. If you didn't want it talked about in the locker room, you better make sure no one found out. If one person found out, it was on.

Teammates talked—and ribbed you—about everything, from whom you dated to what you wore, and from how you talked to anything you could imagine. At one time or another, practically everyone was chastised and criticized—all in good fun—and I certainly recall being the target of the verbal barrage more than a few times.

Perhaps the player I most respected early on in my A&M career was linebacker Dat Nguyen, who was a senior in 1998, which was my sophomore year. In practice, I would find myself standing, watching, and admiring Dat Nguyen on numerous occasions. Dat was a worker! He had a nose for the football and made so many huge plays for us. I didn't play defense, but you didn't have to play on that side of the ball to understand how important he was to our team.

I had played as a true freshman, making some contributions on special teams and catching a few passes as the '97 Aggies won the Big 12 South Division title.

That was a good year. But the real breakthrough year—for me and the team was in '98. Against No. 2–ranked Nebraska in early October, I took a short pass from quarterback Randy McCown and turned it into an 81-yard touchdown that seemed to supercharge Kyle Field.

The first-quarter touchdown gave us a lead we would never relinquish as we recorded our first victory over a top 5 team since 1975.

Our next win over a top 5 team wouldn't take nearly as long to achieve. After winning the Big 12 South for a second consecutive year, we entered the league's championship game in St. Louis as heavy underdogs to No. 1–ranked Kansas State. But we stunned the previously unbeaten Wildcats 36–33 in double overtime.

I ended up leading all A&M receivers with four catches for 99 yards. It felt so good to make a contribution to that championship team. I only had three catches my freshman year, and I may have been questioning my abilities early in the '98 season, especially since I didn't have a catch in the first five games of the year. But that Nebraska game changed a lot for me.

My confidence grew after that long touchdown. From there it took off. I figured that if I could do it against the No. 2 team in the country, I could do it against anybody. That attitude helped me to prove I could make big plays the next two years. My 96-yard touchdown reception against Wyoming in 2000 was the longest play from scrimmage in A&M history. And my six catches for 177 yards against Tulsa in '99 ranked as the sixth-best day by an A&M receiver in school history.

231

But among all my memories at A&M, my fondest is of a game that did not produce many particularly glowing individual moments for me. On November 26, 1999—eight days after the tragic collapse of Bonfire killed 12 Aggies and injured many others—our football team produced one of the most meaningful wins in school history by beating Texas at Kyle Field.

Bonfire was a huge Aggie tradition that tied Aggies together for generations. It was a game that we had to win. There was no way that we were going to lose that game. Being down 16–6 at halftime, every player took it upon himself to do whatever it took to win. We were able to shut Texas out in the second half and win 20–16. That might be the single most important win in Aggie football history. I know it's one I'll never, ever forget.

I ended my career at A&M with 1,316 receiving yards and 83 receptions. I also played in four bowl games (Cotton, Sugar, Alamo, and Independence) and was selected by Pittsburgh in the seventh round of the 2001 NFL Draft. I nearly made the Steelers' final roster but was cut toward the end of training camp. That would not be the last time I dealt with a near miss in the NFL.

After the Steelers let me go, I ended up at Tennessee. I got there in the third week and spent the whole season there. I then signed with the St. Louis Rams, went through training camp, and got cut right at the end again. Then I got picked up by Houston. I made a few stops in the NFL before I ultimately got to Houston. They allocated me to NFL Europe. I actually had a great season in Amsterdam, and it was a blast.

I went over there and led our team in touchdowns and catches. I went back to Houston and went to camp again. For whatever reason, things did not work out at that level again. I got to three NFL training camps and almost made each of those squads. But after I got cut a third time, I closed the book on that chapter of my life. It was time to move on.

After hanging up my cleats for good, I accepted a couple of different jobs. Among other things, I worked at 24-Hour Fitness as a certified personal trainer and then took a position with Klein ISD as a special education adaptive behavior aide. But, ultimately, I felt a calling to return to College Station to make good on a promise to my parents.

When I first earned a scholarship to Texas A&M, my mother was extremely proud, and she strongly urged me to become the first member of my immediate family to graduate from college. It took nearly 12 years from the time I first arrived in College Station until I walked the stage in May of 2009. But it was well worth the wait.

It was kind of surreal to earn my degree, and it was very meaningful for me to have my mom be able to be there. Leading up to going to school, my mom was diagnosed with breast cancer. When I received my diploma, I gave it to my mom. She's been my inspiration for a long time. She understands sacrifice, dedication, and doing things the right way. She set a great example for me, my sister, and my brother.

Now I am trying to set that kind of example for my own kids. As I write this today, I am living in an apartment in Flagstaff, Arizona. Every night when I go to bed, my thoughts drift toward my two kids, who live with my ex-wife back in Houston. (I met my ex while I was an undergraduate at A&M, and we remain on good terms.) My daughter, Mackenzie, started school in 2009. And my son, Cy, was born in September 2006.

I miss them dearly. They are my pride and joy, the focus of my last thoughts at night, along with my first visions in the morning. But they are also the reason I am here in Flagstaff, some 1,200 miles northwest of their home in Houston. I am currently paying my dues as a graduate assistant coach with Northern Arizona University. I am working as a running backs coach at NAU, a member of the Big Sky Conference.

When I was at A&M, some great coaches had a terrifically positive influence on me. Assistant coach Ken Rucker and life skills coordinator Dr. Rick Rigsby were so inspiring in the way they handled themselves and the players.

I'm not saying that our other coaches weren't professional, but those two had a major impact on me. If I had an issue—no matter what it might have been—I was comfortable enough to talk with them about trying to find a solution.

When I first arrived at school and was going through two-a-day practices, I got to a point where I doubted my abilities. We were walking back from Simpson Drill Field, and Coach Ruck put his arm around me and said, "Keep working hard because we are going to need you this year." What perfect timing.

233

I wasn't sure if I was good enough to play at Texas A&M. But those words—no matter how simple they seem—had a lasting effect on my career at Texas A&M. It's been on my heart for many years that perhaps I should pursue the coaching profession to see if I could have a similarly positive impact on today's kids.

I thoroughly enjoyed my first year in coaching. On the other hand, I am hopeful that this is only a temporary stop on a career track that I believe will eventually lead me back to Texas…and will hopefully deliver me to A&M.

The hardest thing about being out here in Flagstaff is that my kids are not here. It's my dream to one day come back and coach at A&M. That is where it started for me as a player, and that is where I would eventually love to coach. But I'm learning as much as I can here, soaking up everything and having a blast working with these great coaches and these players. I know I am doing the right thing, and this is definitely a job I love. It is a major sacrifice to be so far away from my kids, but I believe it will all work out in the end. I think it is important that they understand that Dad is out here chasing his dreams.

Hopefully, I will be back at A&M soon and will be able to share my love for my university with my kids. I remember that I felt like a part of the Aggie family the first time I ran onto Kyle Field against Sam Houston State University in '97.

I had never played in front of a crowd so big or one that loved their football team so much. When I ran out of the tunnel, nothing could prepare me for the feeling that overcame me. I had to stop and just take in the moment. It was unbelievable. Just being a part of that atmosphere was great. It was so great that I am determined to experience it again as a coach.

I think what makes me most proud of being associated with Texas A&M is the tradition and the family environment. Even through the toughest of times at A&M, there is someone there to put his or her arms around you and let you know things will be okay. A&M is a university that stands for something. The traditions here mean something to Aggies all over the world. I know that if I ever need anything, I can pick up the phone and call an Aggie. There is no place I would have rather gone to school and no other place where I would prefer to one day return.

234

Chris Taylor grew up 35 miles from College Station in Madisonville, and he attended many Texas A&M games as a kid. He fulfilled a childhood dream by playing for the Aggies, and he electrified Kyle Field in 1998 by taking a short pass from quarterback Randy McCown and turning it into an 81-yard touchdown pass against Nebraska. Taylor also caught four passes for 99 yards in the 1998 Big 12 title game. His 96-yard touchdown reception against Wyoming in 2000 was the longest play from scrimmage in A&M history. Taylor ended his career at A&M with 1,316 receiving yards and 83 receptions. He played in four bowl games and was selected by Pittsburgh in the seventh round of the 2001 NFL Draft. Taylor earned his degree from A&M in May of 2009. His first coaching job was as a graduate assistant coach with Northern Arizona University in 2009. Taylor has two children—daughter Mackenzie and son Cy.

TERENCE KITCHENS

PLACE-KICKER

1998–2000

WHEN I WAS ASKED TO SHARE some of my experiences from my time at Texas A&M, I was deeply honored. A&M is a very special place to me, and it has helped shape who I am today.

It's difficult to know where to start because there are so many thoughts going through my head. But when people ask me what it was like to play at A&M, all I can say is, "I could try to describe it to you, but you would actually have to run out onto Kyle Field on game day to understand it."

I think many Aggies can relate to that because there is a quote about Texas A&M University that states: "From the outside looking in, you can't understand it, and from the inside looking out, you can't explain it." Playing football at A&M is the same way.

I grew up wanting to be an Aggie. I didn't know why, but when I was in the third grade, I started watching A&M football and became a fan. From then on, I wanted to be an Aggie.

I visited A&M once when I was about 10 years old just to see the campus, but I didn't attend my first football function until I came to the football camp in June 1994. I then attended my first game that season and one more in 1995. I absolutely fell in love with the atmosphere, and I knew this is where I wanted to play.

I was invited to walk on as a kicker in 1996, and I was fortunate enough to receive the opportunity to play. My parents sacrificed a lot for me to go to

Terence Kitchens connected on 73.2 percent of his field-goal attempts from 1999 to 2000, and he left A&M as the most accurate place-kicker in school history.

school at Texas A&M, because I did not receive a scholarship out of high school. I thank them for giving me that opportunity because it changed my life.

During my time at A&M, I experienced a lot of things that made an impact on me. I came to A&M as a wide-eyed little kid from Lumberton, and I left ready to face the real world.

I was fortunate to be surrounded by good people at A&M, which is probably not always the case for other football players at other universities. A&M does a great job of making sure you are surrounded with positive influences, regardless of whether you are walking across campus, sitting in a classroom, studying with tutors, or anything of the sort.

Coach R.C. Slocum talked about being a good person after practice every day. He made us understand that, while we were there to play football, we were also there to become men of integrity and commitment. Dr. Rick

Rigsby, who was the life skills coordinator at the time, made a big impact on my life, as well. His support and guidance helped shape me, and it guided me through some rough times.

One more person who was very influential and instrumental in my development was Fred McClure, a former member of the board of regents of the Texas A&M University system. I became friends with Mr. McClure my freshman year, and we gradually developed a strong friendship and bond that will last a lifetime. He helped me grow as a person and to see what I needed to become.

There are so many things about this school that are meaningful to me, and I could write or speak for hours about the virtues and values that being a part of A&M instills in its students. But there are certain situations that define you and make a huge impact on you that are particularly important.

I think the 1999 Bonfire collapse is one of those. Seeing that tragedy and being part of the school during that time made me closer to other Aggies. It also helped me understand how strong our traditions are and what they mean to so many people. I started to appreciate the traditions, and now I honor them and keep them alive.

I also had an injury during my time at A&M that changed me. I tore my hip flexor in the spring of 1998, and I didn't fully recover for almost a year. I only kicked one extra point my sophomore year, and it was a hard time.

Many people don't know this, but my whole dream at Lumberton High School was to just kick in one game at Texas A&M. I was able to kick off in two games during the 1997 season, and when I injured myself in 1998 and couldn't kick, I almost gave it up.

After putting some serious thought into it, though, I decided to go to physical therapy to rehabilitate my leg. It was a long road. I was very disappointed in 1998 when I didn't get the starting job, and having to sit on the sideline the whole season made me work harder than I ever had the following spring of 1999.

I got my leg stronger than it ever was and won the starting job my junior year. I am so thankful I did, because I ended up earning a scholarship for my last two years and was able to kick for A&M in 1999 and 2000.

The experience of playing on Kyle Field those two years and for this school was an amazing one that shaped who I am. But going through an injury and having to recover from it taught me that if I work hard, I can overcome anything.

Again, I could go on forever regarding my collegiate highlights and memories, from getting my Aggie Ring to all the game-day experiences. But I think I can summarize it all by saying that one of the hardest times in my life was when I graduated. I know it should have been a celebratory time, but being a part of those teams and that university had become an integral part of my life, and I honestly felt lost as a person when I left. That may sound strange, but that's how deeply committed I was to my team and my university.

Now I have season tickets to the football games and try to be involved in as much as I can. I love seeing my old teammates, playing in the Lettermen's golf tournaments, going to the Lettermen's Lounge, working the football camp in the summer, and still being involved. This university gave me so much that I want to keep giving back.

There are many polls and media members that rank different stadiums, traditions, student sections, and atmospheres, but in my mind, there is no doubt that Texas A&M ranks No. 1 in every category. I wouldn't have wanted to play anywhere else and am truly lucky to be in the Aggie family. I also want to thank the student body—the nationally renowned 12th Man—for all they did for us. Representing you and playing for all of you was truly awesome.

I am honored to be able to share some of my experiences about this university. You can obviously tell that I am an Aggie through and through.

In my role as president of USA Fundraisers, I share my love for A&M with everyone I work with and meet. I try to represent the university the best way I can. I hope I can have half the influence on current and future Aggies as people in my past made on me. Thank you, Texas A&M and the special people of Aggieland for everything you have done for me.

Terence Kitchens was invited to walk on in 1996 from Lumberton, Texas, and his career was threatened in 1998 when he tore his hip flexor. He returned from that injury to earn a scholarship and connected on 73.2 percent of his field goals in 1999 and 2000, making him the most accurate place-kicker in school history at the time. Kitchens, now the president of USA Fundraisers, is still a regular at Kyle Field with his season tickets in the north end zone.

JAY BROOKS

SPECIAL TEAMS/DEFENSIVE BACK

1998–2001

LIKE VIRTUALLY EVERYONE ELSE in this book, I bleed maroon. My friends and fellow police officers here in Atlanta occasionally poke fun of me because they know how passionate I am about Texas A&M. They ride me for continually talking about Aggieland, and they give me plenty of grief following an A&M loss.

And, as you can imagine, I was the recipient of plenty of trash-talking following the 2009 Independence Bowl. I may be the loudest Aggie voice in Atlanta, and after Georgia waxed A&M in the bowl game, I had to eat some serious crow. But that's fine. I can handle all the ribbing and verbal abuse that the Atlanta Police Department—as well as all my other friends here in the Peach State—can dish out.

What kills me, though, is seeing the A&M special teams fall apart. The Aggies' loss to Georgia in the Independence Bowl was largely the result of special-teams breakdowns. Special-teams failures also played a huge role in the heartbreaking 2009 loss to Texas on Thanksgiving night. And special-teams deficiencies cost A&M throughout much of the last decade.

That is particularly hard for me to see because I took an enormous amount of pride in trying to make sure that Texas A&M had the best special teams in the country during my days as a player in Aggieland. And for the most part, we were certainly among the premier special-teams programs nationally. We had great punters in Shane Lechler and Cody Scates and a kicker like

Terrence Kitchens. But special-teams excellence involves much more than having good kickers.

Superiority on special teams involves a mindset. You don't have to be the greatest athlete to be a great performer on special teams. But you do have to be willing to sacrifice your body, and you must pay attention to even the smallest details. Special teams is as much about toughness as talent. Some guys don't even want to be on special teams. They just want to play offense or defense.

While I loved playing defensive back, I also coveted my role as a specialist. I knew it could make the difference between winning and losing a big game. And I loved making a play even when our opponents knew I was coming.

I still remember the Oklahoma punt team trotting onto the field early in the first quarter of our 2000 showdown at Kyle Field. More than 87,000 fans inside the stadium were buzzing with eager anticipation. I sensed that everybody wearing maroon began looking for where I was going to line up. So did every member of the Sooners' punt team. Later on, I even discovered that ABC announcer Brent Musburger circled me on the screen so that everyone watching the national television broadcast would know who to watch on this particular play.

"An Aggie to watch is No. 21, Jay Brooks," Musburger said. "He's already blocked three punts this year."

The No. 1–ranked Sooners kept their eyes on me, but there was nothing they could do to prevent me from making the kind of play that earned me the nickname "Big Play Jay." I ran a stunt, looping around a teammate, and I raced up the middle to block a punt that set up our first touchdown. The Sooners eventually hung on for a 35–31 win that propelled them to the national championship, but that play electrified the crowd and gave us a boost we needed to hang with the high-powered Sooners. I lived for those kinds of moments, and I still get a little rush when I watch that on YouTube. It was pure adrenaline.

I guess I am a bit of an adrenaline junkie, which explains why I am now an officer with the Atlanta Police Department. I was sworn in with the department in August 2006, and I immediately was honored with the Special Weapons and Tactics Award for completing the obstacle course with the fastest time. Patrolling the streets of Atlanta is far more dangerous than patrolling the defensive backfield with the Aggies. But there are some similarities, beginning with the adrenaline rush.

Jay Brooks had a knack for making big plays like this one in 1999, when he scooped up a blocked punt against Texas Tech and raced nine yards for a TD. In the 20–16 win over Texas after the collapse of Bonfire in 1999, Brooks helped secure the win by sacking Major Applewhite and stripping him of the football with 23 second left.

When I first got out on the streets, I had four dead bodies and two shootings right away. I was like, *I can't do this.* It was crazy, but after a while, I settled into the job and saw where I could help make a difference. This is the real world. You see that yellow tape and what's behind it. You see evil; you see good; and you see the real deal. It's very interesting, and there's never a dull day.

There are days when the radio is quiet, and you just know something is about to happen. You're just waiting for a call, and you never know if it's going to be a life or death situation. Your heart gets to pumping quickly, and just like football, you better never underestimate any of your enemies. Sometimes the situations you find yourself in can be very intense. That's when it pays to be able to block everything else out and focus on the job at hand. That's like football, too. You can't get all emotional about the crowd or any external factors. You just have to be able to zero in on the job at hand and trust your instincts.

My playing career at Texas A&M really prepared me for this role and sharpened my instincts. Michael Jameson and I arrived in Aggieland in 1997 from Killeen Ellison High School. We both had parents who were stationed at Fort Hood. While Jameson played as a true freshman, I redshirted in '97.

Entering the 1998 season, I was initially projected as a backup in the secondary. But in the week leading up to the 1998 Kickoff Classic against Florida State, Sedrick Curry was slowed by an injury, opening the door for me to start my first collegiate game against the No. 2 Seminoles. My assignment was a challenging one: cover FSU star receiver Peter Warrick.

I was so nervous that it was difficult to sleep leading up to that game, but my performance against the Seminoles eased many concerns among A&M coaches and fans. I had five tackles against FSU and scooped up a fumble late in the second quarter, racing 22 yards for a touchdown to give us a 14–10 lead at the half.

That game and the touchdown I scored is obviously a great memory for me. But I also remember that before the Kickoff Classic that Coach R.C. Slocum made a big deal about how well I had played in practice leading up to that game, and then after that game he made a comparison between me and Kevin Smith in terms of making a big impact as a freshman. That is a great honor that has stuck in my head forever. I had my ups and my downs throughout my career at A&M, but I think I had more ups than downs.

A lot of plays stick out in my mind. In Lubbock in 1999 I scooped up a blocked punt and raced nine yards to give us a 10–0 lead. In the most important game of the '99 season—the 20–16 win over Texas after the collapse of Bonfire—I helped to secure the win by sacking Major Applewhite and stripping him of the football with 23 seconds left, allowing Brian Gamble to recover the loose ball.

In 2000 I was the special-teams MVP after blocking punts against Oklahoma, Iowa State, Texas Tech, and UTEP. And, as a senior in 2001, I helped to wrap up the win at home over Notre Dame with a punt block that was returned for a touchdown by Randall Webb.

I finished my career with 150 tackles, seven quarterback sacks, 18 tackles for losses, and 18 passes broken up. But more than anything else, I always tried to provide energy by coming up with a big play, especially on special teams.

There's a science to blocking punts. Anybody can run out on the field and hit somebody or make an interception because it is just a matter of being in the right spot. But when you are attempting to block punts, you have to study the opponent, find a weakness, and then expose that weakness.

I remember that former assistant coach Shawn Slocum and I would take a lot of time trying to find a weakness in the punt teams we were playing. Some teams were weaker than others, but by my junior and senior years they would be calling my number and name out, saying, "Here he is. Don't let him get through." But if I did my homework right and we executed right, I was still going to block it.

Following my collegiate career at A&M, I signed a free-agent contract with the New York Jets and played in three preseason games. I was released by the Jets and then went to Canada to play in the CFL before an injury cut my north-of-the-border experience short. I then coached defensive backs for a year at Iowa Wesleyan in Mount Pleasant, Iowa.

I liked a lot of the coaching aspects, but I was at the wrong school, I think. Besides, I got the itch to play again and started playing arena football. I played arena for a year, and I got picked up by a couple of different arena teams before ending up with the Georgia Force.

While I was in Georgia, I picked up an application with the Atlanta Police Department and decided to go for it. On the second day I was at the police academy, I got a call from the Columbus Ohio Destroyers of the Arena Football League, offering me a chance to come play the last eight games.

I had to make a decision, and I ultimately decided to start my career as a person in the real world.

It was the right decision. I enjoy Atlanta and my career with the city's police department. But one day I would like to return to Texas. Among other reasons, I want to get back closer to Texas A&M. Hopefully, Coach Mike Sherman can get those guys playing for the name on the front of their jerseys. It means a lot to wear A&M on the front of your chest, and I took tremendous pride in it whenever I suited up in maroon and white.

We've got so many things going for us that Coach Sherman will get it turned around. We just need a little time and a few more players. And we need to dominate in special teams once again.

Jay Brooks was one of the most dominant special-teams performers in Texas A&M history. In 2000 he blocked punts against Oklahoma, Iowa State, Texas Tech, and UTEP. Brooks, also a stellar defensive back, finished his career with 150 tackles, seven quarterback sacks, 18 tackles for losses, and 18 passes broken up. Brooks is currently an officer with the Atlanta Police Department. He was sworn in with the department in August 2006 and immediately was honored with the Special Weapons and Tactics Award for completing the obstacle course with the fastest time.

The
NEW
MILLENNIUM

SAMMY DAVIS

CORNERBACK

1999–2002

BEING A FOOTBALL PLAYER at Humble High School meant that there was a legacy and a tradition to uphold. Bertrand Berry [Notre Dame], David Boston [Ohio State], and David Givens [Notre Dame] all graduated before me and ultimately made it to the NFL. I always was inspired by that kind of tradition and success, and at the end of my junior year of high school, I began experiencing a little of my own.

Following my junior year, I received All-America and all-state honors, as well as being chosen by *USA Today* as one of the top 25 players in the nation. I was quite honored by such recognition, but it also made me anxious about my senior football season.

Fortunately, my senior season was strong enough that it allowed me to be highly recruited. I was again named as one of the top defensive backs in the nation, and I narrowed down my potential collegiate destinations to Nebraska, Michigan, and Texas A&M.

I grew up as a Michigan fan, and I thought I had my mind made up about where I would attend college. I visited Michigan first, where head coach Lloyd Carr offered me a scholarship. After talking with my dad, I decided to wait until my other visits before I officially committed. Although, at the time, I was ready to commit to become a Wolverine.

But I instead decided to go to a game and watch Texas A&M play Nebraska at Kyle Field, and I immediately fell in love with Aggieland and the

Following his six-year career in the NFL, Sammy Davis made it a point to return to Kyle Field to teach his daughters, Taylor and Jaylah, how to Whoop!

game-day experience. It was unlike anything I had ever seen before, and I felt like a little kid on Christmas Day. I couldn't believe the maroon-clad, enthusiastic crowd, the yells, and the overall atmosphere. The Aggies beat Nebraska that day in a victory that helped propel A&M to the 1998 Big 12 championship.

I took my second visit to Texas A&M, when Ja'Mar Toombs was my host. He introduced me to the rest of the team, and I felt as though they accepted me as soon as they met me. I felt like part of the team and as though they wanted me to come and be a part of the Aggie football tradition.

I also met Jarrod Penright, Billy Yates, and Bethel Johnson on my trip. They not only became immediate friends but lifelong friends.

I was scheduled to visit Nebraska on my last recruiting trip, but I canceled that trip. I spent time talking with my parents and family, who are close to me, and I knew in my heart that Texas A&M was the place for me.

I graduated high school at the end of May, and a week later I moved to College Station so I could start the off-season program with the rest of the team. My dad and my brother, Cobbe, dropped me off at Ja'Mar's house, where I stayed for the summer. For the first time, I felt like I was on my own, even if I wasn't too far from home.

248

I spent the summer going through the off-season workouts that were some of the hardest workouts I have ever done. Head strength and conditioning coach Mike Clark would always tell me, "Pace yourself, you are fresh out of high school, and you don't have to try and keep up with the rest of the guys." But I felt like I had something to prove.

I remember my first seven-on-seven drill during the hot summer. One of my teammates, wide receiver Chris Taylor, told the coaches afterward that I would be the next All-America cornerback from Texas A&M, following in the footsteps of great corners like Kevin Smith, Aaron Glenn, Ray Mickens, and Jason Webster. My focus from that point had changed, and I definitely set my standards high.

Some of the best memories of my times at A&M involve hanging out in the locker room and, of course, some of the games. I can remember sitting in the locker room for hours after practice ended and talking to my teammates about classes, girls, practice, and virtually anything else. There were no limits to those conversations. Offensive lineman Andre "Scooter" Brooks, defensive back Terrence Kiel, and Bethel Johnson were some of the funniest guys, who always had an unbelievable story that kept *everyone* entertained.

Playing against Texas my freshman year [1999] was one of the most memorable games because it came right after Bonfire collapsed, killing 12 Aggies and injuring many others. Emotions were high, and it felt like we were playing for a bigger purpose. Thank goodness we won that game.

One of my all-time best games came against Kansas State in 2000. I was lined up against Quincy Morgan, who was one of the top receivers in the nation. I did a good job against him, and after that game, I felt like I could play with the best of the best.

The following year we were playing at Kansas State, and we were up 31–24 late in the fourth quarter. But K-State had all the momentum, as the Wildcats had rallied from a 31–10 deficit. In the closing seconds of the game, K-State faced a fourth-and-2 at our 3-yard line. Kiel came and knocked the hell out of running back Josh Scobey 18 inches short of the first down. We got the ball back and won the game.

And, of course, beating No. 1–ranked Oklahoma at Kyle Field in my senior year was unforgettable. That was the first start at quarterback for Reggie McNeal, and it was a huge win for us!

It is hard to believe that there are times when I can't remember something small like taking out the trash, but I can remember details of so many games I played at Texas A&M. There was an unbelievable amount of talent and tradition, especially among some of the great cornerbacks who played before me.

I can't write about my experiences at A&M without mentioning the coaches who influenced me so much. R.C. Slocum, Shawn Slocum, and Dr. Rick Rigsby are people who have had a huge and positive impact on my life.

R.C. encouraged us to go out and play. He really didn't yell or stay on us too much, as long as we did our job on the field. Shawn was the opposite of that, as he was extremely intense. He always pushed me to be better than what I was and saw the potential in me.

Dr. Rigsby stressed excellence and making a difference in the lives of others. He believed you should stand for something and leave a legacy. I believe that he helped me to become a professional, and he gave me the example and motivation to act like one.

R.C. and Shawn took care of things on the field, and Dr. Rigsby taught us what we needed to know off the field.

My experience at Texas A&M is one that I will always carry with me. Going to A&M obviously helped me to be drafted by the San Diego Chargers in

2003, and the experience I gained in Aggieland helped me to stay in the NFL for six years (with the Chargers, 49ers, and Buccaneers).

Once I made my choice to go to A&M, I immediately became part of the family. The tradition and experience cannot be compared to another school.

I recently went back to watch a game and sat in the stands for the first time. All of the memories came rushing back to me—being on the field, hearing the "Aggie War Hymn," listening to the crowd, and hearing Whoop!

I came back home and taught my daughters, Taylor and Jaylah, how to Whoop! I want them to start learning early.

I am extremely proud to be a part of this university, and I believe it has helped mold me into the person that I have become today. I look back at all of my choices and would not change a thing, I am grateful for Texas A&M, the experiences I had, the friends I made, and the education I received.

Sammy Davis broke up 29 passes from 1999 to 2002, which ranks sixth all-time in the school's record books behind Derrick Frazier and Sean Weston (36), Aaron Glenn (33), and Kevin Smith and Byron Jones (32). Davis was a first-team All–Big 12 performer in 2001. He was a first-round draft pick of the San Diego Chargers in 2003 and played in the NFL for six years with the Chargers, 49ers, and Buccaneers. Davis and his wife have two daughters, Taylor and Jaylah.

TAYLOR WHITLEY

OFFENSIVE LINEMAN

1999–2002

EVEN BEFORE I ACTUALLY ARRIVED at Texas A&M in the summer of 1998, I figured I probably had a lot to learn. I also assumed that I would see some things at a big school like A&M that I had never witnessed before.

After all, I was coming to A&M from Sudan, a town of about 1,100 residents in the Texas Panhandle. I had been a pretty big fish at my Class 1A school, where I was one of 19 players on the 1997 varsity squad.

As an offensive lineman, I had not allowed a single sack in either my junior or senior season. I was also a solid defensive lineman and a pretty decent kicker. And when I wasn't on the football field, I managed to become the Sudan valedictorian and the senior class vice president. I also won three state championships in the shot put and discus.

But for all that I accomplished in high school, I admit that I did not know the first thing about the commitment level required to play big-time college football when I showed up for two-a-day practices in the summer of 1998. I'll never, ever forget my introductory lesson provided by former tight end Dan Campbell, the 1998 Aggie Heart Award winner and the unequivocal leader of the Aggies' only Big 12 championship team.

In the midst of one of the early summer practices, Campbell dropped to the ground, writhing in pain from full body cramps. He cursed and hollered at the top of his lungs. He twisted in agony and rolled on the grass in an attempt to find some kind of relief. Trainers tried to move him off the field,

Taylor Whitley was a part of three bowl teams at Texas A&M and was selected in the third round of the 2003 NFL Draft by the Miami Dolphins. He spent five seasons in the NFL.

but he shoved them away. Coaches initially thought about moving the huddle so that practice could continue away from Campbell, but he would not allow it.

Dan basically stopped practice because he would not allow the first-team offense to run a single play without him in the huddle. He waited until the cramping stopped enough so that he could limp into the huddle.

I remember watching and thinking, *Oh my gosh, these guys are really committed; it's that important to them.* Dan made everybody wait until he could get up and run that play with his boys. The coaches were in awe, too. I remember thinking, *Okay, that's what it takes.* That was the example I needed. He was a grown man, and I was just a boy trying to find my way, but I learned a lot that day. Dan set some kind of standard.

After redshirting in 1998 and serving as a backup to Semisi Heimuli in '99, I broke into the starting lineup in 2000. From that point forward, I tried to set the same kind of example to others that Dan had provided for me. I started the last 36 games of my collegiate career at either guard or tackle.

I was a part of three bowl teams, and I was selected in the third round of the 2003 NFL Draft by Miami with the 87th overall pick. I spent five seasons in the NFL with the Dolphins, Broncos, and Redskins before a broken navicular bone in my right foot abruptly ended my career.

But the fact that I was able to play five years in the NFL proves that I was, indeed, able to learn an awful lot when I was at A&M. I was just a sponge back then trying to absorb anything and everything I could from those older guys and all the great coaches we had.

As I look back on it now, it was really a pretty remarkable time to be at A&M, beginning with winning the Big 12 title my freshman year. I had only been to one A&M game in high school, which was my senior year against Texas in '97. It was raining so hard that day that you really couldn't get a good feel for the atmosphere.

I had been to several A&M games in Lubbock, but my first real taste of a big-game setting at Kyle Field was when we beat Nebraska in '98. I was like, *Whoa, this place is awesome.* The next year was the Bonfire game, which was off the charts in terms of its meaning and the emotion of it all. I was also part of the Red, White, & Blue–Out game in '01, which made me so proud to be an Aggie. So I was part of some really good teams; I played with some great guys, and there were some real memorable games that affirmed to me that I had made a great choice in picking Texas A&M, which probably didn't seem like a logical choice to many people who knew me in high school.

I was born in Baytown and moved to West Texas when I was seven. I set my sights on playing college football when I was eight. My father, Dennis, had played college football at Baylor, and he made a deal with me when I turned 13.

Dad told me that I could either start working to earn money for my college education or that I could start following a rigid strength and conditioning program designed to eventually earn a college football scholarship. I chose the latter plan, although it was certainly not the easy route.

In Sudan, many of the residents still recall how my dad would sit in the family's Bronco while I would push the vehicle across the parking lot in the blazing summertime heat.

When I chose to go after the scholarship, my dad made it clear that that meant I would be lifting weights with him every day. He left me a schedule at 6:00 AM, especially during the summer, that was like a strength and agility schedule. My dad had a presence in Sudan, and he was such a big, yoked-up dude that the recruiters probably didn't know whether to offer me a scholarship or to offer my dad a scholarship. He certainly had a big role in my development.

But my step-grandfather probably played the biggest role in my ultimate decision to attend A&M. My biological grandfather on my mother's side died before I was born. But my grandmother remarried former A&M legend Dick Todd, who still holds the school's career record for punt-return yards from 1936 to 1938.

He was the only grandfather I knew on that side. He always spoke with his A&M buddies, and they were always like a big band of brothers who always looked out for each other. He always brought me A&M T-shirts. That's the first thing that piqued my interest in A&M. The cool thing was that when I played for the Redskins, I learned that my grandfather had quite a presence up there, too. He'd played with the Redskins with Sammy Baugh, and they were very close. I got to hang around Sammy Baugh in junior high and high school.

My older sister went to Texas Tech, which was the backyard choice for West Texas. But it was not for me. I figured A&M was a place I could fit in, and I thought the people were like me. To this day, I say the greatest thing about A&M is that the school is such a relationship-builder.

It's like being in a big family. If nothing else, it takes some courage if you're in the stands to just put your arm around some sweaty, smelly guy next to you to saw varsity's horns off. That takes some trust, especially in early September games when you are crammed into that stadium. If you become involved at A&M, you build relationships, which you don't find so much anymore. A&M facilitates face-to-face interaction, not via Facebook or Twitter or anything like that.

I also developed my most important relationship at A&M with my future bride, the former Shannon Warny, who received her undergraduate degree from A&M in 2002 and then earned her master's degree in hospital administration in '04. She currently is the business manager of the weight management department at Methodist Hospital in the Texas Medical Center in Houston.

I earned my undergraduate degree from A&M in four years and began working on my master's coursework in sports management as a fifth-year senior in '02. I put that on hold while I pursued an NFL career, but I returned to finish my master's degree in the spring of '09.

It was a little weird going back to school because I felt so terribly old. But I've always wanted to get my master's degree. I don't know if I'll ever use that extra degree, but I'm excited that I finished it up.

I am currently dabbling in real estate investments, and I have done well in the industry since retiring from football in 2007. I'm also looking for opportunities where I can buy a business or buy into a business. In a perfect world I would get a job that allowed us to move back to College Station. That would be awesome. Fortunately, the real estate ventures have freed me up to look for the perfect opportunity. I'm not tied to anything particular right now, and I'm open to any possibility.

No matter what line of work I eventually enter, I know the commitment level it will take to succeed. Dan Campbell showed me that a long time ago.

255

Taylor Whitley started the last 36 games of his collegiate career at either guard or tackle. He was a part of three bowl teams and was selected in the third round of the 2003 NFL Draft by the Miami Dolphins. He spent five seasons in the NFL with the Dolphins, Broncos, and Redskins before a broken bone in his right foot ended his career. Whitley, whose father played college football at Baylor, is the step-grandson of former A&M legend Dick Todd, who still holds the school's career record for punt-return yards. Whitley and his wife, Shannon, live in the Houston area, where he is involved in real estate investing. He finished his master's degree at A&M in spring 2009.

TERRENCE MURPHY

WIDE RECEIVER

2001–2004

O NE OF THE THINGS that I've always admired about Texas A&M is the indomitable and spirited resolve of so many of the school's students and former students. It's been my experience that Aggies are particularly appreciative of men and women who display courage under fire and tenacity in even the toughest circumstances.

Maybe that's because A&M was once a military school, where common men were trained to exhibit uncommon valor. Or perhaps it stems from the institution's own humble beginnings. Whatever the case, I truly believe that determination and bravery are paramount qualities that are cherished and celebrated within the Aggie spirit.

Texas A&M promotes perseverance more than most schools I have encountered. You don't always have to win to be honored in Aggieland, but quitting is not an option. Aggies love stories about their own men and women displaying an old-fashioned work ethic and old-school values while overcoming the longest of odds.

Maybe that's why I felt so comfortable at Texas A&M. Perhaps that's why I am back in College Station to build my businesses and eventually raise a family. I also love inspiring stories of courageous men and women overcoming obstacles to achieve their dreams.

In fact, I have a number of stories that fit that description in regard to my own life. It's really not a stretch to say that I have faced long odds from day one. I was born premature on December 15, 1982, at Francis Hospital in Tyler, Texas. On that first day of my life, I stopped breathing several times in my mother's arms.

Although the medical staff was able resuscitate me each time, I developed severe bronchitis. The doctors didn't initially give my mother much hope that I would ever be able to run and play like the other kids.

To make matters worse, I also had developed seizures in my early childhood. And I primarily stayed in the house, on the front porch, or in the hospital for much of my first five years of life.

When I did finally outgrow the bronchitis and seizures, I was cleared to go to kindergarten. But I was so shy and unaccustomed to being away from my mom that I often didn't respond to the teachers or administrators. As a result, when I started kindergarten, the administrators called my mom and told her, "We think your son has some kind of learning disability, or does not want to talk to us."

I eventually took a reading test and did so well on it—as well as some other tests they gave me—that I was placed in honors classes in elementary school and throughout high school. I was also able to eventually prove those doctors wrong. Not only was I able to run and play like the other kids, but I played and learned well enough to eventually earn a scholarship from Texas A&M University, where I became the leading wide receiver in the history of the school.

I then played well enough to be selected in the second round of the 2005 NFL Draft by the Green Bay Packers, where I immediately was among the statistical leaders in the NFC in kickoff returns during the first month of my rookie season. More significant to me, I was beginning to earn Brett Favre's trust in my role as a wide receiver. The coaches and media were taking notice. So were the Green Bay fans. I was beginning to fulfill all my dreams.

But even when I was beginning to reach the pinnacle of my pro football dreams, adversity once again was introduced into my life. As a result, I once again faced long odds.

On the night of October 3, 2005, my life changed in the suddenness of a lightning bolt across the night sky. During the second quarter of our *Monday Night Football* game against Carolina at Charlotte's Bank of America Stadium, our upback, Najeh Davenport, muffed a short kick.

At that moment, I had my whole season, my whole career, and my whole life mapped out. I was going to have a great game on national television;

I was going to eventually become a legend in Green Bay; I was going to become a household name across the NFL; and I was going to use my stardom—and the platform that came along with it—to honor God by spreading the gospel of Jesus Christ. That was my motivation. My heart was really in the right place.

Unfortunately, my head wasn't. It was down.

I had picked up the loose ball and returned it seven yards before being hit by Panthers safety Thomas Davis. It wasn't a cheap shot, but before I could get my head up and my eyes downfield, I was hit. Our helmets collided, and I heard the pop. I heard the roar of the crowd. Then nothing. I couldn't feel my legs. I couldn't feel my arms. I couldn't move. My life forever changed.

As I lay on the spongy green grass on the floor of the stadium, I immediately knew I wasn't going anywhere under my own power. I heard the guy behind me say, "Get up, Murphy," and he went to grab my jersey to help me up. I knew that was not going to happen. Something was seriously wrong. I'd seen enough movies and seen enough serious neck injuries on television to know right away that I shouldn't be moved.

Then a hush fell over the stadium—a stadium that had been rocking and rolling with *Monday Night Football* excitement just moments earlier. It was scary being on the field and not being able to move. For the first five minutes, I was paralyzed from the neck down. The feeling came back to my right side first and then to my left side later at the hospital. But it was very scary for a while.

I was later diagnosed with a spinal stenosis injury and was placed by the Packers on the injured reserve list. To make a long story short, my football career was over after four games in the NFL.

It's difficult to even describe how utterly demoralizing that initially was to me. I had worked so incredibly hard to even have a chance to play in the NFL. But in the blink of an eye, my career—and all my lifelong dreams—was done.

In the aftermath of that life-altering injury, I relied on three things to refocus me, rejuvenate me, and put me back on the right track: my faith in Jesus Christ, my own resolve, and the relationships of so many people who cared for me. All three of those things were strengthened and fortified during my time at Texas A&M. Becoming an Aggie was such a blessing for me in so many different ways.

Cover courtesy of 12th Man Magazine

Terrence Murphy seemed destined for NFL stardom, but a neck injury on October 3, 2005, changed his life and ended his pro career. He and his wife, Erica, now live in College Station, where he is a realtor, real estate investor, and franchise owner.

I thank God daily for sending me down the path that led me to A&M because that school helped to shape and mold me. And it wasn't where I was initially headed.

Even though I had a few hills to climb as a young child, I had some great athletic genes. My mother, Brenda Guthrie, was an outstanding track athlete and softball player during her high school years. My oldest brother, Kendrick Bell, was a four-year letterman at Baylor from 1991 to 1994, where he was an excellent running back.

My mom tells stories about how Kendrick taught me to hold and throw a little plastic souvenir football when I was just six months old. Kendrick was always looking after me and teaching me how to play the game. I was even able to spend significant time around Kendrick and his Baylor teammates when my older brother was in school in Waco.

I looked up to Kendrick in many ways, and I initially planned on following his footsteps to Baylor. I verbally committed to the Bears during the recruiting process. But my stepfather, who had been an assistant coach at A&M, also placed a call to R.C. Slocum. After Coach Slocum examined the highlight tape of me playing quarterback at Chapel Hill, the head coach decided to offer me a scholarship.

260

I thoroughly examined the opportunity and realized I was born to be at A&M, and I got to campus as fast as I could. Not being a very high-profile recruit gave me a lot of incentive. Once I got my foot in the door at A&M, I decided I was going to outwork everybody and prove to all the A&M coaches that they had made the right decision by offering me a scholarship.

I came to campus that summer. I think I was the first signee that summer who was on campus. I used to work with former quarterback Mark Farris. He told me, "Yeah, we're going to need you." That made me feel good. I also heard other players talking, saying, "Murphy is going to come in and help."

That encouraged me to work even harder, and in the opening game of the 2001 season, I think I began to prove I belonged at A&M. In our 38–24 win over McNeese State, I led the team with four catches for 79 yards and the game-winning touchdown.

I would go on to catch a pass in every game but one during the 2001 season, including a 10-reception performance in the Colorado game. I set a freshman school record with 36 catches, erasing the 29-year-old mark of 31 catches by Richard Osborne in 1972.

My success as a freshman made me work even harder the next off-season. I spent countless nights working out by myself into the wee hours of the morning. And I spent the entire summer of '02 relentlessly pumping iron and pounding the pavement. By the time two-a-days started, I had transformed my lean physique to pretty muscular. I was in the best shape of my life and ready for the season of my life.

Shortly after two-a-days began, however, I pulled a groin muscle that caused me to miss the opener against Louisiana-Lafayette. I returned a week later against Pittsburgh, but broke my left thumb in practice the following week. Without any public statement about the condition of my thumb, I played with a small cast underneath my glove against Virginia Tech. That's when I let a few balls drop that I usually catch.

With each ball that slipped through my fingers, teammates and coaches could see that I was pressing harder, as the drops weighed heavily on my mind. I was disappointed because I didn't want to let the guys down, and I knew what I could do at wide receiver. But instead of redshirting, I decided to play through the pain and discomfort of the broken finger. To this day, Coach Slocum tells me that any other kid he knew would have redshirted and sat that season out. Because the most important component a wide receiver needs are his thumbs and fingers. But not me; tribulations are what made me who I am.

Later that season, we beat No. 1–ranked Oklahoma at home. I had five catches for 128 yards and two touchdowns, despite a broken finger. I think the Lord helped me through that and made me realize that anything worthy is achieved through perseverance and faith. I looked at it then as a lesson, and it was preparing me to handle bigger difficulties.

By the time I finished my four years at A&M, I helped to lead our 2004 team back to a New Year's Day bowl game for the first time since 1999. I had accounted for 172 career receptions for 2,600 yards—both school records. I left with the most all-purpose yards by a receiver [3,619] and as the only player in my class to be honored as a three-time Academic All–Big 12 selection.

What pleases me most as I look back on my time at A&M was what I learned about myself during those years. Thanks to some great coaches, teammates, and friends, I learned that I could accomplish amazing things if I put Jesus first. I learned how to set goals, how to sharpen my focus, how to overcome setbacks, and how to build relationships.

I thought all of those lessons would eventually help me make it to the NFL Hall of Fame. Or at least numerous Pro Bowls.

But God had other plans for me. Again, I truly began to really trust Jesus—not just to claim him—during my time at A&M. And that faith, along with all the relationships I developed, really pulled me through some hard times after I was injured.

On the day after I was injured, my mother arrived at the hospital in Charlotte and showed me my cell phone. Within 24 hours of my injury, it contained approximately 250 text messages and more than 200 missed calls. I was so inundated with concerned calls—many from my friends from A&M—that I decided that the only way to let everyone know I was okay was to post a personal message on a website.

I always felt a lot of support at A&M, but the injury really brought it to my attention how much people cared about me. I also came back to College Station after the injury and talked to the guys before an October 15, 2005, game against Oklahoma State.

When I walked into the weight room when the team was warming up, they all went crazy. Everybody ran over and started jumping on me and the coaches had me break it down. It just felt good to be able to come back and still have that effect on my team and stadium. I reminded the guys to play every play like it could be your last one. We all know that, but that injury really brought it home for me.

The Aggies responded to my pregame talk with what was easily the most impressive overall performance of the season, blasting the Cowboys 62–23. But coming back then probably did more for me than it did for the guys.

Coming back to A&M reminded me then that Aggieland is a special place, and that the lessons I learned as a student at A&M—in the classroom, on the field, and just being on campus—were some of the most important of my life.

Being an Aggie helped me learn about the big pictures in life. Being an Aggie strengthened my faith and taught me to look for silver linings even in the midst of the darkest storms.

It's been a while since my injury, and I can now see clearly what I might have missed if I had just kept on playing. I had met a woman named Erica, whom I might never have gotten to know better if I had not been injured. But today she is my wife—the love of my life and the future mother of our children.

We have settled into College Station, where I am a realtor with Keller Williams, a real estate investor, and a franchise owner. I always dreamed of running my own business, and now I am fulfilling those dreams.

I have had some obstacles thrown my way in this lifetime, but I've tried to make the most of every situation. Part of me still wishes that I was representing Texas A&M and Christ in the high-profile world of the NFL. But since I chose my long-term health and future over the NFL, I am exhibiting some of the qualities—perseverance, work ethic, and tenacity overcoming adversity—that Aggies cherish in my post-football career.

Terrence Murphy left Texas A&M as the leading wide receiver in the history of the school. He was selected in the second round of the 2005 NFL Draft by the Green Bay Packers, where he was among the leaders in the NFC in kickoff returns during the first month of his rookie season, before a neck and spinal injury on the night of October 3, 2005, ended his NFL career prematurely. Murphy and his wife, Erica, returned to College Station to begin their successful careers. Murphy is now a franchise owner, real estate investor, and realtor with Keller Williams.

STEPHEN McGEE

QUARTERBACK

2005–2008

I WOULDN'T NECESSARILY SAY I was born to be an Aggie, but as far back as when I was five years old, I would often venture into my yard and play football games by myself. I'd suit up in a Texas A&M uniform that had been given to me by aunts and uncles who had attended A&M, and I would throw passes to myself, dodge imaginary tacklers, and bounce off the ground after being tackled by make-believe linebackers.

I even had a 12th Man towel I would use as my quarterback towel. Before I went out one day, I decided it was going to be a big game and a bloody battle, so I got out my red marker and colored my pants and my towel because I'd seen guys on TV with blood on their pants. I had to have some fake blood on my uniform to make me look authentic.

Little did I know then that I would one day have the opportunity to suit up in a real Texas A&M uniform, and that I would eventually be spilling my own blood on the field as the quarterback for the Aggies. As you can see, it isn't a stretch to say that going to A&M and playing for the Aggies was the fulfillment of a lifetime of dreams for me.

My dad, Rodney McGee, first began taking me to work with him when I was about seven. Dad is now the pastor of a church in Burnet [55 miles northwest of Austin, population 4,700], but he spent 23 years in coaching—first at Edna and later at Burnet. I loved being around the fieldhouse, soaking in the atmosphere of high school athletics, and studying every move the athletes made.

As I grew, I enjoyed all the sports, but I had a particular passion for playing quarterback. Dad encouraged me to follow that passion and to work extremely hard in pursuit of my goals. I took him seriously and devoted 40 to 50 hours a week during the summers trying to get better and accomplish my goals.

The hard work paid off. One of my best friends in Burnet was Jordan Shipley, who went on to be a star wide receiver at Texas. Jordan's father, Bob, was our head football coach at Burnet, and he led us to back-to-back state championship games.

While we did not win a state title, we had plenty of success. In my three years as a starter, we had an overall record of 36–5, including a 28–2 mark during my junior and senior seasons. Jordan and I had envisioned playing collegiate football together. But when it came time to choose a college destination, Jordan jumped quickly at an offer from Texas. I was a huge fan of former Longhorns quarterback Major Applewhite, and I gave some consideration to Texas. But, ultimately, my decision came down to Georgia and Texas A&M.

I followed my heart to Aggieland. But even after I committed to A&M, coaches from other schools tried to convince me that A&M was on a downhill slide.

265

When I was a senior in high school, A&M was 4–8 and got beat 77–0 by Oklahoma. I was living in the backyard of Austin, and Mack Brown was asking me to come to his school. Other coaches were saying this and that to get me to come to their school, but none of those football factors had anything to do with my decision to go to A&M. I wanted to go to Georgia and play for Mark Richt, who is a great coach and a great Christian man. But I felt like God was leading me to A&M.

I prayed about it constantly, and I just felt in my heart that A&M was where God wanted me. After graduating early from Burnet, I first arrived at A&M for the spring semester in 2004. I was immediately struck by the enormous size of the campus and the student body. Remember, my home town had less than 5,000 people in it, while A&M had 48,000 students. The first class I attended—Dr. Ben Welch's management 105—included more than 500 students.

Stephen McGee passed for 2,295 yards and 12 touchdowns and set an A&M single-season school record with a 62 percent completion rate in 2006. *Photo courtesy of 12th Man Magazine*

But one of the remarkable things about A&M was that even though it was a huge campus, it had a friendly, small-town feel to it. People said "Howdy" wherever you went, and even that management class made me feel welcomed.

I will never forget that first week of class. I was sitting way in the back, minding my own business. Dr. Welch was lecturing, and he started talking about something business-related. Then he brought my name up in class and said, "I hear Stephen is in this class. Stephen, can you please stand up and introduce yourself?"

I was beet red, but the guys around me made me stand up and acknowledge the class. Ultimately, it made me feel good that in this large school, folks know who you are, even in a class of 500. You aren't just a lost soul.

On the field, however, I felt pretty lost more than a few times during spring practices in '04. And the following fall as a redshirt was certainly not easy. In fact, it was often quite frustrating.

But by the start of practices for the 2005 season, I was beginning to understand the offense and the speed of the college game. I also developed a very strong relationship with quarterbacks coach and offensive coordinator Les Koenning. His mannerisms, the way he talked, his one-liners, and just about everything else about him made an imprint on my life. One of my best friends, former walk-on quarterback T.J. Sanders, and I still go back and forth, text messaging each other our Coach Koenning's one-liners. Coach was so easy to pick on, and he always picked on us. We spent so many hours with him ribbing each other, and we really got along exceptionally well.

Toward the end of the '05 season, I also got a chance to prove I could play well on game days. In the next-to-last game against Oklahoma, our starting quarterback, Reggie McNeal, went down with an injured ankle in the third quarter. I played the final six quarters of the '05 season—two against OU and all four against eventual national champion Texas.

I didn't do too much in the passing game in those two games, I just tried to play hard-nosed, tough football. It's a contact game, and I never shied away from contact. I never asked any of my teammates to do something that I wasn't willing to do, including taking a big hit in order to gain an extra yard or two.

In those six quarters against Oklahoma and Texas, I rushed for 175 yards and played with reckless abandon. My teammates and fans seemed to appreciate that about me.

Then in 2006 I passed for 2,295 yards and 12 touchdowns and set an A&M single-season school record with a 62 percent completion rate. But the most important thing to me was that we reestablished A&M as a winner. We went 9–3 in the regular season and lost our three games [Texas Tech, Oklahoma, and Nebraska] by a combined total of six points. If one or two plays had gone differently, we could have easily won the Big 12 title. But even after enduring back-to-back one-point losses to OU and Nebraska, our team didn't quit.

Probably my favorite game memory from my time at A&M was the '06 win in Austin. Trailing 7–6 in the fourth quarter, we shoved the ball down Texas' throat, marching 88 yards in 16 plays to score the game-winning touchdown in our 12–7 victory.

We had a lot of people on our backs heading into that Texas game—a lot of naysayers—and it felt great to beat Texas for the first time since 1999. While I was at A&M, we never had the most talented teams in the conference, but that Texas win was an example of what can be accomplished if a bunch of guys band together and fight to the end. It didn't matter what had happened in the past, we just kept pushing forward. It was a pretty special moment.

We had all hoped that the win in '06 would springboard us to a conference championship in '07. But it didn't work out that way. Late in the year, we lost three games in a row to Kansas, Oklahoma, and Missouri, and because of other things that we couldn't control, the heat really intensified on head coach Dennis Franchione.

Fortunately, we ended the regular season by once again playing a great game against Texas. We opened up the offense, and I was able to pass for 362 yards and three touchdowns as we beat the Horns 38–30.

I had very high hopes for my senior season, as Mike Sherman became the head coach of our team for 2008. I learned so much about a pro-style passing attack from working with Coach Sherman. But so many of my plans and dreams for my senior year ended when I was injured early in the second game of the season.

I managed to come back and play some later in the year, but it was a pretty disappointing way to end my A&M career. Nevertheless, I am so thankful for so many things that happened during my time in College Station.

I earned my degree from Texas A&M; I met some great friends whom I will stay in touch with for the rest of my life; I was able to positively impact the lives of others around me; and I developed enough as a quarterback to be selected by the Dallas Cowboys in the fourth round of the 2009 NFL Draft, fulfilling another lifelong dream of mine.

I'm proud to be an Aggie, and I'm proud to be representing Texas A&M in the NFL. Hopefully, I'll receive a chance in the future to play a significant role in leading my team to a championship. My biggest regret from my time at A&M is that I was not able to fulfill that goal.

Nevertheless, I look back on my time at A&M with gratitude. I think about the great traditions—sawing varsity's horns off and watching Kyle Field rock with passion and emotion. And I think about the more solemn traditions like Aggie Muster and Silver Taps.

Those are special traditions, and Texas A&M is a special place that I will always hold dear to me.

I hope Aggies remember me as a young man who sacrificed his body for the greater good of the team. Most of all, though, I hope I am remembered by the A&M community as a man who loved the Lord and lived out his time at A&M passionately in everything I did.

Stephen McGee grew up dreaming of playing quarterback at Texas A&M and earned that chance after leading Burnet High School to back-to-back state championship games and a 28–2 mark as a junior and senior. The gutsy McGee passed for 2,295 yards and 12 touchdowns and set an A&M single-season record in 2006 with a 62 percent completion rate, as he guided the Aggies to a 9–3 record. McGee's toughness was probably used against him, as then–head coach Dennis Franchione turned to an option-oriented offensive attack in 2007. He was injured in 2008 in Mike Sherman's first season as head coach but was selected by the Dallas Cowboys in the fourth round of the 2009 NFL Draft. He served as a backup quarterback in his rookie season with Dallas.

MARK DODGE

LINEBACKER

2006–2007

EVEN BEFORE THE 2006 SEASON BEGAN, I sensed that I might receive some media attention for what I had done in the past. Not because of what I had done in the past in a football uniform, but rather, because of where I had been in a military uniform.

After all, 2006—my first year as a junior-college transfer linebacker at Texas A&M—marked the five-year anniversary of the terrorist attacks on the World Trade Center and the Pentagon. I was an Army soldier in the Pentagon on September 11, 2001, filling out paperwork and watching coverage of the World Trade Center attacks when hijacked American Airlines Flight 77 slammed into the other side of the complex. I evacuated and joined my unit, which assisted in search-and-recovery efforts.

Because of that background, I anticipated some attention—even if I never emerged as a big-time player at A&M. But I was floored by how much attention I received around the anniversary of the terrorist attacks. Newspapers from across the country told my story. So did TV stations and magazines. I was even featured prominently on ESPN's *College GameDay*.

It was overwhelming. I did interviews for at least two weeks leading up to 9/11, and I can't even count how many stories were done. It was an honor because I felt like I was representing all those guys in my platoon and, to a larger extent, all the people who participated in the military efforts in the aftermath of the attacks. But after a while, I finally had to put an end to

271

Prior to pursuing his college football dreams, Mark Dodge was an Army soldier in the Pentagon on September 11, 2001, when American Airlines Flight 77 slammed into the other side of the complex. In 2006 he sealed a 12–7 road win over Texas with a fourth-quarter interception in Austin. *Photo courtesy of 12th Man Magazine* the interviews so I could really concentrate on my current mission at the time: restoring the defensive reputation of Texas A&M.

I am so proud to be an Aggie. Unlike many other greats in this book, I didn't grow up in Texas with a vast knowledge of Texas A&M and its awesome traditions. I also didn't arrive in Aggieland as an 18-year-old kid who was intent on sewing wild oats.

When I enrolled at Texas A&M in January 2006, at the start of the spring semester, I became the oldest player on the Aggies' roster at 25. But in terms of my overall optimism and youthful enthusiasm, I was probably more excited than a kid on Christmas morning.

My football career easily could have ended many years earlier when I left high school in Nevada—where I had been a 170-pound receiver and safety. At that point in my life I decided to join the Army. During my four years in the Army, I grew up in a lot of ways and bulked up my body. Among other things, I was selected to serve in the Presidential Honor Guard. While stationed at Fort Meyers, Virginia, I happened to be inside the Pentagon on September 11, 2001, and I was fortunate enough to have survived one of the deadliest days in U.S. history.

When I left the Army, I decided to give football one more chance. I was in such good shape physically that I figured it was at least worth a shot. But even when I made the decision to begin my collegiate football pursuit at the junior-college level, I ran into more barriers than I had ever seen on a military obstacle course.

I called 30 junior colleges along the West Coast, seeking an opportunity to continue my collegiate dreams. I received no return phone calls. Not a single call back. I can't say I blamed them, either. Who wanted a former military guy who has been playing in company flag football leagues? I know a lot of guys probably would have given up right then.

Not me, though. I continued to make phone calls and discovered that Feather River [California] Community College featured a good neighbor enrollment discount for Nevada residents. So, without an invitation from the football coaches, I enrolled in school and showed up for the first day of football conditioning drills in the spring of 2004.

By the time Feather River began spring practices, I had impressed my coaches enough that I was named as a starting linebacker. I then recorded 86 tackles, six sacks, 12 tackles for losses, two forced fumbles, two fumble recoveries, and one blocked punt in my debut season.

In 2005 I earned Mid-Empire All-Conference honors after registering 144 tackles, two sacks, five forced fumbles, four fumble recoveries, and one interception. Suddenly, I was no longer the guy that no junior college wanted to consider. I was actually a prospect among Division I-A schools.

It was amazing how things worked out. After my freshman year, I started getting phone calls from schools like BYU and the University of Nevada. Then A&M was the first big school that contacted me, and shortly after that it just kind of blew up. I had about 10 or 15 offers from major schools before my senior season even started.

But I was most intrigued by A&M. With the school's military tradition and defensive reputation, I didn't even need to visit College Station before committing. Then when I arrived in January '06, I was amazed by everything A&M offered. The facilities at A&M were incredible; so were the coaches; and so were the guys on the team.

And that's just the football aspect of it all. I will never forget the way the people at A&M made me feel so welcome right away.

My second week there—long before we had started playing football or anybody else knew my background story—I was able to live as a normal student, and I discovered the most amazingly unique thing about A&M. While it is a huge school of nearly 50,000, the student body is there for each other. It's amazing how the students are so connected to each other. If you were stuck on the side of the road, someone in College Station would stop and help, I guarantee it.

Even if you just had an Aggie sticker on your car anywhere in Texas, another Aggie would stop and help. Your race, religion, sex, etc. made no difference. If you were an Aggie, you were bonded to all other Aggies. You were part of the family. I immediately felt the same type of bond at A&M that I felt in the military. You have that team-oriented bond not just in the locker room, but also in the classroom.

I loved A&M right from the start, and I wanted to do my part to bring respect to my university. I felt like I did that in a little way by the attention I received surrounding the 9/11 coverage. But I was also very proud that, toward the end of my first season, I began to make a name for myself because of what I was doing, not solely because of what I had done.

In mid-November 2006 I recorded 17 tackles and an interception against Nebraska, earning Big 12 Defensive Player of the Week honors. Then versus Texas, I stopped a fourth-and-1 play in the first quarter with the Longhorns at our 8. That proved to be a big play in our win over Texas. I was also able to seal the 12–7 win in Austin with a fourth-quarter interception to earn another Big 12 Player of the Week honor.

I finished that first season with 51 tackles and two interceptions. Then, as a senior in '07, I started all 12 games and led my team with 117 tackles. I was also honored with the Pat Tillman Patriot Award during the season.

More important to me, though, was that I helped lead my team to back-to-back bowl games. We also beat Texas both years I was in school at A&M—something I quickly discovered was a top priority for many Aggie fans.

Beyond football, I feel so lucky to have been accepted into the Aggie family and to have met so many wonderful friends whom I will keep in touch with for the rest of my life. The relationships I developed at A&M are the most memorable aspect of my time in Aggieland, especially the one I developed with a beautiful coed named Courtney, who became my wife on August 1, 2008.

In the summer of 2006, I was living with former Aggie wide receiver Cody Beyer. We were moving from an apartment to a duplex, and in the interim, we were crashing at Cody's girlfriend's house. As fate would have it, my future wife was living in the house during a three-month rental as she attended summer school.

I was just some crazy guy sleeping on the couch. She came home the first night, went to her room, locked the door, and called her mom to tell her there was some scary guy on the couch. But I eventually convinced her I wasn't too scary, and we ended up going out after that. Thankfully, we've been together ever since.

I also owe my current job to being an Aggie. As I write today, I'm the operations manager for Dallas-based Trinity Industries. I came out of college in December '07 and began this job in January.

We manufacture railcars, inland barges, wind towers, highway safety products, and concrete. I was originally a plant manager of a railcar axle shop. But late in 2009 I was moved to corporate headquarters. Now I'm an operations manager for 17 different facilities.

It's a great job that I landed because of A&M connections. One of the senior vice presidents of Trinity, Mark Stiles, has a daughter who attended A&M. For numerous reasons, he likes to recruit military guys or A&M grads.

He went to an A&M game with one of the vice presidents of development and heard my story. He then contacted Troy Kema in our academic office and asked for my contact information. An interview was eventually scheduled, and I ended up committing to them even before my senior year started.

So I essentially owe my life as it is today to my time at Texas A&M. I loved being a student at A&M, and I will forever hope to promote and represent my school in the most positive light that I can imagine.

I didn't come to A&M like so many others did. But like most everyone else, I instantly knew that being an Aggie was something to cherish. When you become part of Texas A&M, you become part of something much bigger than yourself. The spirit in Aggieland is amazing, and I feel so blessed to have had the opportunity to play football at Texas A&M.

Mark Dodge was an Army soldier in the Pentagon on September 11, 2001, when hijacked American Airlines Flight 77 slammed into the other side of the complex. After four years in the Army, he walked on at Feather River (California) Community College, where he earned Mid-Empire All-Conference honors. Dodge arrived at A&M in January 2006 and finished his first season with 51 tackles and two interceptions. Then, as a senior in 2007, he started all 12 games and led the Aggies with 117 tackles. He was also honored with the Pat Tillman Patriot Award during the season. Dodge met his wife, Courtney, while at A&M. He is now the operations manager for Dallas-based Trinity Industries.

BOYD · ROY BUCEK · JESSE "RED" BURDITT · BILLY PETE HUDDLE

SIMONINI · BUBBA BEAN · PAT THOMAS · CHARLES L. "TANK" MA

ARTHUR · LOUIS CHEEK · DAVID COOLIDGE · AARON WALLACE ·

ARDSON · KEVIN SMITH · DERRICK FRAZIER · QUENTIN CORYA

· KYLE BRYANT · DAT NGUYEN · RICH COADY · RANDY McCOWN

OR · TERENCE KITCHENS · JAY BROOKS · SAMMY DAVIS · TAYLO

O · ROY BUCEK · JESSE "RED" BURDITT · BILLY PETE HUDDLESTON

NINI · BUBBA BEAN · PAT THOMAS · CHARLES L. "TANK" MARSH

UR · LOUIS CHEEK · DAVID COOLIDGE · AARON WALLACE · MICK

ON · KEVIN SMITH · DERRICK FRAZIER · QUENTIN CORYATT · M

E BRYANT · DAT NGUYEN · RICH COADY · RANDY McCOWN · MA

TERENCE KITCHENS · JAY BROOKS · SAMMY DAVIS · TAYLOR WH

BUCEK · JESSE "RED" BURDITT · BILLY PETE HUDDLESTON · J

NINI · BUBBA BEAN · PAT THOMAS · CHARLES L. "TANK" MARSH

UR · LOUIS CHEEK · DAVID COOLIDGE · AARON WALLACE · MICK

ON · KEVIN SMITH · DERRICK FRAZIER · QUENTIN CORYATT · M

E BRYANT · DAT NGUYEN · RICH COADY · RANDY McCOWN · MA

TERENCE KITCHENS · JAY BROOKS · SAMMY DAVIS · TAYLOR WH

BUCEK · JESSE "RED" BURDITT · BILLY PETE HUDDLESTON · JACK